ATI TEAS 6 Prep 2020-2021

680 Questions and Detailed Answer Explanations for the Test of Essential Academic Skills (4 Full-Length Practice Exams)

Table of Contents

Chapter 1: The Fundamentals of the ATI TEAS VI Test

The ATI TEAS VI test is a standardized test administered by the Assessment Technologies Institute (ATI), an organization that handles education for nurses in the US. This exam, the Test of Essential Academic Skills, includes reading, English language skills, mathematics and science. The ATI administers this exam weekly at designated centers across the United States and Canada, some of them within nursing schools.

Every person who wants to pursue a career in nursing in the US needs to take the ATI TEAS VI test first, as passing the exam is a preadmission requirement for most of the nursing courses offered in these countries. It has been observed statistically that the TEAS test is great at predicting whether a candidate is capable of succeeding in a nursing course.

Candidates should know that there is nothing in the test that is entirely new to a person who has graduated from high school. This test will assess your knowledge at the entry-level. When the time comes for you to apply for admission to a nursing school in the US, you will be required to submit your TEAS VI results before your application will be considered.

How the TEAS VI is Different from the TEAS V

Although material prepared for the TEAS V may, to some extent, help prepare for the TEAS VI, it is not sufficient. A new curriculum for nursing programs has been adopted, and the TEAS has been modified to ensure that aspiring nurses can handle the new demands of these courses. Anyone who passed the TEAS V or any of the earlier versions of the test can no longer use those results when applying for admission to a nursing program.

One of the differences between the test version V and VI is that candidates can now use four-function calculators for the mathematics section of the exam. This type of calculator performs only the basic functions of addition, subtraction, multiplication and division. You will be provided with such a calculator at the testing center.

Additionally, you will be given scrap paper on which to do your calculations. It is important to note that both the calculator and any paper you use should be left behind as you leave the exam room. Upon completion, leave all scrap paper and return your assigned calculator to an exam proctor.

As for which version of the TEAS is tougher, there is no difference; they are both at the same level. However, there were some adjustments made to ensure that what is being tested currently corresponds to the standards of academics taught in high school and to the level of understanding students are expected to have as they graduate from high school.

Items You Should Bring With You to the Exam Center

On the day of the test, you should take with you a state-issued ID like a driver's license. If you are taking the exam at the school you have been attending, you can present your student ID. You must also turn in a confirmation that you are scheduled to take the test. Those are the only items you are allowed to take with you to the exam center, and they are for the purpose of identification.

The Format of the TEAS VI

The ATI TEAS VI is entirely multiple-choice and timed. To ensure you can complete the test within the time allowed, you must do plenty of timed practice tests before you take the actual exam. This guide provides you with four full practice tests.

It is also important that you pay close attention to the explanations given in the answer section of this study guide. The answers give you a pretty good idea of what kind of information you need to include in your answer to earn a good score.

As you practice with the tests in this guide, you'll be able to isolate areas of strength and weakness. Work on improving your weaknesses, using this guide as one way to help.

Number of Questions and Time Allocated

The ATI TEAS VI has four sections. Although the length of the TEAS exam has remained unchanged from previous versions of the exam, the time allocated to each particular section is now slightly different.

Reading section – 53 questions, 64 minutes

Only 47 questions will be scored.

Mathematics section – 36 questions, 54 minutes

Only 32 questions will be scored.

Science section – 53 questions, 63 minutes

Only 47 questions will be scored.

English and Language Usage – 28 questions, 28 minutes

Only 24 questions will be scored.

In total, the test comprises 170 multiple-choice questions. You will have 209 minutes (3½ hours) to take the full exam.

Scoring of the ATI TEAS VI

The total number of questions scored is 150, while the other 20 questions are meant to help the ATI improve on future versions of the exam by assessing the kind of questions best included in the TEAS and which ones appear excessively challenging.

You will receive your scores within 48 hours of taking the exam. The scores will automatically be sent to the nursing program of your choice.

Significance of the TEAS Scoring System

Generally, the TEAS score serves as a dependable tool in the evaluation of a candidate's suitability for admission to a given nursing program. The nursing program's admission panel will compare your performance to the demands of its curriculum to decide whether or not you are a good fit for the program. The test's scoring highlights both your strengths and weaknesses for each section. This way, a nursing program can tell, for example, if English is your strongest area, while math is your weakest. The test also has a total score, in addition to individual scores for each section.

Chapter 2: English & Language Usage Section

In this chapter, you will learn the requirements of the English Language & Usage section of the test, and the nature of the questions you should anticipate.

English & Language Usage

English & Language Usage is similar to other standardized tests you may have previously taken, but this test does not require you to write an essay.

If you're wondering why English and language skills are pertinent to a nursing career, it comes down to communication. In the medical field, you will communicate on a day-to-day basis with a wide range of people, mainly patients and your colleagues. Whether you are filling out a patient's chart, reading a medical order, explaining a procedure or treatment to a patient, etc., clear communication is absolutely critical, as miscommunication can cost a patient his or her life. Clear communication means being able to speak and write clearly and coherently in response to the variety of situations you will encounter daily while on the job.

Vocabulary

In this category of English & Language Usage, you should anticipate questions that test your reading comprehension. Questions in this category seek to gauge how good you are at defining words within given contexts. You will be expected to know how to restructure a given piece of text and be able to present it in a manner that makes it easier for a reader to comprehend.

You will be tested on your knowledge of prefixes and suffixes, and the effect they have on various root words. You will also be tested on vocabulary, punctuation, spelling and other general writing conventions.

Parts of Speech

As a candidate aspiring to join a nursing program, you need to be able to recognize nouns, pronouns, verbs, adverbs, adjectives, conjunctions and prepositions within a sentence. Consider how some sentences can have their meaning drastically altered depending on how a conjunction is used, and you will understand the purpose of this part of the test. In nursing, accurate delivery of information is of paramount importance. That requires you to be able to clearly communicate both verbally and in writing.

Some of the questions asked in the TEAS VI seek to establish if you can identify when the subject-verb agreement is incorrect. Other questions assess whether you can differentiate a dependent clause from an independent one. You will also be tested on the use of formal versus informal language.

How to Approach the English & Language Usage Section

Bear in mind that you cannot afford to take more than a minute on any question in this section. With that in mind, consider the following tips.

Analyze the Content

If there's a passage to read, first, quickly skim through it and making a few mental notes of information you already know. For instance, you may automatically notice certain grammatical errors. Then read the passage thoroughly, followed by the test questions.

You should be able to identify clues within the context. Not all words are used literally. Sometimes you have to be able to read between the lines to capture their full meaning. Punctuation marks may also be used in ways to indicate that the writer wants you to focus on something specific, such as when a word or phrase is italicized or in quotation marks. Be aware that test questions may ask you to infer an answer, rather than to find one that is written word-for-word in a text.

To do well in this section, you need to practice a lot on punctuation, spelling and sentence construction, with a particular emphasis on the use of conjunctions.

Know How to Use Graphics

You may be presented with a graphic and then asked to answer a question based on it. For this reason, you need to practice gathering information from bar charts, pie charts, graphs and other such diagrams.

You will be tested upon your ability to read patterns in a graph and/or on how well you can use a map key. When, for example, a question is asked about forested areas, and the key shows that forests are indicated by a single tree, you should be able to locate the trees on the map and interpret the desired information.

You could be asked to state the distance between two locations, based upon a scale. This means you should be able to determine if 1 cm on a map represents 100 km on real land, and what the distance is, for example, between a town and a hospital that are 2.5 cm apart on the map.

Predict the Answer

Multiple-choice questions can be tricky. They're designed to not always give you the answer clearly. For this reason, it helps to already have an answer in mind for a particular question before you skim through the choices given.

Imagine that you are being tested on the conventional layout of a textbook. The question might require that you know where to find an alphabetical list of definitions. Even though the term "glossary" may not instantly come to mind, your mental image should flash to the end of a textbook, where such a list is normally provided. Then, when you're looking through the choices, seek out one that matches that initial answer in your head.

Assess All Answer Choices

Once you have decided on an answer, make sure you still read all the choices, just to double-check that you haven't been hasty in your decision.

Chapter 3: The Reading Section of the TEAS VI

Reading comprehension is a vital skill, particularly in a field where you'll regularly be reading complex documents and must then interpret the information to share with patients and/or to create a care plan.

The reading section of the ATI TEAS VI contains a variety of passages drawn from historical, scientific or academic material. You should be able to differentiate between when an author is presenting facts, narrating events or providing a personal opinion.

Text Sources

Primary Sources

Primary sources are firsthand documentation of events. This includes diaries, emails, letters, works of art and literature, statistical information presented in different forms, including graphs, publications such as journals, census records and other such sources.

Other primary sources include witness accounts, interviews, speeches or lectures, photographs, drawings, paintings and news reports.

Secondary Sources

Secondary sources interpret material received from the original or primary source. Such material is often written by people who never witnessed the events they are writing about, but who have taken the initiative to analyze the primary sources. Such authors then proceed to draw their own conclusions based upon the information contained in the primary source.

Secondary sources include literary criticism, biographies, historical and political analyses and essays.

Tertiary Sources

Tertiary sources are lists or compilations of primary sources as well as secondary sources of material. You should not anticipate finding any fresh material from tertiary sources. Tertiary sources can be best exemplified by encyclopedias, bibliographies, textbooks and almanacs.

Evaluating Sources

Some of the best ways to evaluate information sources include establishing the purpose for a particular passage. Once you know why something was written, it becomes easy to recognize any biases therein.

At the same time, it may help to know the background of the writer to establish his or her credibility. For example, a medical piece written by a doctor will be more reliable than a medical piece written by someone who has never practiced medicine. In the passages used in the TEAS, it helps to focus on if the author was an eye witness or participant in an event, or if the author is reporting something based on other people's information.

As you read, ask yourself the following questions:

- Are the sources current?
- If the sources are secondary, do they rely solely on primary sources, or are there secondary sources used?
- Is the writer a specialist in the field he/she is writing about? If not, has he/she cited expert sources?
- Is there bias in the author's tone or manner of conveying information?
- What stance has the author taken on the issues highlighted?
- Has the author presented varied points of view?
- Has the author provided content that concurs with information on a similar topic from reliable writers or sources?

It also helps to take note of where the information was previously published because some sources have more credibility than others. For example, information sourced from academic papers or journals can be considered credible because such sources are known to be meticulous and to maintain very high publication standards. Even the internet has a range of credible sources as long as you know how to identify them. For example, the Centers for Disease Control and the Food and Drug Administration are reliable sources.

Information Based on Opinion

Sometimes the passages on the test won't contain statistics or other factual information but will just be based on the opinions of people interviewed or read about. Or, the passage could strictly be the author's opinion. An opinion is a person's own judgment of an issue. You must be able to differentiate between opinion and fact.

Information Based on Biases or Stereotypes

Sometimes, opinions provided by an author or by specific characters in the text may be biased based upon strong beliefs or stereotypes held by the author or the narrator. It is important to appreciate that such information may influence a person's capacity to make fair observations or judgments. That can impact how a situation is narrated or reported upon. Thus, being able to identify an author's bias is key to reading comprehension.

When people have strong opinions or beliefs about something, their judgment is likely to be clouded, and it is up to you, as a competent reader, to deduce what the unbiased judgment would be.

The reason you want to pass the TEAS VI is to gain admission to a nursing program, and in the course of your nursing career, you are bound to encounter people who have stereotypical ideas on why, for example, certain modes of treatments are better than others. Thus, being able to recognize bias and stereotypes, whether in person or in writing, is an important part of clear communication.

Kinds of Questions to Anticipate

The questions in this section seek to test integrated knowledge as well as ideas mainly associated with research and fact-finding. That is why you should anticipate questions that require you to interpret myriad sources. Other questions test if you can identify how evidence can be used effectively to support a particular line of thinking or a given argument. Some questions test if you can decipher what argument, specifically, is being presented.

Other questions, in this section, seek to establish if you can identify types of information, and any relationship that may exist between those different source types. There are also questions in this section whose purpose is to test your capacity to infer information, identify authorial intent, note whether an author's conclusions are subjective or objective and your ability to make reasonable deductions.

Be prepared to be asked to read and/or interpret bar charts, pie charts, graphs and different forms of diagrams.

Finally, you will be tested on word usage, grammar and language mechanics. As you read through any passage, you should be able to assess how individual sentences fit into the overall passage. To that end, being able to identify a text's structure and purpose is important.

Simple Reading Techniques

To do well in this section of the test, consider the following tips.

Avoid making assumptions

Do not answer what you think the examiner *wanted* to ask; rather, address what the examiner *actually* asks. In other words, answer the question as it actually is, not as you *think* it might be. Similarly, avoid making assumptions about passages you are reading. Assuming is different from inferring in that you don't need facts to back up an assumption. Inferring, which is what you will be asked to do for many questions, does require you to carefully read a passage and find evidence to support your inference based on context.

Distinguish facts from opinions

Make sure you understand the difference between a passage that is giving an opinion on, for example, a certain historical event, versus a passage that is clearly detailing the facts of the event as it is known to have happened.

Be patient as you read the question

A simple question may sound difficult if read too fast or, conversely, it may appear too simple if you read so fast that you skip over a key word. Read each question carefully and completely. If you're struggling to decide between two answers, reread the question.

Apply the elimination method

Figure out the answers that you know are wrong, and work your way toward determining the ones that can be right until you've eliminated everything except the correct answer.

Notice wording

Pay attention to the words an author uses. They can lead you to notice sarcasm, irony and skepticism, all of which can point to bias.

Be able to identify text types

As you read a passage, you should quickly be able to determine whether it's an index, a glossary, a text from an encyclopedia, etc.

Writing Types

The reading section has a good number of passages, and not all of them are the same type. While there is no writing for you to do in the exam, it helps to understand the categories of writing, and how they are different from one another. The more you understand about textual structure and purpose, the better your comprehension. In short, you need to be able to determine whether a passage is narrative, expository, persuasive, entertaining, etc.

You should also be able to distinguish when the author is using the first person, second-person or third person. These three perspectives are denoted by the use of "I," "you" and narration, respectively.

Narrative Essay

A narrative tells a story, and each event typically builds from the next. A narrative has some center around which the story is woven. If you read a piece of text where all characters and events keep revolving around one theme, you are most likely dealing with a narrative. A narrative essay usually adopts the five-paragraph format.

In a narrative, a writer will often share personal experiences. You should expect to find details that the author provides to help you understand those experiences better. Sometimes, this might involve flashbacks or other similar stylistic devices that you should be able to identify.

A narrative text often states its point (purpose) in the very first sentence of a passage.

Narratives will include a plot, characters, settings and conflicts, all moving steadily toward a climax and an ultimate resolution of events.

A narrative is told from a given viewpoint; it makes a point and supports it; it has many details and makes use of clear verbs, adjectives and other modifiers. Narratives may or may not be told sequentially. Sometimes they include dialogue.

Expository Essay

In an expository essay, the author introduces a topic and explains it, while providing a foundation to help you understand the ideas later presented.

The term "expository" is derived from the verb "expose." Expository (explanatory) writing includes essays, articles, instruction manuals, textbooks, etc. The goal of all these texts is always to explain something to a reader. This may include providing necessary definitions, examples, comparing and contrasting, and analyzing cause and effect.

Structurally, an expository essay often starts with a thesis statement and then proceeds to methodically prove the thesis.

Persuasive Essay

In a persuasive essay, the author goes all out to convince you to accept his/her position as valid. This kind of writing makes careful use of words, choosing the ones with the greatest impact so that, hopefully, at the end of the essay, a reader is convinced of the author's point of view.

Good persuasive essays are well researched, and so you should be able to identify these facts even as you note biases, which clarify what is influencing the writer's thoughts. You should be able to identify both sides of the argument the author makes, knowing what the author stands for and what he/she is against. At the end of the reading, you should be able to succinctly summarize your own opinion on whether you agree or disagree. In other words, were you persuaded by the essay?

Persuasive writing can be found in editorials, newspaper columns, magazines, marketing material, etc. Authors could be trying to persuade you about a particular political stance, for example, or they could be trying to get you to buy something.

Technical Essay

A technical essay conveys information that is precise and often on a specified topic. You can usually identify a technical essay from the formality of the writing style, which is usually geared towards teaching something specific and issuing instructions, directions or guidelines that are very specific.

Authors of technical essays have purposes that are entirely different from those of authors of narratives, persuasive essays, etc.

Technical essays are often found in journals, reports and briefs. Common topics of technical essays include engineering, biotechnology, aerospace developments, manufacturing, etc.

Technical essays don't necessarily have to be lengthy. They could be emails, policy statements, press briefs, etc. If the text you are reading teaches you how to perform a task or how to use something, it is very likely to be a technical piece of writing.

Chapter 4: The Science Section of the TEAS VI

In this chapter, you will learn about the questions in the science section of the ATI TEAS VI. This will help you determine what material you need to study for the test.

Need for Science in the Medical Field

Obviously, science is central to the medical field. Nurses handle medications on a daily basis. Whether calculating dosages, considering interactions between medications or interpreting scientific research, a sound knowledge of science is vital to the field.

Areas of Science Tested

In the science section of the TEAS VI, candidates are tested on things that a person pursuing nursing should know. For example, people in the nursing profession are expected to know anatomy.

Your knowledge of science must be broader than just topics related to human beings. You must have a strong working knowledge of other living organisms and the environment they live in. This is because there are principles of nursing that cannot be understood in isolation, and which can only be understood in the context of the ecosystem as a whole.

You can understand this better if you think of instances of disease outbreak, whether it is a known disease or one that is entirely new, like COVID-19. People in the medical profession need to have some knowledge of how different or similar organisms are and how they relate. Without this knowledge, it can be difficult to predict the likely implications of a disease outbreak in a certain environment or the possibilities of curbing spread.

Nurses are expected to stay abreast of new publications in the medical field so that they can be of help when supporting doctors, researchers and other medical professionals. Nurses are the professionals nearest to the patients most of the time, and someone with a good science background is more likely to understand patients' changing vitals, for example, and to know how to react accordingly.

With that understanding, you should be prepared to find questions in this section related to anatomy, body systems and other topics pertaining not only to biology but also chemistry.

Kinds of Questions to Anticipate

The science section of the test includes Anatomy & Physiology; Scientific Reasoning and Life & Physical Sciences. The Anatomy & Physiology questions relate to processes of a biological nature that take place in a person's body, how various body systems function individually as well as together. You will be tested on things like the cardiovascular system, respiratory system, skeletal system and immune system.

The questions related to Life & Physical Sciences address different disciplines of science, particularly those associated with the natural environment. That includes chemistry, biology and physics.

In the science section, many questions require that you remember facts. If you are faced with such a question, note the keywords. For example, if the question asks about anything regarding the pumping of oxygenated blood, the keyword "oxygenated blood" should send a quick signal to your mind, reminding you that this question probably has to do with circulation and the heart.

Some other questions ask that you draw a conclusion based upon an experiment described. On the test, whenever there is a reference to an experiment, or you are required to make a deduction, relevant data is provided, sometimes in prose within the question itself, and other times in tabulated form. Other forms of diagrams, such as a graph or a map, can also be used, depending on the nature of the question.

A question on the effect that human behavior has on the habitat, for example, may require an answer based on some geographical features. Remember that as a person looking forward to joining the medical profession, you are expected to have a broad knowledge of various topics and must be able to understand how they interconnect.

Summary on How to Answer Science Questions

When faced with a science question, identify the facts and the keywords. After you have done this, identify the topic under which those facts and keywords are likely to fall. Reread the question part that spells out what the examiner wants you to answer.

If you are required to carry out an evaluation of a given experiment or must make a deduction, certain data will have been provided or a process of the experiment will have been explained. Make sure you read that information carefully when formulating your answer.

Chapter 5: The Math Section of the TEAS VI

Science and math go hand in hand. That's a given. Sometimes the numerical information you need can be as basic as the vitals of a patient, or as central as the exact dosage a patient requires for some specific treatment. As such, in the TEAS VI, a whole section is dedicated to math questions.

Kinds of Questions to Anticipate

The math questions in this section largely cover Measurement & Data and Numbers & Algebra.

Measurement & Data deals with data of a quantitative nature. This data is sometimes in the form of different kinds of measurement units and varying tools of data presentation as well as numerous properties and principles of geometry and statistics.

Under Numbers & Algebra, the questions test your understanding of the properties of an algebraic or numerical nature. This can include word problems, ratios and proportions, estimation, percentages and arithmetic.

Areas Tested in Math

Anyone aspiring to join the nursing profession should be able to read, understand and analyze data. On the test, you must be able to translate actual or real-life situations mathematically so that the examiners know you will be able to find solutions to real-life issues.

Sometimes, as a nurse, you will be required to read the test results presented in graph form and must be able to calculate the dosages of medication. Other times you will be required to interpret the results of research studies. You must be able to work with numbers, to calculate, analyze and derive conclusions.

For these reasons, you need to apply mathematical skills to solve word problems, interpret diagrams, use statistics and understand relationships between given numbers. You must be able to calculate geometric figures or values and appropriately apply measurements. You should also be able to convert values from a given unit into other units.

How to Approach Math Questions

The most important way to handle math questions is to be systematic. The following are tips to help you approach the test questions in this section:

Analyze information & data provided

Mathematics should not scare you when it comes to the questions you will be asked on the test. For starters, you are always provided with pertinent data and information. Sometimes it is provided in tables, figures or other forms. The answer options also have helpful information. Calmly analyze the question and any graphics or data provided.

Be strategic in your approach

Read the question and place it mentally under the topic to which it belongs. This is helpful because if you can identify the topic being tested, all the rules to be followed will come to mind, making it that much easier to answer the question. For example, you need to be able to identify a problem that falls under algebra as opposed to ratios or proportions. That knowledge clues you into what direction you should take to solve the problem.

Establish right away what the question requires

Sometimes students spend time doing careful calculations, only to find out at the end that they solved a question that wasn't being asked. Even when a question looks easy at a glance, like one that begins with 2x = 4, read the entire question carefully. Do not assume the examiner wants you to find the value of x. If you read carefully, you may realize the question demands that you actually find the value of 1/2x. Always answer what the question asks—not what *you* think it asks.

Reevaluate the question

If your answer does not match any of the answer options, reread the question and refer back to any data provided. You are likely to realize you made an error such as putting a decimal in the wrong place when making a calculation, for example.

Subjects Tested in the Math Section

Fractions, Decimals & Percentages

On the test, you will be assessed on your knowledge of fractions, decimals and percentages. With regards to these topics, you need to familiarize yourself with various terminologies used when dealing with numbers, quantities and algebra as a whole. You should be able to differentiate a rational number from an irrational number, positive from negative numbers, integers from non-integers, even numbers from odd numbers and Arabic numerals from Roman numerals. You should also be conversant with squares versus square roots and must be able to identify a perfect square.

Rational Numbers & Arithmetic Operations

The test will contain arithmetic operations involving the use of rational numbers. You need to be able to work with both associative and commutative properties. A good example of an associative process is addition. Among the terms you should know are sum, addend, difference, minuend, subtrahend, product, divisor and quotient.

Comparison & Ordering of Rational Numbers

Just to refresh your memory for the sake of the TEAS math section, positive numbers constitute any number greater than zero. These are the numbers mostly encountered on a day-to-day basis. Nurses will encounter these numbers when performing tasks such as taking patients' vitals, recording dosages prescribed if requested by a doctor and so on.

In math, these numbers are used in addition, subtraction, multiplication and division. A positive is written as it is. i.e., 88. There is no positive or negative sign in front of it.

Negative numbers are below or lesser than zero. They are rarely used in day-to-day operations, although in science you can find them when measuring temperature. A temperature of minus 10 degrees, for example, should be written as -10°C. Notice the minus sign in front of the number, indicating a negative.

Another example of negative numbers used in daily life is at the bank. If you had $20 as your bank balance, but you withdrew $35, your bank balance will show -$15 because $20 − $35 = -$15. Whenever you subtract a number from a smaller number, the outcome will always be negative.

Solving One-variable Equations

Under this topic, you are required to be well-versed in solving equations that have one unknown variable, where the term 'variable' refers to the number within an algebraic equation whose value is not known.

The math involved in such equations is not beyond any high school graduate. For instance, calculations of inverse mathematics require that you exchange two given functions. For example, addition's inverse mathematic calculation is simply subtraction, and conversely, subtraction's inverse mathematic calculation is addition. In the same manner, multiplication is paired with division.

You must practice how to work with different algebraic expressions whose notations include power or exponents; coefficients; terms; operators; variables like x, y, z; and constants.

To solve an algebraic calculation, first, separate the known values from the variables whose value is unknown. Put these on opposite sides, with the equal sign in the middle. Ordinarily, the unknown variable is represented by the letter "x," although any letter can be used.

Shift the numbers whose values are known, the constants, to the right side of the equal sign. You now have the unknown variable on its own, to the left of the equal sign.

Finally, do some inverse mathematical calculation so you are left with only a single unknown variable. For example, if you had 2x, you divide that by 2 to get x after the 2x cancels out.

Multi-Step Calculations Involving Rational Numbers

In addition to being able to solve mathematical problems that require a single step, you are also expected to have the skills to tackle problems that require more than one step. To be able to accomplish this, you need to, first of all, understand what rational numbers are when compared to irrational numbers, which information is necessary, and which is extraneous and what it means for information to be erroneous. All these are terms mostly used in word problems.

There is the potential for any word problem to include information that is extraneous or erroneous; you need to be able to identify it so that you can discard such information. Once you have gotten rid of these two types of information, you can focus on information that is important for solving the question being asked.

Percentage-based Questions

You will be tested on your understanding of percentages. You should understand that a number is deemed a percentage when it is compared to 100. For example, 10 percent, which compares 10 to 100, is written as 10%. You can also have percentages such as 0.25%.

You should be able to convert fractions to decimal numbers and vice-versa, as well as ratios to percentages and vice-versa. Just to recap how to work with percentages, here are some examples.

Just as 10% means 10/100 or 10 ÷ 100, in which case the answer in decimal form is 0.1, 125% means 125/100 or 125 ÷ 100. That remains the principle, irrespective of how big the number being compared to a hundred is.

Working out such fractions is like converting the percentages to decimal form, the same way 10% becomes 0.1. For ease of calculation, keep in mind that any time you divide a number by 100, you need to shift the decimal point two steps to the left. If you are dealing with a whole number like 10, the assumption is that the decimal number is on the extreme right, so that if it were to be indicated, the number would be 10.0. Since the value of the number does not change in such a case, the zero is redundant and is omitted.

If you convert 125% to a decimal number by following the convention of shifting the decimal number two steps to the left, your answer should be 1.25. You should anticipate such questions based on real-life situations like when you buy an item on sale and are given the percentage discount. Such a question may demand that you calculate the new price or the original price, depending on what figure you are given as the "known."

How to Estimate and Round off Numbers

Sometimes you will need to approximate an answer. In such a case, you need to know how to make estimates that do not drastically change the expected outcome and to know the best time to either round up or round down a number. In this regard, you need to practice front-end estimation involving simple addition, subtraction and multiplication. It is also important that you review the rules of rounding off numbers.

Seeking Solutions to Proportion Problems

You must familiarize yourself with terminologies used in this topic like "ratio" and "proportion." You also should understand how the two are related. For example, whereas 1:2 is a ratio that is read as "one to two," proportions are used when there is a need to compare different ratios.

Take a ratio like 4:3. It could represent a situation where 7 students are representing the same school in a competition, out of which 4 are boys and 3 are girls. The same ratio could represent a situation where there is a basket with 7 fruits, 4 apples and 3 oranges. In fact, the same ratio could represent a compound with 7 rental houses, 4 of them with 3 bedrooms and 3 of them with 2 bedrooms.

What these three scenarios demonstrate is that one ratio can provide an infinite amount of information. The reason for this is that a ratio on its own does not convey information on the number of boys or girls representing their school, the number of apples or oranges in the basket, or the number of 3-bedroom or 2-bedroom houses in a compound. All you have is the ratio "four to three" (4:3), which could mean many different things.

For example, if the school sent 12 boys and 9 girls, the ratio would still be 4:3. All you need to do is simplify 12:9 by dividing either side by 3, and the answer will be 4:3.

Varied Ways to Express a Ratio

Using the ratio 1:3 as an example, you can express it in three different ways, and its meaning will remain unaltered. You can express it as 1/3, 1:3 or 1 to 3.

Comparison of Ratios

Whenever you want to compare ratios, write them in the form of fractions. If those fractions are unequal, it means they cannot be taken to constitute a ratio. A good ratio is 1/2 or 2/4 because if you write both in their simplified forms, they will be the same, 1/2.

Ratios & Change Rates

Considering you already know what a ratio and proportion are, you also need to be able to find out what rate of change means in mathematics. In simple terms, the rate of change stands for the relationship between two different numbers, or the qualities they have, and the way those change with respect to one another.

The rate of change is expressed either as a ratio or as a fraction while factoring in the given amount or degree of change. This amount of change is added to those numbers that comprise the ratio. The TEAS often has questions that deal with change rates, frequently involving time and distance, as well as speed. Other math problems under this topic require that you calculate the new price after factoring in a change rate in sales tax.

Translation of Phrases & Sentences into Inequalities, Expressions & Equations

You should be able to mathematically understand what an inequality is, what an equation is, and what an expression is.

An equation is a phrase indicating that two given expressions are mathematically or arithmetically equal. Normally you have one expression on one side and the other on the other side of an equal sign (=).

As for an expression, it is a composition of mathematical or arithmetic numbers, variables or symbols put in a series and grouped meaningfully to bring out some value.

Equalities simply denote that the referenced items have equal value, while the term "inequalities" means the items referenced are unequal.

Chapter 6: How to Prepare for the TEAS VI

As much as it is important to have your science facts right, your math formulas at your fingertips and to be good at English, it also matters how you prepare yourself psychologically. One way of doing this is to ensure you know the TEAS VI exam schedules, the location of the testing center and what is required of you on the test day.

Since the exam is administered every week, throughout the year, you can schedule it whenever it is convenient for you.

Cost & Scheduling

The TEAS VI costs $115 for the test, and if, for some unfortunate reason, you fail to make it to your appointment, you will have to pay the same amount to take the test later, plus an additional $27.

It is important to note that although ATI provides an opportunity for you to take the TEAS VI at any time, some nursing programs monitor the number of times individuals have attempted the exam. Some programs limit the number of times you can take the test while still remaining a viable candidate for their program.

Nursing School Programs' Requirements

It is easier to plan your studies when you know the requirements of the exam. This book will help you with that objective.

The national average for scores is 65% to 75%. Nevertheless, some schools will only admit candidates whose composite score is at least 85%. Keep in mind that the requirements of the school of your interest may not be similar to those of the average school or any other school you know about. Make sure you talk to your desired program or school before you take the test, so you are aware of the score requirements.

Your Options if You Do Not Make the Score

If you do not meet the score for the nursing school or program you applied for, and the school does not accord candidates a second chance, you have two options: one of them is to send your application to a different nursing school, and the other is to choose an entirely new program of study.

Many schools require candidates to wait at least 30 days before retaking the test. Other schools require a wait of two and a half months to two years.

While these requirements may sound tough, there is the advantage that you will have time to study for the test and thereby excel when you eventually retake it.

Exam Day

The TEAS VI is three and a half hours long. You will receive a 10-minute break after completing two sections.

If you need to use the restroom, raise your hand and wait to be granted permission. Be aware that any time you take outside of the official break will count against the time you have to take the exam. Hence, it is to your advantage not to leave the room until you have completed the test.

Practice Test 1: Questions

Reading Section – Test 1

Read the following passage and answer the two questions that follow.

Do you want to contribute to the community to which you belong but have no idea how to begin? One of the finest ways to invest in your community's future is by assisting in the education of youngsters. Schools suffer from underfunding, and teachers are beset by increasing pressure to help students with very scarce resources. We have numerous teacher-designed programs in need of funding. Teachers are best placed to understand what is required to effectively assist students. You rarely get an opportunity to know precisely where your donation goes after you have made your contribution. Send your donation today and participate in changing the lives of students within your own community.

(1) Which of the answers listed below is a unique advantage of the group-based funding program?

(A) Helping to train additional teachers

(B) Knowing exactly where your donation goes

(C) Your donation being tax-deductible

(D) Having your donation help other people

(2) The word "beset" as used in the passage means _____.

(A) Overwhelmed and stressed

(B) Able to excel in spite of the obstacles

(C) Determined to persevere

(D) Likely to give up

Read the following passage and answer the two questions that follow.

Nancy,

I feel it is a good time that we open one more location. This is something we have talked about over and over, and if we fail to fulfill that wish now, we will never do it. I'm aware such a move is risky, but we can only grow our business by taking a calculated risk or two.

Business is booming at the moment, and data based on our particular focus demographic indicates that people in Seattle want to have our store in their biggest mall there. If this is handled well, our business can double its profits. I'd like to hear what your take is on this.

Thanks,

Carol

PS: I'm thinking we could even make the announcement regarding our expansion soon after that funny piece on Channel 4, so we can capitalize on the attention.

(3)   Going by the tone in the memo you have just read, identify the answer with the best description of Nancy and Carol's relationship.

(A)   Carol is Nancy's boss

(B)   Nancy is Carol's boss

(C)   Carol and Nancy belong to the human resources department

(D)   Carol and Nancy are business partners

(4)   The aim of the author is _____.

(A)   To rejuvenate a floundering business

(B)   To expand an already successful business

(C)   To make herself appear as the leader with more clout

(D)   To convince her colleague of the need to do due diligence with a view to opening a second location

Read the following passage and answer the three questions that follow.

Teachers all over the country have begun to notice how important it is to incorporate films within the classroom. Movies are no longer viewed as just babysitting students while their teacher continues work at his or her desk.

Films as teaching mediums are versatile, and they can play the role of textbooks, literary pieces or even art pieces with the capacity to introduce a fresh dimension to students' learning. The teachers who support this position are aware that in order to effectively teach a film, one has to carefully prepare lessons based upon it.

The teacher can decide to turn out the lights and tune into the initial twenty minutes of *Saving Private Ryan* by Steven Spielberg to help support a lesson on World War II. The teacher can then use one lesson to analyze a particular scene with the students, highlighting the way Spielberg develops anxiety and apprehension, along with the way he helps his audience feel attached to characters they are yet to meet.

(5)   With regard to teachers making use of films in class, the author concludes _____.

(A)   Using movies in the class is not helpful to students

(B)   Teachers should be encouraged to show students a scene from *Saving Private Ryan*

(C)   Students can benefit greatly from the use of films as teaching tools if the films are properly utilized

(D)   Films only come in handy as teaching tools for slow learners.

(6)   According to the passage, *Saving Private Ryan* can be used as an effective teaching tool in class. Choose the answer that supports that premise.

(A)   It can help students to enhance their analytical skills as well as their critical thinking

(B)   *Saving Private Ryan* is not helpful when a teacher uses it to babysit students while he or she grades papers

(C)   Too many teachers refuse to use movies in the classroom

(D)   Another good movie to use in teaching a class is *Jaws*

(7) From the context of the passage, the closest meaning of "versatile" is ____.

(A) Something with a heavy rhythm

(B) Something based on reality

(C) Something prone to misinterpretation

(D) Something with multiple uses

Read the following passage and then answer the five questions that follow.

Mahatma Gandhi inspired many people across the world because he was a leader who sacrificed a lot for the Indian people. He led the Indian National Congress, a group that comprised thirteen men within the government of India, who were steadfast in fighting against discrimination and the government's unfair practices of taxation that were oppressive to farmers as well as laborers in urban areas.

Gandhi, alongside his ardent followers, boldly resisted the control the British had over the lives of Indians and chose to rebel against the laws and policies that were unfair and discriminatory. The Gandhi-led group's rebellion irked the British.

In response to the resistance, the British increased their military personnel in India, and that often resulted in people losing their lives. While Gandhi was intent on gaining freedom for Indians, the government of Britain was determined to suppress his struggle and often did that violently.

Due to his resistance, Gandhi was subsequently imprisoned for his "radical" beliefs in 1942. He later captured international interest for going on a hunger strike until the British changed their unfair policies.

(8) Which of the following is an apt description of Gandhi?

(A) Positive-thinking but prejudiced

(B) Positive-thinking and also objective

(C) Negative-thinking and also prejudiced

(D) Negative-thinking but objective

(9) After reading the passage, the most logical deduction is that ____.

(A) Although Gandhi was courageous, he finally failed in his search for justice

(B) The British ended up changing their unfair policies

(C) In the mind of Gandhi, violence as a means of disobedience was only a last resort

(D) Gandhi's followers were very loyal to him and always supported him

(10) Which of the choices listed below indicates the opinion the author held toward the British authority that Gandhi was revolting against?

(A) Bold

(B) Shy

(C) Dangerous

(D) Unfair

(11) The basic argument the author advances in the passage is _____.

(A) Gandhi employed nonviolent methods of rebellion and managed to successfully draw the world's attention to the unjustified practices the British used against India, his homeland.

(B) Gandhi's protests became extreme and the British rulers in India ended up sending him to prison.

(C) Gandhi formed the Indian Congress in order to pass the legislation necessary to amend the country's unreasonable labor policies.

(D) Gandhi employed hunger strikes more successfully than any other world leader.

(12) Which of the answers below represents an opinion expressed in the passage?

(A) The move by the British government to increase its military presence within its colony, India, resulted in the deaths of many people.

(B) Gandhi courageously used civil disobedience of a nonviolent nature to oppose Britain's unjust discrimination of Indians.

(C) Gandhi became internationally famous because of his hunger strikes.

(D) Gandhi took over India's National Congress in 1921.

Read the following passage and then answer the two questions that follow.

When it is time for scientists to perform an experiment, they follow the scientific method. This is a method whose experimentation structure ensures the data is valid. In employing the scientific method, the people carrying out the experiment must begin by stating their purpose. What problem exists? They need to highlight the question under exploration. So as to be certain their experiment is worth being carried out, the people involved are required to first carry out research with a view to establishing if someone else has previously gathered data on the subject of interest.

The people interested in carrying out the experiment can make use of any readily available data to help them come up with a hypothesis. Once they have stated the parameters and expectations of the experiment, they can then carry out the experiment, gather data and make deductions. If people fail to adhere to this scientific procedure, they risk having their data corrupted and drawing conclusions that are not accurate.

(13) The passage has a structure that can be described as _____.

(A) Problem and solution

(B) Sequence

(C) Cause and effect

(D) Compare and contrast

(14) The point of view of the author can be best described as ____.

(A)   We all apply scientific methods on a daily basis although we may not be aware of it

(B)   Too often, researchers apply scientific methods blindly and fail to explore different options

(C)   If the results of an experiment do not provide verification for the experimenter's hypothesis, the experiment has failed

(D)   Making use of scientific procedures is the most appropriate way of ensuring the data you use in your experiment is accurate and valid

(15) After reading the instructions below, answer the question that follows.

From Point A, walk one block west. Next, walk three blocks north. Finally, walk two blocks east. What is your new position?

(A)   Two blocks west; two blocks north

(B)   Two blocks east; two blocks south

(C)   Two blocks south; one block west

(D)   Three blocks north; one block east

(16) If you are reading about China's first emperor, and you wish to establish where the Terracotta Army is referenced within the book, you should look at the ____.

(A)   Afterword

(B)   Table of contents

(C)   Glossary

(D)   Index

Read the following memo and then answer the two questions that follow.

Dear Milli,

I wish to congratulate you for winning the 2018 Employee of the Year award. All of us appreciate your effort and dedication to this company. During the meeting to discuss the potential recipients of the award, members identified you as an obvious frontrunner, based on the long hours you put in and the fact that the team you lead has enabled the world sales to increase by about 11% even while the economy has been slowing down.

The award you have won qualifies you for an entirely different parking spot, a bonus to the tune of $5,000 and a plaque to be put on display close to the company's entrance to the office. Please talk to Wei Loh as soon as possible, to have an official photo taken.

Thank you for your wonderful work,

Mrs. Sheila Mohamed, Human Resources Director

Cabro Construction, Inc.

(17) Going by the information provided in the passage, which of the following statements is factual?

(A) Milli's team achieved an 11% global sales growth

(B) Mrs. Mohamed appreciates all the work Milli does

(C) Milli is committed to the company that employs her, Cabro Construction, Inc.

(D) Milli's new parking space is bound to be far better than the one she used before

(18)   Which of the following answers provides a good description of the author's viewpoint?

(A)   People normally work as a team when conducting business, and it is important that individual effort be recognized

(B)   For people not to leave a company, it is advisable to offer them huge monetary bonuses

(C)   Everyone who puts in hard work and succeeds amid obstacles deserves a reward

(D)   When the economic environment is harsh, the only way a business can survive is if it lays off people

Read the following passage and then answer the three questions that follow.

A spacesuit is made up of many different pieces. The astronaut's chest is covered by its hard upper torso. The spacesuit's arm assembly is meant to cover the astronaut's arms and provide a link with the gloves. Then there is the helmet and extravehicular visor assembly, whose design is meant for protection of the head even as it allows the astronaut to have as wide a view as possible.

The spacesuit's lower torso assembly is meant to cover the astronaut's feet and legs. The parts of the spacesuit that are flexible comprise numerous strata of material, with each of those layers performing a different function. The functions include maintenance of oxygen inside the astronaut's spacesuit and protection of the spacesuit from dust.

Beneath their spacesuits, astronauts wear a garment filled with liquid for cooling and ventilation. There are tubes woven to form a clothing piece that fits tightly and covers the astronaut's whole body except for his/her hands, feet and head. There is water flowing through the tubes to keep the astronaut cool as he/she takes spacewalks.

At the spacesuit's back is a pack referred to as the primary life support subsystem. It contains oxygen to be used by the astronauts as they take spacewalks. The pack is also responsible for the removal of carbon dioxide after the astronaut exhales. Additionally, the pack supplies the suit with electricity. There is a fan that moves oxygen through the astronaut's spacesuit and life support system. Also, there is a tank that holds water meant for cooling as it flows via the liquid cooling and ventilation garment.

(19) Identify the paragraph that explains the manner in which a spacesuit prevents overheating when the astronaut is taking a spacewalk.

(A)   The first paragraph

(B)   The second paragraph

(C)   The third paragraph

(D)   The fourth paragraph

(20) An astronaut suit's _____ helps him/her breathe properly.

(A)   Liquid cooling and ventilation garment

(B)   Hard upper torso

(C)   Primary life support subsystem

(D)   Lower torso assembly

(21) Which of the following answers provides a good summary of the passage?

(A)   There is more to a spacesuit than its capacity to serve as a piece of clothing for the astronaut during spacewalks

(B)   NASA's inaugural spacewalk happened when the Gemini program was ongoing

(C)   Astronauts don an orange advanced crew escape suit both when launch is taking place and as the space shuttle lands

(D)   NASA is in the process of determining the requirements for the spacesuits that will be used when it is time for astronauts to take trips to Mars

Read the information provided below, and use it to answer the question following it.

Esther is older than Rachael. Elsa is older than Rose. Rose is younger than Esther.

(22) The answer which shows Esther, Rachael and Rose in their correct descending order of age is ____.

(A) Elsa, Rose, Esther, Rachael

(B) Esther, Rose, Elsa, Rachael

(C) Rachael, Elsa, Esther, Rose

(D) Esther, Rachael, Elsa, Rose

Read the following paragraph and then answer the two questions that follow.

Doctors normally recommend a blood glucose test, otherwise referred to as a fasting PG test, when a patient hasn't eaten for a minimum of eight hours. This test is generally considered reliable, and its results are not dependent on the age of the patient or how active or inactive the person is. The reason doctors like to use this testing method is that it is not only easy and fast, but also inexpensive.

(23) Choose the answer which means "reliable" in the context of the given text.

(A) Considerable

(B) Benign

(C) Important

(D) Accurate

(24) Very likely, when doctors use the fasting PG test, they want to _____.

(A) Encourage patients to consume less sugary foods

(B) Identify particular blood disorders

(C) Measure the level of glucose in the plasma

(D) Help patients by using less expensive tests

Read the following passage and answer the five questions that follow.

Thomas Paine cannot be considered well-known in comparison to most other well-known founding fathers of our country. Actually, a good number of Americans have not heard of Paine, a corsetiere's son, born in 1737. A corsetiere is a tailor who specializes in making corsets alongside other innerwear. Paine was brought up in rural Thetford in England. When he was young, Paine did several jobs, including being a corsetiere, a sailor and a minister. However, he realized what his real calling was after moving to the British colonies in America.

Paine's unsavory reputation began when he was *Pennsylvania Magazine's* editor, and his prominence rose during the period of political chaos that pervaded the British colonies. In 1776, Paine had a book anonymously published. The book, *Common Sense*, advocated passionately for Britain to grant independence to America. Its popularity grew widespread, and within no time, 200,000 copies were in circulation. When the war started, Paine released several pamphlets referred to as *The Crisis*. The pamphlets that came as the bloody war raged helped to boost the troops' morale. The name "The United States of America" is attributed to Thomas Paine.

As a writer, Paine was extremely gifted, and even Thomas Jefferson and John Adams derived inspiration from his work as they drafted the Declaration of Independence. Later in his lifetime, Paine published other works that were greatly controversial. He ended up being exiled from his motherland, England, and being sent to prison in France because of his publications. In his final significant work, *Agrarian Justice*, published in 1796, Paine suggested a young and elderly people's social security system.

(25) Which of the following answers logically concludes the opening paragraph of the given passage?

(A)   Paine is among the country's founding fathers

(B)   Not only was Paine a gifted writer, but he also ignited the American Revolution

(C)   Were it not for the role Paine played, the Declaration of Independence would never have been written

(D)   It is possible that Paine was able to advance his political standpoints due to his vast range of experience in different jobs

(26) The inference one can draw from the passage's second paragraph pertaining to *Common Sense* is that ____.

(A) It can be considered the most tangible contribution Paine made to the American Revolution

(B) It was responsible for inspiring King George to swear to take revenge against Paine

(C) For inspiration, Paine depended greatly on his experience as a minister

(D) It served to catalyze the American Revolution

(27) The basic argument the author makes in the passage is that ____.

(A) There would have been no American Revolution without Paine

(B) It is important to remember Thomas Paine because of the role he played in the American Revolution

(C) The work Paine did later had more impact than the work he began with

(D) Since Thomas Paine published his works anonymously, he does not deserve to be recognized for his accomplishments

(28) It is easy for the reader to infer that the source of the passage is ____.

(A) A political treatise

(B) A history textbook

(C) A guide for tourists

(D) A history-based novel

(29) Focusing on the last sentences in the third paragraph, the reader can infer that
____.

(A) *Common Sense* was an inspiration to many people

(B) Thomas Paine became a criminal in his later life

(C) The writings of Thomas Paine still influence people in America today

(D) Thomas Paine published his best works later in life

Read the following passage and then answer the two questions that follow next.

Wolfgang Amadeus Mozart was just five years old when he completed his first music compositions. So what are you waiting for? If you want to do something great during your lifetime, it is best that you begin immediately. The world only rewards the people prepared to take some risks. By the time Mozart was five years of age, he had already begun his journey toward becoming a legend; what is stopping you from becoming one in your own right?

(30) Which of the following answers supports the argument presented in the passage's opening paragraph?

(A) According to Stanford researchers, if you follow your passion, you will have less success in your life

(B) At the age of about 30 years, Wolfgang Amadeus Mozart started to become deaf, and by the time he was 40 years old, he was totally deaf

(C) Pablo Picasso's first words were "piz, piz," which is short in Spanish for "pencil." By the time he was seven years old, Picasso had already started to formally receive training in oil painting as well as figure drawing

(D) Children whose talent is discovered early in their lives do not often fulfill their potential

(31) If this passage had been advertising either a college or a school, which of the
following answers would have been a suitable conclusion to the passage?

(A)   The world needs doctors; as such, you ought to begin trying to become one

(B)   Irrespective of what your wish in life is, you must attend school

(C)   Mozart did not hesitate; you also should not

(D)   Come and join our school today and achieve your dreams

Read the following passage and then answer the six questions that follow.

The One-Hundred-Dollar Bill

Susan quickly glanced at her watch as she cycled fast. The clock tower indicated it was
10:57, and that sent panic through her spine. She kept bending even more over the bike,
hoping her legs would pedal faster. Soon, she came to an abrupt halt before a huge
restaurant that bore a bright blue neon sign. Her ears rang and sweat seeped out of her
skin. She locked the bike in a rush and pushed in through the front entrance, whose
heavy doors were made of glass.

"You're late."

Susan stopped for a moment and turned toward her boss, who looked at her sternly,
with lips forming a line. Shaking her head apologetically, Susan said, "I'm really sorry,
Peter. The tires of my bike went flat and I had forgotten my official badge. I had no
choice but to go back for it—"

Peter raised his hand to cut her off. "Just ensure it does not happen another time."

Susan made a ponytail of her hair and hoped the day would get better. Nearly running to
her very first table for that day, she feigned a smile and said hello to her customers. She
politely responded to the questions they posed, although she was still preoccupied with
the disappointment Peter had shown as she walked in the front door.

In spite of her earlier mistakes, Susan put in a lot of effort and tried to be cheerful and
upbeat as she answered questions from customers as best as she could. She forced
herself to keep smiling even when she felt her eyes glazing with tears.

As the first customers departed, Susan's eyes met those of an elderly man who was
within that first group. He gave her a wink and proceeded out the entrance doors. Susan

was confused, and as she started to collect the dishes that were on the table, her eyes landed on a $100 bill. She allowed a stream of tears to fall at last. It was evident her day had begun to get better.

(32) The kind of writing "The One-Hundred-Dollar Bill" exemplifies is _____.

(A) Biography

(B) Educational

(C) Essay

(D) Narrative

(33) From the second and third paragraphs, it is possible to tell the kind of relationship that exists between Susan and Peter. Which option best represents it?

(A) Susan is stressed to see Peter disappointed

(B) Peter is an unfair boss

(C) Peter has a habit of treating Susan badly

(D) Peter is not interested in what Susan does

(34) Which of the following indicates what the passage's main topic is?

(A) How generous people are within society

(B) The kind of relationship Peter and Susan have

(C) The challenges of having a bike as one's sole means of transport

(D) The successes and challenges of Susan's ordinary workday

(35) The main purpose of the passage is _____.

(A) To issue a warning against laziness

(B) To educate the readers about proper work etiquette

(C) To narrate a story of hope based on a waitress who seemed unlucky

(D) To persuade readers to be generous with their tips

(36) From the passage, one can infer that ____.

(A) Susan's work trouble is because of laziness

(B) Peter is the one who caused Susan trouble

(C) Susan's job is the only way she can pay her bills

(D) The man who tipped Susan generously was her friend

(37) Which of the following best describes the role of Susan in the passage?

(A) The antagonist

(B) The narrator

(C) The protagonist

(D) The heroine

Read the following passage and then answer the four questions that follow.

To the person concerned,

After a comprehensive review of the piece of work you submitted, we are of the opinion that the work does not fulfill the requirements for the literary journal. We are delighted you showed interest in contributing to the journal and urge you to review our guidelines and resubmit a piece of writing next year.

We hope to receive a piece of work from you again in the near future. Best of luck!

– Midland School Review Panel

(38) What purpose does the passage serve?

(A) To let students know it is not easy to have work accepted in a literary journal

(B) To let a student know his work was not accepted for publication

(C) To inform a student he has been accepted for a journalism internship

(D) To persuade students to submit pieces of work for publication

(39) From the supporting explanation in the passage, one can infer that the work the student submitted _____.

(A) Was too long for the journal

(B) Contained inappropriate content

(C) Did not meet all the requirements of the journal

(D) Should've been reviewed prior to resubmitting

(40) For the student to have his work accepted the following year, he must _____.

(A) Write another poem from scratch

(B) Submit the same work again but to a different member of staff

(C) Submit his work to a different journal

(D) Read the guidelines for the journal again and then submit work that complies with them

(41) The letter can be categorized as _____.

(A) Fiction

(B) Persuasive

(C) Nonfiction

(D) Expository

Read the passage and then answer the three questions that follow.

Edna and Beatrice each bought a bike in preparation for college. Considering the price of gas was on the rise, they reasoned that their purchases were justified and that as they would be staying on campus, there would be no need for cars. However, their mother had a different opinion, feeling that they would be better off having a car to share, so she gave them one as a present. Subsequently, Edna and Beatrice decided to return one of their bikes so that they had one bike and one car to share between them. By keeping one bike, they reasoned they could still save some money.

(42) The main topic of the passage is ____.

(A) The benefits public transport has over cars

(B) The transport-related decisions made by Edna and Beatrice as they headed to college

(C) How to be successful in completing one's college freshman year

(D) Edna and Beatrice's mother

(43) Edna and Beatrice's mother would agree with which of the following statements?

(A) It is optional to have a car in school

(B) The university encourages students to have personal cars

(C) A car is unnecessary for students

(D) A car is necessary for students

(44) The type of structure used in the passage is ____.

(A) Compare and contrast

(B) Sequential

(C) Cause and effect

(D) Descriptive

Read the next passage and then answer the nine questions that follow.

Education on political matters has many purposes. It can be said to be the rehearsal a citizen undergoes to become a responsible person who can participate in his or her country's national endeavors until the country attains its socio-economic goals. The main socioeconomic goals India has are bringing poverty to an end as well as modernizing society.

During the colonial era, the leadership within the Indian congress made an argument regarding the importance of political education, emphasizing that it was a crucial part of the country's education. Congress refused to embrace the official standpoint that it is not suitable to mix education with politics. However, in 1947 when it was their time to take the reins, the policy they adopted was similar to that of the British. They labeled politics as 'defiling' education.

Nevertheless, despite this call, politics had a way of infiltrating the sector of education considering every politician competes against the others to win the minds of not just the teachers but also of students. Those academicians who were wise tried to attract political assistance while still guarding against the interference of a political nature. The reality is that the sector of education has received endless political meddling with extremely little sincere political help. This manner in which political parties influence the sector to gain mileage cannot in any way be considered educating people politically, and when one considers how elitism is growing everywhere, it is not surprising that true political tutoring in the country's school system, meaning development towards social change, has become even milder than during the colonial era.

In that era, the fight to gain freedom ended and with that came the disappearance of the main non-official agency that advocated for political education. Though the press provided a bit of political education, it did not make maximum use of the chance they had, continuing instead to be dominated by parties with a vested interest. That was the same case with the various political parties as well as every other institution and agency beyond the education arena, which one would have considered suited to offer political education.

With everything considered, one can see clearly that progress has not been made at all in real political education after the post-colonial era, and this education has instead retrogressed in some respects. This is evident from the way the country's education environment now favors the elite, and patriotism is not rewarded. The nation's founder offered us the boldness to resist government if ever it is found doing wrong, but in a respectable manner and based on principles. Now, even that courage to resist the fundamental values, while maintaining a dignified manner, is non-existent, and what has become prevalent is confrontational politics and chaos, for the aggrandizement of individuals, groups or parties.

Of late, the system of education has continued to encourage dominancy of the advantaged groups as the poor become domesticated. This state of affairs is not going to change unless we undertake rigorous measures to offer effective political education to an adequate level. This constitutes one among those major reforms required in education, and in case its implementation is missed out, continuing to expand the formal system of education on a linear scale will just help to entrench the dominance by the privileged and suppression of the disadvantaged even as it hampers radical social change.

(45) Identify the word whose meaning is almost the opposite of "defiling" in the context of the passage.

(A) Sanctification

(B) Disparagement

(C) Degenerating

(D) Forging

(46) Based on the passage, state the major role political education plays.

(A) To bring up a generation that is highly intelligent

(B) To continue the goals of elitism

(C) To develop an egalitarian society

(D) To make quality changes across the whole education sector

(47) After India's independence, what relationship did politics and the country's educational institutions develop?

(A)   The institutions received political help but no interference from politicians

(B)   The institutions were interfered with but did not receive any meaningful political help

(C)   The institutions received political help and also were interfered with by politicians

(D)   The institutions neither received political help nor were interfered with by politicians

(48) According to the passage, the main problem in the current Indian education system is _____.

(A)   It encourages dominance by the privileged minority

(B)   It is greatly hierarchical yet still egalitarian

(C)   It mimics the model used in Britain

(D)   It is generally representative of the disadvantaged groups in the country

(49) Identify the word from the list below whose meaning is the opposite of "hampers."

(A)   Fosters

(B)   Accelerates

(C)   Initiates

(D)   Envisions

(50) Which of the following words has the same meaning as the word "rehearsal" as used in the opening line of the passage?

(A) Politics

(B) Grilling

(C) Preparation

(D) Wooing

(51) In place of the phrase "colonial era," the author could have written _____ to mean the same thing.

(A) Colonial celebration

(B) Colonial education period

(C) Pre-independence

(D) Post-independence

Read the next sentence and then answer the question that follows.

"However, in 1947, when they took over power, the policy they adopted was almost similar to that of the British."

(52) Who does the pronoun "they" stand for in the passage?

(A) The British

(B) The Indians

(C) The Queen of England

(D) The teachers

(53) The phrase "aggrandizement of individuals, groups or parties" as used in the passage means _____.

(A)   Individuals, groups and parties took actions that were self-serving

(B)   Individuals, groups and parties were glad to work together

(C)   Individuals, groups and parties built grand apartments all over India

Individuals, groups and parties all became political agitators

Math Section – Test 1

(1) What is 8 – 27?

(A) 0

(B) -35

(C) 19

(D) -19

(2) What do you get from 1,078 + 0?

(A) 2,156

(B) 1,078

(C) 1,079

(D) 0

(3) Calculate the following: 3 + 1 – 5 + 2 – 6.

(A) 17

(B) -9

(C) -5

(D) 0

(4) What do you get when you divide 762 by 127?

(A) 8

(B) 9

(C) 6

(D) 4

(5) Using ЛI as 3.14, calculate the circumference of a coin if its area is 11 mm². Round off your answer to the nearest 1/10 of 1 mm.

(A) 5.7

(B) 11.9

(C) 17.0

(D) 11.4

(6) Which of the following decimals is the smallest?

(A) 0.687

(B) 0.786

(C) 0.768

(D) 0.876

(7) Solve the unknown in the following equation: $3(y + 1) + 2(y + 1) > 5(3 − y) + 4(y + 2)$

(A) $y > 1$

(B) $y = 0$

(C) $y > 3$

(D) $y > 2$

(8) Solve the unknown in the following equation: $-6x = 36$

(A) 30

(B) -216

(C) 42

(D) -6

(9) Calculate the ratio of blue cars to red or blue cars if there are 120 red cars and 230 blue cars.

(A) 35:23

(B) 23:35

(C) 12:35

(D) 12:23

(10) Calculate the acceleration rate of a truck if its initial speed was 60 mph and the final speed was 100 mph.

(A) 40%

(B) 67%

(C) 33%

(D) 17%

(11) If Jack's house is situated at coordinates (15, 30) and Mike's house is 100 meters away from Jack's house, what are the coordinates for Mike's house?

(A) (115, 30)

(B) (115, 15)

(C) (15, 30)

(D) (30, 15)

(12) Calculate the height of a right triangle in inches if the base is 6 inches, the hypotenuse is 10 inches and the triangle's area is 24 inches squared.

(A) 6 inches

(B) 4 inches

(C) 10 inches

(D) 8 inches

(13) Calculate a company's total loss or profit in a week if it reported a $300 loss each day on Tuesday and Wednesday, a $100 loss on Monday, a $400 profit on Saturday and a $600 profit each day on Thursday and Friday.

(A) $1,400

(B) $600

(C) $2,300

(D) $900

(14) Calculate the average points in a ball game if the points for the 10 turns played were recorded as -5 points, 4 points, -7 points, -2 points, 0 points, 3 points, 5 points, -6 points, -4 points and 2 points.

(A) -1

(B) 2

(C) -2

(D) 1

(15) If the lowest point of a hill is recorded as -80 ft and the highest point is recorded as 1,450 ft, calculate the difference between the two points.

(A) 1,430 feet

(B) 1,370 feet

(C) 1,5670 feet

(D) 1,530 feet

(16) Convert 19:20 hrs into 12-hour time.

(A) 7:20 a.m.

(B) 6:20 a.m.

(C) 7:20 p.m.

(D) 6:20 p.m.

(17) Convert 18 m to mm.

(A) 1,800 mm

(B) 18,000 mm

(C) 180,000 mm

(D) 180 mm

(18) Calculate the following: 2/3 · 5/8

(A) 10/12

(B) 12/8

(C) 5/12

(D) 5/24

(19) Calculate the value of 3.5 · 0.4

(A) 1.4

(B) 0.14

(C) 13.5

(D) 14

(20) What is the decimal form of 33/80?

(A) 0.345

(B) 0.4125

(C) 4.125

(D) 0.0412

(21) If a pack of tissue is selling at $26.50 from an initial price of $25, what is its percentage price increase?

(A) 0.6%

(B) 60%

(C) 6%

(D) 35%

(22) Calculate 0.3 – 0.03.

(A) 0.3

(B) 0.027

(C) 2.7

(D) 0.27

(23) Simplify $(6 + 9)/(6 \cdot 9)$ to its simplest fraction form.

(A) 5/18

(B) 1/9

(C) 0.277

(D) 15/54

(24) Express 9/40 in percentage form.

(A) 2.25%

(B) 22.5%

(C) 0.0225%

(D) 0.225%

(25) Express 48 cm² in m².

(A) 0.48 m²

(B) 0.048 m²

(C) 0.0048 m²

(D) 4800 m²

(26) What time does a 1 hr 25 min-long art class finish if it starts at 09:40 am?

(A) 8:15 am

(B) 11:40 am

(C) 10:55 am

(D) 11:05 am

(27) Calculate the initial cost of a dress whose price after a 40% discount was $42.

(A) $105

(B) $70

(C) $72

(D) $58.80

(28) If 1 kg of sugar costs $3.40, what amount of sugar can you buy using $12?

(A)   35 kg

(B)   3.53 kg

(C)   6.3 kg

(D)   0.35 kg

(29) What is 5.6 expressed as a percentage of eight?

(A)   70%

(B)   25%

(C)   75%

(D)   4.48%

(30) If a 5-cm line is used to represent 4 km of road, what length of road is represented by 8 cm?

(A)   64 km

(B)   10 km

(C)   20 km

(D)   6.4 km

(31) Find y:x if 6y = 7x

(A)   7:6

(B)   6:7

(C)   42:6

(D)   7:42

(32) Find x if x:12 = 4:10

(A) 5/24

(B) 12/5

(C) 5/12

(D) 24/5

(33) If you pour 42.8 liters of oil into two containers in the ratio 7:2, how much oil will be in the smaller container?

(A) 9.51 liters

(B) 21.4 liters

(C) 0.856 liters

(D) 12.22 liters

(34) If Stella, Mike and Carol divide 60 sweets among themselves using a ratio of 4:5:6, what is the number of sweets that Mike took home?

(A) 24

(B) 16

(C) 20

(D) 3

(35) What is 2/7 expressed to the nearest hundredth?

(A) 0.29

(B) 0.3

(C) 3.5

(D) 0.285

(36) Calculate the following: 0.07 · 0.4.

(A) 28

(B) 2.8

(C) 0.028

(D) 0.28

Science Section – Test 1

(1)   Which of the following is a vitamin that a person's body synthesizes?

(A)   Vitamin E

(B)   Vitamin C

(C)   Vitamin A

(D)   Vitamin D

(2)   Trypsinogen is one enzyme that the pancreas secretes, and is then converted to trypsin by another enzyme, _____, within a person's duodenum.

(A)   Hydrochloric acid

(B)   Pepsin

(C)   Protease

(D)   Enterokinase

(3)   _____ is/are responsible for the production of the follicle-stimulating hormone, which enables ovary follicles to mature.

(A)   The ovaries

(B)   The corpus luteum

(C)   The pituitary gland's posterior lobe

(D)   The pituitary gland's anterior lobe

(4)   When a chemical reaction is taking place, as illustrated here, what does X represent?

Sulfuric acid + X = salt + water + carbon dioxide

(A)   Potassium

(B)   Copper (II) oxide

(C)   Sodium carbonate

(D)   Magnesium hydroxide

(5)   There is a ball tied to a pole using a rope, and it is making a circular movement at a speed that is constant. Which of the following statements is true regarding the ball?

(A)   No acceleration is involved

(B)   The force is moving away from the circle's middle

(C)   The force is moving toward the circle's middle

(D)   The force is moving at a circle's tangent

(6)   Which of the following constitutes a fat molecule?

(A)   A single carbon, a single hydrogen and a single oxygen molecule

(B)   3 fatty acid molecules and a single glycerol molecule

(C)   A single molecule of glycerol and 3 molecules of stearic acid

(D)   3 glycerol molecules and a single fatty acid molecule

(7)   Identify the best answer to complete the sentence.

"Enzymes are ____ which work best while at ____ pH or even temperatures."

(A)   Chemical substances, moderate

(B)   Biological catalysts, optimum

(C)   Organic catalysts, lowest

(D)   Inorganic catalysts, maximum

(8)   Which of the following statements is true about the process of fermentation?

(A)   It is an aerobic procedure whereby a solution of sugar is acted on by yeast and releases oxygen as well as alcohol

(B)   It is an anaerobic procedure whereby a solution of sugar is acted on by yeast and releases carbon dioxide as well as alcohol

(C)   It is an anaerobic procedure whereby a solution of protein is acted on by bacteria and produces carbon dioxide as well as alcohol

(D)   It is respiration by tissue whereby carbohydrates are acted on by yeast and produce oxygen as well as alcohol

(9)   Which of the following is true about oxygen debt emanating from strenuous exercise?

(A)   Oxygen debt develops due to lactic acid buildup within a person's liver, requiring storage of massive amounts of oxygen

(B)   Oxygen debt develops following acetic acid buildup within a person's muscles, requiring oxidation of high levels of oxygen

(C)   Oxygen debt develops following lactic acid buildup within a person's muscles, requiring oxidation of high carbon dioxide levels

(D)   Oxygen debt develops owing to lactic acid buildup within a person's muscles, requiring oxidation of high levels of oxygen

(10) Which of the following is true when related to facilitated diffusion within the membrane of a cell?

(A) It constitutes a type of active transportation requiring trans-membrane or carrier proteins

(B) It constitutes a type of active transportation requiring protein pumps

(C) It constitutes a type of passive transportation not requiring trans-membrane or carrier proteins

(D) It constitutes a type of passive transport, meaning one where energy is not directly consumed like in ATP hydrolysis, requiring trans-membrane or carrier proteins

(11) The bones known as phalanges are found in the _____.

(A) Fingers and toes

(B) Fingers

(C) Ears

(D) Skull

(12) Which of the following pertains to the human joints known as ball and socket?

(A) These joints are bi-axial; they are mobile and allow movement within two different planes

(B) These joints are uni-axial; they are mobile and allow movement within one axis and one plane

(C) These joints are uni-axial; they are greatly mobile and allow rotation, where movement is around one central axis

(D) These joints are multi-axial; they are greatly mobile and allow movement within several axes as well as planes

(13) A ball and socket, hinge, pivot and plane all can be described as ...

(A)   All these joints are synovial

(B)   Apart from the synovial ball and socket, all the others are fibrous joints

(C)   While the ball and socket and the pivot are synovial, the plane and hinge are cartilaginous joints

(D)   All these joints are cartilaginous

(14) Which of the following are features of cardiac muscles?

(A)   Striated and involuntary with no intercalated discs

(B)   Striated and voluntary with intercalated discs

(C)   Striated and involuntary with intercalated discs

(D)   Unstriated and involuntary with intercalated discs

(15) Choose the answer with the best words to fill in the gaps within the sentence.

"The function of a person's hepatic portal vein is to carry blood that is ____ and _____ from his/her _____ to his/her _____."

(A)   Deoxygenated, nutrient-filled, liver, stomach

(B)   Deoxygenated, nutrient-lacking, liver, intestines

(C)   Deoxygenated, nutrient-filled, intestines, liver

(D)   Oxygenated, nutrient-filled, intestines, liver

(16) Brachiocephalic veins are created when two different veins, the ____ and the ____, unite.

(A)   Internal jugular veins, subclavian veins

(B)   External jugular, internal jugular veins

(C)   External jugular veins, subclavian veins

(D)   Common carotid, subclavian veins

(17) A person's lymphatic system has two major vessels that are formed after the uniting of his/her large lymphatic trunks. These two major vessels are the ____ and _____.

(A)   Right lymphatic duct, left subclavian vein

(B)   Thoracic duct, superior vena cava

(C)   Left lymphatic duct, thoracic duct

(D)   Right lymphatic duct, thoracic duct

(18) Which of the organs listed below cannot be considered lymphoid?

(A)   Liver

(B)   Spleen

(C)   Tonsils

(D)   Thymus

(19) Which of the following does not belong to the central nervous system?

(A) The spinal cord

(B) The tract

(C) The cranial nerves

(D) The brain

(20) Which of the following structures is not part of a person's rib cage?

(A) The lumbar vertebrae

(B) The costal cartilage

(C) The sternum

(D) The thoracic vertebrae

(21) Which of the following is considered the heart's pacemaker?

(A) AV node

(B) SA node

(C) Muscle fibers of the atria

(D) Cardiac plexus (nerve fibers)

(22) In between a person's left atrium and left ventricle is a valve known as the ____.

(A) Tricuspid valve

(B) Pulmonary valve

(C) Mitral valve

(D) Aortic valve

(23) Which of the following has a skin layer which contains hair follicles, nerves and sweat glands?

(A) The dermis

(B) The basal layer

(C) The epidermis

(D) The subcutaneous layer

(24) Which of the following is necessary for thyroxine to be produced normally?

(A) Iodine

(B) Calcium and vitamin D

(C) Magnesium

(D) Phosphorus

(25) Fill in the gaps in the sentence with the appropriate word choices.

Vitamin A, also referred to as ____, is a _____ vitamin, and a deficiency of the vitamin can easily cause _____.

(A) Calciferol, fat-soluble, osteoporosis

(B) Retinol, fat-soluble, night blindness

(C) Ascorbic acid, water-soluble, night blindness

(D) Retinol, water-soluble, osteoporosis

(26) Which of the following exemplifies an illness associated with malnutrition due to a lack of protein?

(A) Scurvy

(B) Kwashiorkor

(C) Anemia

(D) Rickets

(27) The process by which food movement takes place within a person's gastrointestinal tract is known as _____.

(A) Voluntary muscles' peristalsis

(B) Contractions' voluntary waves

(C) Peristalsis involving the circular and longitudinal muscles

(D) Peristalsis involving just the longitudinal muscles

(28) In the human body, amylase has the function of _____.

(A) Breaking down starch to become a simpler form of sugar

(B) Breaking down fat to become glycerol

(C) Breaking down proteins to become amino acids

(D) Breaking down fat to become fatty acids

(29) Which of the following statements about the gastrointestinal tract is untrue?

(A) The large intestine does not produce enzymes

(B) Villi present within the large intestine take in water as well as mineral salts

(C) Villi have lacteals meant to absorb fat

(D) The ileum takes in vitamin B12 as well as bile salts

(30) Choose the answer that most correctly completes the sentence.

"Red blood cells have a life span of ____, and when they break down they produce ____."

(A) One year, oxyhemoglobin

(B) Six months, ammonia

(C) Four months, bilirubin

(D) Two months, biliverdin

(31) Choose the answer that most correctly completes the sentence.

"T cells develop and mature within the _____."

(A) Spleen

(B) Bone marrow

(C) Lymph nodes

(D) Thymus gland

(32) Which of the following is a false statement about blood cells?

(A)   Once red blood cells mature, they become oval bi-concave discs whose life span is 120 days

(B)   Once red blood cells mature, they become bi-concave discs with a central nucleus and can live for an extended period of time

(C)   The white blood cells are bigger and much fewer than the red blood cells

(D)   The most prevalent white blood cells are phagocytes and lymphocytes

(33) Some changes take place in a person's diaphragm as he/she inhales. Which of the following correctly describes those changes?

(A)   There is a contracting of abdominal muscles that makes the diaphragm move upward

(B)   There is a contracting of the diaphragm muscles in an upward direction

(C)   There is a contracting of the diaphragm in a downward direction

(D)   The diaphragm relaxes and becomes dome-shaped

(34) Choose the answer that most correctly completes the sentence.

"There is still some air which remains within a person's lungs after he/she has exhaled; that air volume is termed ___ and it is around ___."

(A)   residual volume, 1.2 liters

(B)   vital volume, 2 liters

(C)   tidal volume; 2.4 liters

(D)   residual volume, half a liter

(35) Which of the following has a pyrimidine base only present in RNA?

(A) Guanine

(B) Cytosine

(C) Adenine

(D) Uracil

(36) Spinal muscular atrophy is a recessive disorder described as autosomal. On the basis of this knowledge, what is the percentage of possibility that if a child's parents are carriers of the disorder, the child won't have a recessive allele?

(A) 50%

(B) 0%

(C) 25%

(D) 100%

(37) If Tom is lying on his belly, his position is _____.

(A) Lateral

(B) Posterior

(C) Prone

(D) Supine

(38) Which of the following is true about boiling but not about evaporation?

(A)   The smaller the liquid surface area, the slower the process

(B)   The cooler the liquid, the slower the process

(C)   Boiling always happens at a particular temperature

(D)   Gas forms on the liquid's surface

(39) The point at which a substance melts or boils is affected by impurities. Which of the following correctly reflects that fact?

(A)   The impurity has the effect of lowering both the boiling point and melting point

(B)   The impurity has the effect of lowering the boiling point and raising the melting point

(C)   The impurity has the effect of raising both the boiling point and the melting point

(D)   The impurity has the effect of raising the boiling point and lowering the melting point

(40) Which of the following is untrue with regard to isotopes?

(A)   Isotopes possess a similar number of protons and electrons in every atom, yet have a varying number of neutrons within their respective nucleus

(B)   Isotopes possess atoms of a similar element but with varying mass numbers

(C)   Radioisotopes are isotopes that have unstable nuclei which release radiation

(D)   An element's isotopes have similar chemical and physical properties

(41) Which of the following is an incorrect statement about the periodic table?

(A) Densities and melting points increase across all groups

(B) With groups of non-metallic substances, reactivity decreases going down all groups

(C) With groups of metals, reactivity increases going down all groups

(D) Atomic size increases going down any group and also across any period

(42) Which of the following properties is seen in any simple covalent compound?

(A) A high melting point and high boiling point

(B) The capacity for conducting electricity even when molten or dissolved in water

(C) Being crystalline solid while at room temperature

(D) Being soluble while in organic solvents such as ethanol

(43) The Law of Conservation of Mass states that _____.

(A) The entire mass of a chemical reaction's products equals the entire mass of its reactants collectively

(B) The entire mass of a chemical reaction's products exceeds the entire mass of its reactants collectively

(C) The entire mass of a chemical reaction's products is independent of the entire mass of its reactants collectively

(D) The entire mass of a chemical reaction's products is less than the entire mass of its reactants collectively, because part of the mass changes to energy in the course of the reaction

(44) When an object made of zinc is immersed in a solution of copper (II) sulfate, _____.

(A) The copper in the solution of copper (II) sulfate is displaced by zinc

(B) Sulfur dioxide is liberated

(C) The copper in the solution of copper (II) sulfate is displaced by zinc, but the blue coloration that was in the original solution remains

(D) There is no change or reaction in the solution as zinc reacts less than copper

(45) Which of the following statements is correct?

(A) Oxidizing agents add oxygen to, or extract electrons from, other substances

(B) Reducing reagents add oxygen to, or extract electrons from, other substances

(C) Oxidizing agents extract oxygen or electrons from other substances

(D) Reducing agents extract oxygen or electrons from other substances

(46) Which of the following causes a body in motion to resist any change?

(A) The body's inertia

(B) The body's acceleration

(C) The body's speed

(D) The body's momentum

(47) Whenever there is a change in the body's gravitational field, it affects one of the body's properties. Which is that property?

(A) Volume

(B) Weight

(C) Mass

(D) Temperature

(48) Which of the following physical quantities is only scalar?

(A) Mass, time and speed

(B) Time, force and velocity

(C) Mass, acceleration and velocity

(D) Speed, acceleration and weight

(49) In a power station fired by coal, changes in energy occur. Which of the following represents the sequence in which some of those major changes normally occur?

(A) Kinetic, heat, electrical, chemical

(B) Heat, chemical, kinetic, electrical

(C) Chemical, heat, kinetic, electrical

(D) Chemical, electrical, heat, kinetic

(50) The sun's center produces a massive quantity of energy through a phenomenon known as _____.

(A) Radioactive decay

(B) Nuclear fission

(C) Nuclear fusion

(D) Chemical reaction

(51) Which of the following is an organ that comprises epithelial tissue?

(A) The heart

(B) The skin

(C) The brain

(D) The liver

Read the next passage and answer the two questions that follow.

The pea plant has the capacity to pollinate itself, which means its sperm and eggs are all from one single plant. Besides self-pollinating, the pea plant can also cross-pollinate, which means the sperm and the eggs are not from the same plant. This information was applied by Gregor Mendel in his study on heredity. He discovered that when he used one plant with the capacity to only produce yellow peas and cross-pollinated it with another plant with the capacity to only produce green peas, the resulting offspring were always yellow peas.

When Mendel didn't interfere with the offspring and allowed them to self-pollinate, his second generation of offspring had yellow and green plants mixed at a 3:1 ratio. As such, it was possible for Mendel to show that there are various traits that are essentially dominant or recessive.

(52) When carrying out experiments in genetics and heredity, why was it crucial for Gregor Mendel to use plants in huge numbers?

(A)   When using many plants, it was possible to show that his results were not accidental

(B)   The pea plant is susceptible to various diseases, and there was a need for many of them to survive to maturity so Mendel could draw the necessary conclusions

(C)   Plants don't have as many genes as animals

(D)   It was not actually important; the pea plant produces a lot of seeds, and Mendel planted all of them so as to observe their behavior

(53) The human mouth has an enzyme known as "salivary amylase" which is contained in the saliva; it is responsible for the breaking down of starch into sugar. Where else in the body, apart from the mouth, is this enzyme found?

(A)   The pancreas

(B)   The small intestine

(C)   The liver

(D)   The large intestines

English and Language Use Section – Test 1

(1) Which of the choices below is a compound sentence?

(A) Although Jane and Mary wanted to dine at the Hilton, they could hardly afford the meal prices.

(B) Because Mary left her purse at home, she could not take Susan out for lunch as promised.

(C) Susan put a lot of effort into her work.

(D) Mary studied geography, but Susan chose to pursue economics instead.

(2) Choose the correctly spelled word to fill in the blank space in the sentence.

Considering the child's symptoms, it is safe to say she ___ has an infection.

(A) Definitively

(B) Defanately

(C) Definitely

(D) Defiantly

(3) Write the sentence in the active voice.

"Many records were broken by African athletes in one season."

(A) African athletes broke many records in one season

(B) We broke many African records in one season

(C) Many African records were broken in one season

(D) Although it was just one season, Africans broke many records.

(4)   Identify the right word to complete the sentence.

"Peter, Tom and Ida collaborated well on ____ final project."

(A)   They're

(B)   There

(C)   Their

(D)   They

(5)   "The students traveled to school by bus."

"Traveled" is a/an _____.

(A)   Adverb

(B)   Noun

(C)   Adjective

(D)   Verb

(6)   "After seeing how meticulous the teacher had been in correcting her essay, Jane concluded that his style of teaching was extremely pedantic."

Identify the meaning of the word "pedantic" from the sentence context.

(A)   A tendency to be lazy

(B)   A tendency to mistakenly identify errors

(C)   A tendency to grade easily

(D)   A tendency to focus on even the smallest of mistakes or details

(7) Identify the verb in the appropriate tense to complete the sentence.

"Victor ___ to Vancouver only once before."

(A) Drove

(B) Has driven

(C) Had drove

(D) Has drove

(8) Identify the type of error found in the following sentence:

"Jane and Jake danced at the party, Jane's mother served as the photographer."

(A) Compound sentence

(B) Incomplete sentence

(C) Comma splice

(D) Fragmented sentence

(9) Which of the following sentences is correctly punctuated?

(A) Tim did not eat fruits: resulting in scurvy.

(B) Lucy attended class regularly however because she did not take notes she scored poorly on the exam.

(C) This morning an elephant walked past the school as lessons continued.

(D) Susan, no matter how often she cooks, James does not eat.

(10) Which of the following compound words is incorrectly hyphenated?

(A) Mother-in-law

(B) Stock-broker

(C) Ex-husband

(D) Twofold

(11) Which of the following has a subject-verb agreement error?

(A) Napoleon's fashion collection is not as popular as before.

(B) The behavior of boys and girls is often shaped by their parents' behavior.

(C) The partying teenagers was getting too rowdy for the local community.

(D) Four scouts were responsible for maintaining order at the camp where a hundred pupils were residing.

(12) Identify the word that gives the best meaning of "egregious" as used in the sentence.

"The CEO was sacked for her egregious error of omission.'"

(A) Unpredictable

(B) Misunderstood

(C) Terrible

(D) Minor

(13) Identify the option whose pronoun-antecedent agreement is correct.

(A) Julia Roberts is considered a great actress. She shot to fame with her role alongside Richard Gere in *Pretty Woman.*

(B) The car was sleek. She was glossy blue on the exterior.

(C) A student must be committed to consistent study in order to pass exams. It cannot afford to miss classes or continuous assessment tests.

(D) The play was very entertaining. They kept us on the edge of our seats.

(14) Which of the words listed below has a plural form that is irregular?

(A) Table

(B) Mouse

(C) Giraffe

(D) Hotel

(15) Which of the following is incorrectly capitalized?

(A) "Is this illness treatable, Doctor?" the worried child's mother asked.

(B) President Nicholas spends a lot of time on airplanes.

(C) Donald Trump, the President of the United States, addressed the press regarding the coronavirus.

(D) He is eager to see the Tower Bridge once he gets to London.

(16) Identify the antecedent in the sentence.

"The Hilton has maintained its popularity in Chicago, Nairobi and several other cities. The hotel is known for hosting dignitaries."

(A) Chicago

(B) Nairobi

(C) The Hilton

(D) Several

(17) "Jubilant, Kipkemboi strode leisurely towards the finish line as he waved to the cheering fans."

In the sentence, the word "leisurely" is a/an _____.

(A) Noun

(B) Adjective

(C) Verb

(D) Adverb

(18) Choose the combination of subject and verb that correctly completes the sentence.

"Jennifer's relationship with her ____ ____ when the latter became a principal at her school."

(A) Brother, built

(B) Brother, grow

(C) Father, improved

(D) Father, improves

(19) Which of the following is in past perfect tense?

(A) Will see

(B) Saw

(C) Has seen

(D) Had seen

(20) The best way to define the word "juxtaposition" is ____.

(A) Similarities between two items

(B) Two items are positioned close together

(C) One item is much larger than the other

(D) Differences between two items

(21) A homophone is a word used to describe similar-sounding words that are different in meaning. Identify the homophones that best complete the sentence.

"If you bake with rich ___ and decorate each cake with a beautiful _____, you will make the elderly visitors very happy."

(A) Floor, flour

(B) Flour, flower

(C) Floor, flower

(D) Flower, flour

(22) Among the few irregular plural words below is the plural form of the word "ox." What is the plural of "ox"?

(A) Oxes

(B) Oxi

(C) Oxen

(D) Oxs

(23) If you combine the words "over" and "worked," you get a compound word written as ___.

(A) Over-worked

(B) Over worked

(C) Worked-over

(D) Overworked

(24) Which of the following is correctly spelled?

(A) Recommendation

(B) Temperacher

(C) Recieved

(D) Conveniense

(25) Which of the following is correctly punctuated?

(A)   Lucy, Penny and Sasha, forgot for a while that studying is vital to obtaining good grades.

(B)   Alex bought his wife, a bible for their wedding anniversary; Richard had no idea what to buy his wife.

(C)   Jane, Lucy and the rest of the team camped at the park for a whole week.

(D)   Susan called her father, to inform him, the semester was to end sooner than expected.

(26) Which of the following correctly capitalizes 'doctor' or 'Dr.'?

(A)   Dr. Bernard was a well-respected surgeon. Nevertheless, his colleagues had no idea the good doctor was destined for fame.

(B)   The Doctor always wears a bright white coat.

(C)   The mother was addressing Dr. Patel, but the Doctor was focused on the crying child.

(D)   "Hello, Doctor," Susan said shyly. The Doctor replied with a smile.

(27) Which of the following is a compound sentence?

(A)   Pamela walked her dog across the neatly mowed park.

(B)   Following his early morning appointment, the professor could not give the first lecture.

(C)   People think Jack and his wife misunderstand each other because the latter only learned English recently.

(D)   James watched TV on Sunday morning and he watched a movie in the afternoon.

(28) Which of the following is written in active voice?

(A)   The vehicle's registration number was discovered to be forged.

(B)   The worms in the grass were eaten by the birds.

(C)   The doctor followed up on the patient's progress until she recovered fully.

(D)   The boy's jacket was bleached when it was still new.

Practice Test 1: Answers

Reading Section – Test 1 Answers

(1)   The correct answer is: (B) Knowing exactly where your donation goes.

The answer is explicit from the sentence, "You rarely get an opportunity to know precisely where your donation goes …" As for (A), this information is not available in the passage. (C) and (D) are advantages common to charitable donations in general, hence, not unique.

(2)   The correct answer is: (A) Overwhelmed and stressed.

The reason (A) is correct is that it aptly describes the feeling experienced by teachers who want to do a good job, yet are unable to do so because they don't have the necessary resources. (B) and (C) express the teachers' resilience, but that is not what the word "beset" represents. (D) is factually incorrect.

(3)   The correct answer is: (D) Carol and Nancy are business partners.

(D) is correct because it portrays a relationship of mutual respect between Carol and Nancy. The use of the word "we," a collective pronoun, indicates that whatever decision needs to be taken is the responsibility of both parties. This argument then renders (A) and (B) incorrect. (C) is incorrect as Carol and Nancy are business partners, based on the decisions they're making, not employees.

(4)   The correct answer is: (B) To expand an already successful business.

(B) is the correct answer because the opening sentence says, "I feel it is a good time that we open one more location." (A) is incorrect as it is said that the business is booming. (C) is incorrect as the language of the passage portrays a position of equals. (D) is incorrect as information is disclosed about data from research already carried out on the business focus demographic.

(5)   The correct answer is: (C) Students can benefit greatly from the use of films as teaching tools if the films are properly utilized.

According to the passage, films can be just as helpful as textbooks and other teaching tools. There is no message like those in (A) and (D) in the passage, and as for (B), *Saving Private Ryan* is just an example of one film among many that can be used as teaching aids.

(6)   The correct answer is: (A) It can help students to enhance their analytical skills as well as their critical thinking.

(A) supports the reasoning behind the use of films as teaching aids, using *Saving Private Ryan* as an example. Although (B) sounds logical, it actually counters the manner in which the use of films is implemented rather than supports its use. (C) and (D) have no link to *Saving Private Ryan*, therefore, they cannot be correct.

(7)   The correct answer is: (D) Something with multiple uses.

The writer explains some of the ways in which films can be used in the sentence, "Films as teaching mediums are versatile, and they can play the role of textbooks, literary pieces, or even art pieces ..." (A), (B) and (C) have no bearing on the passage.

(8)   The correct answer is: (B) Positive-thinking and also objective.

(B) is correct because the author justifies whatever is said about Gandhi, including his disobedience against the British. The author also explains that Gandhi rebelled so that all Indians would be treated better by the British. The resilience the author portrays Gandhi as having is an indication that Gandhi was positive and hopeful about the outcome of his actions.

(9)   The correct answer is: (B) The British ended up changing their unfair policies.

(B) is supported by the passage's closing sentence, "He later captured international interest for going on a hunger strike until the British changed their unfair policies." (A) is incorrect and (D) is not supported in the passage. As for (C), there is no indication Gandhi would have entertained violence under any circumstances.

(10) The correct answer is: (D) Unfair.

The author describes the British policies that Gandhi rebelled against as "unfair and discriminatory." It is the author's opinion, therefore, that the behavior of Gandhi and his followers toward the British was justified. (A) and (C) are used in reference to the oppressed and not the oppressors. The author has mentioned that the group of 13 men, led by Gandhi, "were steadfast in fighting against discrimination and the government's unfair practices of taxation", therefore, (B) is incorrect.

(11) The correct answer is: (A) Gandhi employed nonviolent methods of rebellion and managed to successfully draw the world's attention to the unjustified practices the British used against India, his homeland.

(A) captures the essence of the passage, encompassing Gandhi's advocacy for nonviolent resistance, and his success in getting the unjust policies amended. Although Gandhi was a member of the Indian National Congress and the British imprisoned him, (B) and (C) do not comprehensively cover the passage's main concept. (D) is an opinion and is not supported by the passage.

(12) The correct answer is: (B) Gandhi courageously used civil disobedience of a nonviolent nature to oppose Britain's unjust discrimination of Indians.

(B) is correct as an opinion expressed in the passage, and though the ideas in (A), (C) and (D) are correct, they are factual and not opinions.

(13) The correct answer is: (B) Sequence.

(B) is correct because the text is sequential; it highlights the first step in the process, followed by the second and the next in that order.

(14) The correct answer is: (D) Making use of scientific procedures is the most appropriate way of ensuring the data you use in your experiment is accurate and valid.

(D) is the correct answer since the writer mentions how important it is to apply scientific methods of experimentation. According to the author, it is the only way to get accurate data and therefore be able to draw a credible conclusion. All the other suggestions are not supported by facts from the passage.

(15) The correct answer is: (D) Three blocks north; one block east

Visualize. Once you make one shift to the west, vertically you are still at point zero. When from that one west position you make three shifts to the north, you will still be one west, but now three north. In the final step, shift one takes you back to zero horizontally, and step two takes you one east.

(16) The correct answer is: (D) Index.

An index is a list that has individual words or phrases mentioned in a book, and the page number where each can be found. A glossary does not incorporate the location of individual words or phrases in the book. It only explains their meaning.

(17) The correct answer is: (A) Milli's team achieved an 11% global sales growth.

The reason (A) is correct is that the growth of 11% is quantitatively verifiable data. (B) and (C) do not offer factual information, and so they are opinions. As for (D), the passage does not indicate that the newly allocated parking space will be better; it can only be assumed.

(18) The correct answer is: (C) Everyone who puts in hard work and succeeds amid obstacles deserves a reward.

One of the reasons (C) is the best answer is that it is indicated in the memo that the aim is to congratulate Milli for having won the award for Employee of the Year. It is also noted that Milli's team succeeded in increasing sales revenue when the economy was in a downward spiral.

(19) The correct answer is: (C) The third paragraph.

The sentences that provide the answer are, "Beneath their spacesuits, astronauts wear a garment filled with liquid for cooling and ventilation. There are tubes woven to form a clothing piece ..." The paragraph provides a vivid description of how water flows via tubes within a tight-fitting garment, and effectively keeps the astronaut cool.

(20) The correct answer is: (C) Primary life support subsystem.

The reason (C) is the correct answer is that, in the last paragraph of the passage, it is explained that the primary life support subsystem is the part of the astronaut's spacesuit that helps him/her breathe when taking a spacewalk.

(21) The correct answer is: (A) There is more to a spacesuit than its capacity to serve as a piece of clothing for the astronaut during spacewalks.

The reason (A) is the most suitable answer is its sole focus on the spacesuit and the suit's importance in making the astronaut's trip possible. The first paragraph delves into the make-up of the spacesuit, while the second, third and final paragraphs explain the functions of the various parts of the spacesuit.

(22) The correct answer is: (D) Esther, Rachael, Elsa, Rose.

Place the names of the four people in age sequence. Esther being older than Rachael means you write Esther first and then Rachael. Then move to the fact that also refers to Esther, which is Rose being younger than her, but before writing down Rose write the name of Elsa, who is older than Rose. Or use the elimination method.

(23) The correct answer is: (D) Accurate.

The reason (D) is correct is that the results of the test do not vary according to the age of the patient or any other personal factors. For this reason, doctors find the test accurate and reliable.

(24) The correct answer is: (C) Measure the level of glucose in the plasma.

(C) is the best answer because it is stated in the opening sentence of the paragraph that it is common for doctors to recommend the blood glucose test. This is the only answer that mentions glucose in plasma, so it has to be right.

(25) The correct answer is: (A) Paine is among the country's founding fathers.

In the opening sentence of the passage, Thomas Paine is said to be an American founding father, although he may not be as well-known as many others. The rest of the paragraph is about him as a person, how he grew up and also how he moved to the British colonies in America and became a very influential author.

(26) The correct answer is: (D) It served to catalyze the American Revolution.

In this paragraph it is made clear how strongly Paine felt about America deserving its independence. There is a discussion of the impressive number of copies that his pamphlet sold, which means people were inspired by it as the wave of revolution swept across the land.

(27) The correct answer is: (B) It is important to remember Thomas Paine because of the role he played in the American Revolution.

The author of the passage opens by indicating that Thomas Paine is not well-known, yet he is among the founders of America. The author explains Paine's numerous accomplishments, and the important part he played in the American Revolution.

(28) The correct answer is: (B) A history textbook.

The passage is an extract from a history textbook because it is informative and factual. Had the source been a political treatise, the passage would have been dominated by opinions, and if it was a historical novel it would have contained fictitious information.

(29) The correct answer is: (C) The writings of Thomas Paine still influence people in America today.

Towards the end of the passage, it says that Paine had a great influence on America's social security system. This means people still make use of his ideas when making crucial decisions that affect society as a whole.

(30) The correct answer is: (C) Pablo Picasso's first words were "piz, piz," which is short in Spanish for "pencil." By the time he was seven years old, Picasso had already started to formally receive training in oil painting as well as figure drawing.

The reason (C) is most appropriate is that it reflects the gist of the example given of Mozart in the passage, where a person who recognized his talent early in life pursued it right from the beginning.

(31) The correct answer is: (D) Come and join our school today and achieve your dreams.

The reason (D) is the correct answer is that it serves as a call for you to act in response to the advertisement.

(32) The correct answer is: (D) Narrative.

The passage exemplifies a narrative. Its storyline is linear and is about a fictional character. In contrast, a biography is a story about the life of a real person, while educational work is meant to teach.

(33) The correct answer is: (A) Susan is stressed to see Peter disappointed.

It is clear from the way Susan is distracted as she serves her first customers that she is stressed that her tardiness has disappointed Peter. (B) and (C) are incorrect because although Peter expressed his disappointment at Susan's tardiness, there is nothing to indicate he is unfair or that he treats her badly.

(34) The correct answer is: (D) The successes and challenges of Susan's ordinary workday.

The reason (D) is the correct answer is that the main theme in the passage revolves around Susan's workday, with her source of sadness explained, as well as her source of joy.

(35) The correct answer is: (C) To narrate a story of hope based on a waitress who seemed unlucky.

The passage opens by describing a waitress who was down on her luck as she rushed to work in near panic due to her tardiness. The passage then depicts how Susan's day improves as she is generously tipped by a man. So the passage is about a waitress who, at first, appeared unlucky.

(36) The correct answer is: (C) Susan's job is the only way she pay her bills.

One reason (C) is the correct answer is that it is evident Susan is afraid she may anger her boss if she's tardy, which (we can infer) might mean she will lose her job and not be able to pay her bills.

(37) The correct answer is: (C) The protagonist.

(C) is correct because Susan is the story's main character. (A) is incorrect as Susan is not a character opposing the protagonist. As a character being discussed in the third-person, she cannot be the narrator. (D) is incorrect as Susan hasn't fulfilled any extraordinary feat.

(38) The correct answer is: (B) To let a student know his work was not accepted for publication.

The reason (B) is the correct answer is that the writer explains the details of why the student's work was not accepted, even as he proceeds to ask the student not to give up but to try again the following year. There are no facts to support the other options.

(39) The correct answer is: (D) Should've been reviewed prior to resubmitting.

The reason (D) is correct is that, in closing, the writer of the letter advises the student to ensure his piece meets the submission guidelines next time.

(40) The correct answer is: (D) Read the guidelines for the journal again and then submit work that complies with them.

The reason (D) is correct is that it is clearly spelled out that the student's work failed to meet the journal requirements, and at the end, the student is told, "We are delighted you showed interest in contributing to the journal and urge you to review our guidelines and resubmit a piece of writing next year."

(41) The correct answer is: (D) Expository.

The reason (D) is the correct answer is that the main reason the letter was written was to explain matters to the student in question.

(42) The correct answer is: (B) The transport-related decisions made by Edna and Beatrice as they headed to college.

(B) is correct because the passage dwells on the decisions and actions of Edna and Beatrice pertaining to the best mode of personal transport once they get to college. Their mother is only mentioned as a facilitator and does not feature prominently. The major topic is not about public transport or someone's freshman year.

(43) The correct answer is: (D) A car is necessary for students.

It is true that Edna and Beatrice's mother believes it is necessary for students to have a car at university, but that is not the view of the university, nor is it stated in the passage as a fact. Whether having a car is optional or not is not discussed in the passage.

(44) The correct answer is: (B) Sequential.

The reason (B) is the correct answer is that events are explained in the passage in sequence. Edna and Beatrice buy bikes, their mother offers them a car and they return one bike in preparation to share one bike and one car.

(45) The correct answer is: (A) Sanctification.

The word "defiling" connotes being foul or dirty. Since sanctification means purification, (A) is the correct answer because the question seeks the word with the opposite meaning. "Disparagement" means to slight someone; "degenerating" means to worsen in quality and "forging" means to reproduce something fraudulently.

(46) The correct answer is: (C) To develop an egalitarian society.

The role of political education, based on the passage, is to allow citizens to achieve the country's socioeconomic goals, which include ending poverty while creating a democratic modern society. A society that is egalitarian believes that everyone is equal and deserves the same rights and opportunities.

(47) The correct answer is: (B) The institutions were interfered with but did not receive any meaningful political help.

(B) is correct because people who led the education sector could not resist the pressure from political leaders and parties, and their support was not reciprocated for the benefit of the education sector. This point is encompassed in the sentence, "The reality is that the sector of education has received endless political meddling with extremely little sincere political help."

(48) The correct answer is: (A) It encourages dominance by the privileged minority.

(A) is correct as the passage indicates the current system of education in India encourages dominance by the privileged while subjugating the disadvantaged. The exact sentence where that answer is found towards the end of the passage is, "Of late, the system of education has continued to encourage dominancy of the advantaged groups as the poor become domesticated."

(49) The correct answer is: (A) Fosters.

(A) is correct because the word "hampers" means "hinders," so that something that was to succeed ends up facing challenges and ultimately not succeeding, while the word "fosters" means "enhances advancement."

(50) The correct answer is: (C) Preparation.

The word "rehearsal" is used in reference to the political education process that one undergoes so as to become knowledgeable and responsible enough to be able help the country succeed in its socioeconomic goals. For a person to be ready to do something, he or she must be prepared or well-rehearsed.

(51) The correct answer is: (C) Pre-independence.

(C) is correct because "pre-independence" means before independence and the colonial period existed before India gained its independence from Great Britain.

(52) The correct answer is: (B) The Indians.

(B) is correct because the passage is about the behavior of Indian leaders after the country gained its independence from British rule. The answer cannot be (A) because the British were already in power, and it cannot be (C) because the British authorities acted on behalf of the crown. Teachers were not a political class.

(53) The correct answer is: (A) Individuals, groups and parties took actions that were self-serving.

The passage states that the education system did not become better even after independence, as the political leadership did not provide the support necessary to make the education sector a place for learning. Everyone involved wanted personal benefit.

Math Section – Test 1 Answers

(1) The correct answer is: (D) -19.

In this problem, 8 is less than 27, so subtraction will not directly apply. Instead, apply the rule of $x - y = -(y - x)$ to get $8 - 27$ is equal to $-(27 - 8)$. When you apply that algorithm, you get $27 - 8 = 19$ which means that $-(27-8)$ is -19.

(2) The correct answer is: (B) 1,078.

In basic subtraction and addition problems, adding any given value to 0 should give you that same number.

(3) The correct answer is: (C) -5.

To solve this problem you should use the BEDMAS rule which states that you should first solve parentheses, then exponents, then multiplication, then division and then addition and subtraction. i.e., $(3+1) - 5 + 2 - 6$ will give you -5.

(4) The correct answer is: (C) 6.

This is a problem that can be solved with division. In this case, since 127 is greater than 7 and 76, you should start the division using all three digits.

(5) The correct answer is: (B) 11.9.

The circumference of a circle is ЛI, which is 3.14 multiplied by the diameter of the circle. We are not given the diameter, but the area is given as 11 mm², so $Лr^2$ or $3.14 \times r^2 = 11$ mm². When you solve this you get r = 1.9. Therefore, the circumference is $3.14 \times 2 (1.9)$, which is 11.932.

(6) The correct answer is: (A) 0.687.

To identify the smallest decimal, look at the tenths value of each decimal since the decimal with the lowest value in its tenth place is the smallest number. In this case, 6 is the least among the tenth-place values, so 0.687 is the answer.

(7)   The correct answer is: (C) y > 3.

First solve the equation on both sides: $3(y + 1) + 2(y + 1)$ will be $3y + 3 + 2y + 2 = 5y + 5$ and on the other side $5(3 - y) + 4(y + 2)$ when solved is $15 - 5y + 4y + 8 = 23 - y$, so $5y + 5 > 23 - y$. Combine the like terms to get $6y + 5 > 23$ and then subtract 5 from 23 to get $6y > 18$. Divide each side by 6 and get $y > 3$.

(8)   The correct answer is: (D) -6.

6 and 36 are both divisible by a common number. Divide both sides by 6. So $-6x = 36$. Dividing this by 6 on both sides will give you $x = -6$.

(9)   The correct answer is: (B) 23:35

The first part of your ratio should indicate the 230 blue cars and the second part of your ratio should indicate the total sum of blue cars and red cars, 120 + 230. The ratio should therefore be 230:350. When simplified, you get 23:35.

(10) The correct answer is: (B) 67%.

First get the difference between the two speeds. 100 mph, the final speed, minus 60 mph, the initial speed, gives you 40 mph. To get the acceleration rate, divide 40 mph by 60 mph. Then multiply by 100 to get 66 2/3. When rounded off, this is 67%.

(11) The correct answer is: (A) (115, 30).

Mike's house is 100 meters away from Jack's house, whose coordinates are (15, 30). 15 represents the x coordinate and 30 represents the y coordinate. Add the 100 to the x coordinate, so 100 + 15 = 115.

(12) The correct answer is: (D) 8.

In a right triangle, the height is always given as "a," the width as "b" and the hypotenuse as "c." The area of a right triangle is (a × b) /2. The area is 24, so (a × 6)/2 = 24. When we solve for "a," we get 6a/2 = 24. So 3a = 24. Therefore a = 8.

(13) The correct answer is: (D) $900.

The first thing you should do is create an expression using the information we have been given. -$300 dollars + -$300 + -$100 + $400 + $600 + $600 will give you $900 in profit.

(14) The correct answer is: (A) -1.

Add all the points together, then divide the sum by the number of turns played (10). When you add -5 +4 + -7 + -2+ 0 +3 +5 + -6 + -4 +2 you get -10. So -10/10 is -1.

(15) The correct answer is: (D) 1,530 feet.

To get the difference between the two points, subtract -80 from 1,450. So, 1,450 – -80 should give you the difference. When you have two negative signs before a number, that number becomes positive, so 1,450 feet + 80 feet = 1,530 feet.

(16) The correct answer is: (C) 7:20 p.m.

To convert time from 24 hr clock time to 12 hr clock time, deduct 1200 from that given time. Therefore, to convert 1920 hours into the 12-hr clock time you will subtract 1200 from 1920 to get 7:20 p.m.

(17) The correct answer is: (B) 18,000 millimeters.

In conversion, 1 meter is equal to 1,000 millimeters. To determine how many millimeters are in 18 meters, multiply 18 meters by 1,000. So, 18 × 1,000 will give you 18,000 millimeters.

(18) The correct answer is: (C) 5/12.

First, multiply the numerators. 2 · 5 = 10. Next, multiply the denominators. 3 · 8 = 24. Your answer is 10/24, which gives you 5/12 when simplified.

(19) The correct answer is: (A) 1.4.

A simple way to solve this problem is to first remove the decimals and deal with the figures as 35 · 04 or 35 · 4, which will give you 140. Next, add the number of decimal places, and since they were 2, move the decimal two places from the right to get 1.4.

(20) The correct answer is: (B) 0.4125.

To convert a fraction into decimal form, divide the numerator by the denominator. In this question, the numerator is 33 and the denominator is 80. 33/80 gives you 0.4125.

(21) The correct answer is: (C) 6%.

First, identify the increase by subtracting the new selling price from the initial one. $26.50 − $25 = $1.5. Next, divide that increase by the initial price: $1.5/$25 = 0.06. Multiply by 100 to get the percentage. 0.06 · 100 = 6%.

(22) The correct answer is: (D) 0.27.

Ensure that the decimals are lined up when using column subtraction or addition. To make it easy to subtract, add a 0 in 0.3 to read as 0.30 since the other number has two decimal places. Then subtract normally. 0.3 − 0.03 = 0.27.

(23) The correct answer is: (A) 5/18.

First, find the value of the numerator and the denominator separately and then simplify the fraction. Solve the numerator. 6 + 9 = 15. Then solve the denominator: 6 · 9 = 54. The fraction will be 15/54, and when simplified you get 5/18.

(24) The correct answer is: (B) 22.5%.

To convert a fraction into a percentage requires multiplying that fraction by 100%. In this question, the calculation will involve dividing 9 by 40 to get 0.225. Once you multiply this by 100%, you shift the decimal two spaces to the right because of the 100, and you end up with 22.5%.

(25) The correct answer is: (C) 0.0048 m².

The first thing you need to identify is how many cm² make 1 m². If 100 cm make 1 m, then to get the value in square units you should square both units. So (100 cm)² is equal to (1 m)², which gives you 10,000 cm² = 1 m². So 48 cm² is equal to 0.0048 m².

(26) The correct answer is: (D) 11:05 am.

Convert the 1 hr 25 min into 24-hour time to get 0125, then add this time to the 0940 hours, which is when the class started. 0940 + 0125 = 1065. Here 1065 can also be written as 10 hr + 1 hr + 5 min. When added together you get 11 hr 5 min or 11:05 am.

(27) The correct answer is: (B) $70

If there is a 40% discount, then the new cost of the dress is 60% since 100% − 40% = 60%. Find out what 1% represents by dividing 42 by 60, and the result will be 0.70. If 1% = 0.70, it means 100%, which should be the original price = 0.70 x 100 = 70.

(28) The correct answer is: (B) 3.53 kg.

First, find out how much $1 can buy. 1 ÷ $3.40. If $1 buys (1 ÷ $3.40), $12 can buy (1 ÷ $3.40) x $12; which is the same as (1/ $3.40) x $12/1. Multiply numerators and denominators to get $12/$3.40 = 3.529 kg. Rounded, it is 3.53 kg.

(29) The correct answer is: (A) 70%.

To get this percentage, first divide 5.6 by 8 and then multiply by 100%. 5.6/8 x 100%. works out to 560/8 %. Once you simplify, you get 70%.

(30) The correct answer is: (D) 6.4 km.

5 cm represents 4 km. Hence, 1 cm represents 4/5 km. To find out how many kilometers are represented by 8 cm, multiply what is represented by 1 cm by 8. That should be 4/5 km x 8, which is the same as (4/5 x 8/1) km. Multiply the numerators and then the denominators. 32/5 km = 6.4 km.

(31) The correct answer is: (A) 7:6.

A ratio can also be written as the first portion divided by the second; so y:x is also y/x. Put y/x on one side. Divide both sides of the equation by 6 to get y on one side. 6y/6 = 7x/6 becomes y = 7x/6. Move x across by dividing both sides by x; hence, y/x = 7/6. In ratio form this is y:x = 7 : 6

(32) The correct answer is: (D) 24/5.

Write the ratio as a fraction to make it easier to solve so x/12 = 4/10. Next, cross-multiply the equation so (x × 10) = (4 × 12) will give you 10x = 48. Then solve x by multiplying both sides by 10 to get x = 48/10. Simplify this fraction by dividing the numerator and the denominator by 2 to get x = 24/5

(33) The correct answer is: (A) 9.51 liters.

First convert 7:2 into fractions. To do this you need a denominator which you will get by adding the two portions together. 7 + 2 = 9. The equation can then be written as 7/9 + 2/9 ≈ 42.8. To get the value of 2/9, first get the value of 1/9, which will be 42.8/9 = 4.755. Therefore 4.755 × 2 = 9.51

(34) The correct answer is: (C) 20.

First write this ratio in fraction form. To get a common denominator for each ratio, add the three ratios together. So 4 + 5 + 6 is 15. The portions in fraction form will therefore be 4/15: 5/15 : 6/15. Mike got 5/15 of the 60 sweets, which means that he got 5/15 · 60 = 20 sweets

(35) The correct answer is: (A) 0.29.

The fraction 2/7 means 2 ÷ 7. This gives you 0.285. To give the answer to two decimal places, consider the third place value after the decimal. Since it is 5, cancel it and add one to the second place value to get 0.29.

(36) The correct answer is: (C) 0.028.

First remove the decimals to avoid confusion, then add them after calculating. Your problem will now be 7 × 04 = 28. We had a total of three decimal places, so include them by adding the decimal point three places to the left of 28. This gives you 0.028.

Science Section – Test 1 Answers

(1)   The correct answer is: (D) Vitamin D.

The reason (D) is the correct answer is that vitamin D is the only vitamin the human body synthesizes, and the process of synthesis takes place within the person's skin. At the time this vitamin is inactive, and what makes the process successful is the presence of sunlight.

(2)   The correct answer is: (D) Enterokinase.

(D) is correct because that enzyme, which is also known as "enteropeptidase," is responsible for converting trypsinogen that is not yet active to its active form, which is trypsin. Enterokinase is produced by the duodenum's lining. Hydrochloric acid, pepsin and protease are all incorrect answers.

(3)   The correct answer is: (D) The pituitary gland's anterior lobe.

The reason (D) is the correct answer is that it is the pituitary gland's anterior lobe that is situated right at the bottom part of the brain and supplies the FSH, which then enters the bloodstream and penetrates the ovaries, causing follicles to mature.

(4)   The correct answer is: (C) Sodium carbonate.

The reason (C) is the correct answer is that acids are known to react when mixed with carbonates and they end up producing salt and water as well as carbon dioxide. Considering there is a production of carbon dioxide during the reaction, it means that the substance 'X' represents can only be a carbonate. The other choices have no carbonate.

(5)   The correct answer is: (C) The force is moving toward the circle's middle.

The reason (C) is correct is that the present centripetal force happens to be directed at the circle's center. If the velocity or direction changes, it has to involve some acceleration. If the body were moving in a straight manner and also at a constant speed, acceleration would not be involved.

(6)   The correct answer is: (B) 3 fatty acid molecules and a single glycerol molecule.

(B) is the correct answer because there are three organic acid molecules required in the formation of a fat molecule. This organic acid is commonly referred to as a fatty acid. These three molecules in combination with a single glycerol molecule make up a single fat molecule.

(7)   The correct answer is: (B) Biological catalysts, optimum.

The best definition of a catalyst is a substance of a chemical nature that has the capacity to accelerate a reaction while not being spent or changed. As for enzymes, they are catalysts of a biological or organic nature, made of living cells, and they hasten various body reactions.

(8)   The correct answer is: (B) It is an anaerobic procedure whereby a solution of sugar is acted on by yeast and releases carbon dioxide as well as alcohol.

Bacteria and yeast, as well as muscle cells, have the capacity to carry out a metabolic procedure known as fermentation. During the process, sugar is converted to gas, alcohol and/or acid. A good example is fermentation resulting from yeast producing alcohol from glucose represented by carbohydrates, with no oxygen; hence, an anaerobic environment. Carbon dioxide is also released.

(9)   The correct answer is: (D) Oxygen debt develops owing to lactic acid buildup within a person's muscles, requiring oxidation of high levels of oxygen.

As a person exercises, pyruvic acid builds up within the muscles at a faster rate than the rate of oxidation. This acid is converted into lactic acid. Even when the person has ceased to exercise, a high oxygen level is still needed for the purpose of oxidizing the lactic acid produced.

(10) The correct answer is: (D) It constitutes a type of passive transport, meaning one where energy is not directly consumed like in ATP hydrolysis, requiring trans-membrane or carrier proteins.

Facilitated diffusion can be defined as the movement made by substances across a biological membrane, making use of the trans-membrane's integral proteins. Substances end up moving down along the gradient of concentration without directly using ATP hydrolysis as energy.

(11) The correct answer is: (A) Fingers and toes.

(A) is the correct answer because the fingers and toes have phalanges. Phalanges are not found in the skull or ears.

(12) The correct answer is: (D) These joints are multi-axial; they are greatly mobile and allow movement within several axes as well as planes.

(D) is the correct answer because the ball and socket have a spheroidal surface, and that surface moves while inside another bone's socket, providing mobility to the maximum extent possible among all the other joints—circumduction, abduction, adduction and such.

(13) The correct answer is: (A) All these joints are synovial.

(A) is correct as synovial joints have the capacity to move freely, and they have articulating bones linked by a joint capsule that has articular fluid and synovial fluid. The main types of synovial joints are plane joints and hinge joints; saddle and condyloid joints; ball and socket and pivot joints.

(14) The correct answer is: (C) Striated and involuntary with intercalated discs.

(C) is correct because cardiac muscles are heart muscles with striations showing, and they are not voluntarily controlled. They also possess intercalated discs in between the muscle fibers.

(15) The correct answer is: (C) Deoxygenated, nutrient-filled, intestines, liver.

The reason (C) is correct is that each person has a hepatic portal vein carrying deoxygenated blood that is rich in nutrients from the intestines all the way to the liver. The term deoxygenated blood means that oxygen has been removed from the blood.

(16) The correct answer is: (A) Internal jugular veins, subclavian veins.

The reason (A) is the correct answer is that it is accurate to say a person's internal jugular and subclavian veins comprise the brachiocephalic veins after they have united. These resulting veins are posterior to the sternoclavicular joint.

(17) The correct answer is: (D) Right lymphatic duct; thoracic duct.

(D) is correct because the right lymphatic duct and the thoracic duct are formed after the big lymph collecting vessels unite.

(18) The correct answer is: (A) Liver.

The reason (A) is correct is that the lymphoid organs in the body are responsible for producing lymphocytes, but a liver has no role like the thymus, tonsils and spleen that can produce lymphocytes. Hence, the liver is not one of the lymphoid organs.

(19) The correct answer is: (C) The cranial nerves.

The reason (C) is correct is that the major organs that comprise the central nervous system are a person's brain and spinal cord, and the tract is made up of nerve fibers or axons. As for the cranial nerves, they are peripheral to the central nervous system.

(20) The correct answer is: (A) The lumbar vertebrae.

The reason (A) is the correct answer is that the lumbar vertebrae is located in the lower back. They are not an extension of the rib cage, unlike the sternum, thoracic vertebrae and costal cartilage.

(21) The correct answer is: (B) SA node.

(B) is the correct answer because the sinoatrial node (SA) is responsible for initiating and regulating impulses so as to trigger the heart's contractions about 70 times each minute on average for an adult.

(22) The correct answer is: (C) Mitral valve.

The reason (C) is the correct answer is that the mitral valve is responsible for regulating the blood flow that starts from a person's left atrium moving up to the left ventricle. This valve possesses two cusps, which are the anterior and posterior. The heart has three other valves, namely the tricuspid, pulmonary and aortic.

(23) The correct answer is: (A) The dermis.

The reason (A) is the correct answer is that the dermis is the central skin layer that has blood vessels, lymph vessels, hair follicles, nerves and sweat glands. It also has bundles of collagen and additional structures. The basal and subcutaneous layers as well as the epidermis do not have all these structures.

(24) The correct answer is: (A) Iodine.

The reason (A) is the correct answer is that a person's thyroid gland requires iodine in order to produce the hormone known as thyroxine. Another hormone that is produced by the thyroid gland is triiodothyronine, and both of these hormones help to regulate metabolism.

(25) The correct answer is: (B) Retinol, fat-soluble, night blindness.

The reason (B) is the correct answer is that retinol, basically vitamin A, is a vitamin that is soluble in fat, and if one does not have it in sufficient amounts, there is a chance of developing eye problems such as night blindness (nyctalopia).

(26) The correct answer is: (B) Kwashiorkor.

The reason (B) is correct is that kwashiorkor refers to malnutrition that develops when a person has not been consuming sufficient amounts of protein. The other answers are incorrect as one develops scurvy from vitamin C deficiency, anemia from iron deficiency and rickets from a vitamin D, phosphorus or calcium deficiency.

(27) The correct answer is: (C) Peristalsis involving the circular and longitudinal muscles.

The reason (C) is correct is that contraction waves are responsible for moving food downwards through a person's alimentary canal, as the gastrointestinal tract's circular and longitudinal muscles go through peristalsis. Peristalsis is involuntary muscle movement in the form of alternating constriction and relaxation.

(28) The correct answer is: (A) Breaking down starch to become a simpler form of sugar.

The reason (A) is the correct answer is that amylase, which is produced within a person's salivary glands and pancreas, is responsible for converting starch into disaccharides and trisaccharides. These are then processed by different enzymes to become glucose.

(29) The correct answer is: (B) Villi present within the large intestine take in water as well as mineral salts.

The reason (B) is correct is that it is an untrue statement. Villi do not exist in the large intestine. They are only found inside the ileum, which is essentially the small intestine.

(30) The correct answer is: (C) Four months, bilirubin.

The reason (C) is the correct answer is that red blood cells remain alive for 120 days (four months). When the red blood cells' hemoglobin breaks down, what is produced is bilirubin, and this is eliminated or excreted via the bile.

(31) The correct answer is: (D) Thymus gland.

The reason (D) is the correct answer is that the despite the fact that production of a person's T lymphocytes (T cells) takes place within the bone marrow, their development and maturation happens within that person's thymus gland.

(32) The correct answer is: (B) Once red blood cells mature, they become bi-concave discs with a central nucleus and can live for an extended period of time.

The reason (B) is the correct answer is that red blood cells have no nucleus and they can only live for around 120 days.

(33) The correct answer is: (C) There is a contracting of the diaphragm in a downward direction.

The reason (C) is correct is that the diaphragm moves down as a person inhales air because the thoracic volume increases, and pressure reduces. The reason it is easy for air to move in is that the thoracic pressure within the lungs is low; the lungs consequently expand.

(34) The correct answer is: (A) residual volume, 1.2 liters.

The reason (A) is the correct answer is that there is always a residual volume of air amounting to 1.2 liters that remains in a person's lungs at all times. This residual air prevents the lungs from entirely collapsing.

(35) The correct answer is: (D) Uracil.

The reason (D) is the correct answer is that uracil is found in RNA; the others are bases present in DNA.

(36) The correct answer is: (C) 25%.

The reason (C) is the correct answer is that genes always exist in pairs, and where there is an autosomal recessive disease like SMA, each of the parents has one gene that is affected and one that is not affected. As such, the chances of the child not carrying the disease are 25%.

(37) The correct answer is: (C) Prone.

(C) is correct because the belly-down position is referred to as the prone position, while lying on one's back is referred to as the supine position. Lying on one's side is termed a lateral position.

(38) The correct answer is: (C) Boiling always happens at a particular temperature.

The reason (C) is correct is that whereas evaporation occurs at different levels of temperature, boiling can only happen at a very specific level of temperature known as the liquid's boiling point.

(39) The correct answer is: (D) The impurity has the effect of raising the boiling point and lowering the melting point.

(D) is correct because a pure substance has a tendency to melt as soon as its normal melting point is reached. Nevertheless, an impure substance can have its melting point fall within a broad temperature range owing to the different elements in it. This is because impurities lower the pressure of the vapor.

(40) The correct answer is: (D) An element's isotopes have similar chemical and physical properties.

The reason (D) is correct is that an element's isotopes possess similar properties chemically but have some variations with regard to properties of a physical nature, such as density.

(41) The correct answer is: (D) Atomic size increases going down any group and also across any period.

(D) is correct because the radius or atomic size increases going down a group, and decreases when moving across a period. The reason for this pattern is that as the nucleus gets protons added to it, it gets electrons brought nearer to it. This decreases the radius of an atom.

(42) The correct answer is: (D) Being soluble while in organic solvents such as ethanol.

The reason (D) is correct is that a covalent compound is soluble when put in an organic solvent like ethanol. The properties contained in (A), (B) and (C) do not apply to covalent compounds, therefore, they are incorrect.

(43) The correct answer is: (A) The entire mass of a chemical reaction's products equals the entire mass of its reactants collectively.

The reason (A) is the correct answer is that all the mass is conserved as the chemical reaction takes place. The mass before and after the chemical reaction remains equal.

(44) The correct answer is: (A) The copper in the solution of copper (II) sulfate is displaced by zinc.

(A) is correct because zinc is more reactive than copper, and so it ends up displacing the copper and taking its position in the solution. The result is the formation of reddish-brown copper deposits on the piece of zinc. Effectively, therefore, the solution's original blue color fades.

(45) The correct answer is: (A) Oxidizing agents add oxygen to, or extract electrons from, other substances.

The reason (A) is the correct answer is that it is possible for oxidizing agents to have double functions. One can be transferring atoms that are electronegative, usually oxygen, to another compound. The other function can be removing electrons from different substances during oxidation; reactions of reduction.

(46) The correct answer is: (A) The body's inertia.

The reason (A) is the correct answer is that every single body has inertia, and that inertia is change-resistant while the object or body is in motion. The body's acceleration, speed or momentum in (B), (C) and (D), respectively, do not help the body resist change while in motion.

(47) The correct answer is: (B) Weight.

The reason (B) is the answer is that gravitational force is the result of mass times gravitational acceleration, and that weight declines as altitude increases; meaning as the altitude drops, weight increases.

(48) The correct answer is: (A) Mass, time and speed

The reason (A) is correct is that scalar quantities are only associated with magnitude and not direction.

(49) The correct answer is: (C) Chemical, heat, kinetic, electrical.

The reason (C) is the correct answer is that chemical energy in the coal plant is converted into the water's heat energy, and that is then converted into steam's kinetic energy. That kinetic energy becomes electrical energy.

(50) The correct answer is: (C) Nuclear fusion.

The reason (C) is the correct answer is that nuclear fusion stands for the process where energy is produced through the conversion of mass. This process can be found in the sun and stars. Therefore, (A), (B) and (D) are incorrect.

(51) The correct answer is: (B) The skin.

The reason (B) is the correct answer is that a person's skin is composed of epithelial tissue. This layer is also known as the epidermis, and it gets support from connective tissue.

(52) The correct answer is: (A) When using many plants, it was possible to show that his results were not accidental.

(A) is correct because Mendel used a big sample to ensure the experiment's outcome was not arrived at by chance. Repeating an experiment and getting results that are similar makes the experiment repeatable. Also, the use of a big sample size provides sufficient data for testing if the variations observed can be considered statistically significant.

(53) The correct answer is: (B) The small intestine.

Salivary amylase is found both in the mouth and small intestine. It is contained in the saliva and is responsible for initiating the digestion of carbohydrates, acting as a catalyst for the conversion of polysaccharides into disaccharides. Then the major task of digesting carbohydrates takes place in the small intestine.

English and Language Use Section – Test 1 Answers

(1)   The correct answer is: (D) Mary studied geography, but Susan chose to pursue economics instead.

The reason this sentence is considered to be compound is that it is a combination of two independent clauses or sentences, each of which can be understood on its own, and they are joined by the conjunction "but." (A) and (B) have one dependent clause each, while (C) is a simple sentence.

(2)   The correct answer is: (C) Definitely.

(C) is the correct answer as it has a similar meaning to "certainly" and therefore fits correctly into the sentence.

(3)   The correct answer is: (A) African athletes broke many records in one season.

The sentence is in the passive voice, which means that the thing/person, in this case "records," affected by the main verb, serves as the sentence subject. A sentence in the active voice has the doer of the main action/verb, as in the case of (A), "athletes." Though the subject and object change places, the meaning of the sentence should not change.

(4)   The correct answer is: (C) Their.

The word "their" is a possessive pronoun used for plural nouns in the third-person. Here it shows that the project belonged to the three people. "They're" is a contraction of "they are" and would be wrong for the sentence. "There" is an adverb of place while "they" is a third-person plural pronoun.

(5)   The correct answer is: (D) Verb.

The word "traveled" is a verb, and it is in the past tense. It represents the action taken by the subject of the sentence, "students." An adverb is a word that describes a verb, while an adjective is a word that describes a noun.

(6)   The correct answer is: (D) A tendency to focus on even the smallest of mistakes or details.

The part of the sentence that helps to identify the meaning of "pedantic" is "how meticulous the teacher had been in correcting." This means that the teacher combs through every detail of an assignment, including those details that others are likely to find insignificant.

(7)   The correct answer is: (B) Has driven.

The correct verb form used is the present perfect. Using "drove," which is in the simple past tense, would be wrong because that tense is used when you have a specific timeline in mind. e.g., He drove to Toronto this morning. (C) and (D) are grammatically incorrect.

(8)   The correct answer is: (C) Comma splice.

When a comma is used to link two independent clauses or sentences, it is erroneous, and the error is referred to as a comma splice. Such sentences should be connected using a conjunction. For example: "Jane and Jake danced at the party while Jane's mother served as the photographer."

(9)   The correct answer is: (C) This morning an elephant walked past the school as lessons continued.

Although there are no punctuation marks within the sentence, the period at the end is sufficient. In (A), the colon should be replaced with a comma. In (B), if the sentence has to remain as one then it requires a semicolon after the word "regularly." It also needs a comma after "however." (D) needs a change of punctuation and structure.

(10) The correct answer is: (B) Stock-broker.

The correct way to write the word is "stockbroker." It is in the same category as "twofold," which has been correctly written without a hyphen. The other hyphenated words, "mother-in-law" and "ex-husband," are correctly written.

(11)   The correct answer is: (C) The partying teenagers was getting too rowdy for the local community.

Since the word "teenagers" is plural, the verb that follows should be plural as well as, in this case, "were." In (A), "fashion" is singular, and so "is" is correct. In (B) the subject is "behavior"—not "boys and girls"—and so "is" is correct. In (D), "scouts" is plural and matches the verb "were."

(12)   The correct answer is: (C) Terrible.

When identifying meaning within context, check for words to give you a clue, rather than for dictionary meanings. Here, "sacked" gives a hint that the error cannot have been unpredictable or minor. It is also likely there was no misunderstanding. Sacking is the ultimate punishment for a terrible mistake.

(13)   The correct answer is: (A) Julia Roberts is considered a great actress. She shot to fame with her role alongside Richard Gere in *Pretty Woman*.

The second sentence in (A) begins with "she" as the pronoun, and its antecedent is "Julia Roberts," a woman. So the pronoun-antecedent agreement is correct. This is different from the other answers. As for (B), though some people use "she" in reference to their cherished cars, yachts, etc., it's incorrect grammatically.

(14)   The correct answer is: (B) Mouse.

The reason (B) is the correct answer is that the noun "mouse" in its plural form is "mice." It does not conform to the general rule where "s" is added at the end of the singular form. The other nouns, "table," "giraffe" and "hotel," become "tables," "giraffes" and "hotels" in their plural forms, respectively.

(15) The correct answer is: (C) Donald Trump, the President of the United States, addressed the press regarding the coronavirus.

The sentence begins with the proper noun, "Donald Trump," and so "President of the United States," is just a descriptive phrase and should not have the word "president" capitalized. Nevertheless, "United States" remains capitalized as it is the name of a country, hence, a proper noun.

(16) The correct answer is: (C) The Hilton.

"The Hilton" is the hotel in the second sentence referred to by the pronoun "it," and that makes it the antecedent. The Hilton is the thing said to be known for hosting dignitaries. The other nouns—Chicago, Nairobi and cities—can serve as antecedents in different sentence structures.

(17) The correct answer is: (D) Adverb.

An adverb describes how the action represented by the verb took place. In the sentence, the verb "strode" is modified or described further by the word "leisurely." A word that modifies the noun is an adjective, and so "jubilant" in the sentence is an adjective.

(18) The correct answer is: (C) Father, improved.

(C) is the correct answer because the accompanying verb matches the tense of the rest of the sentence as indicated by the word "became." You cannot say the relationship "improves" or "grow" or "built" when the father became president. The verb must be in the simple past tense.

(19) The correct answer is: (D) Had seen.

"Had seen" is in the past perfect tense. This means the action happened in the past and was completed by the time another event took place. For example, "The teacher had seen a girl entering the room with a glass of water before a tall boy came out with a wet shirt."

(20) The correct answer is: (B) Two items are positioned close together.

The word "juxtaposition" refers to two objects directly beside one another. It can also be used to describe related concepts and not just tangible items.

(21) The correct answer is: (B) Flour, flower.

The reason (B) is the correct answer is that the word "flour" fits the first gap while the word "flower" fits the second gap, completing the sentence in a logical manner. While flour is the major ingredient in baking, a flower is the beautiful part plucked from a plant for decoration. Floor is the ground.

(22) The correct answer is: (C) Oxen.

The correct plural of the word "ox" is "oxen." An ox is a male mammal that has been domesticated for the purpose of manual work like pulling ploughs. Two or more of these animals are referred to as "oxen."

(23) The correct answer is: (D) Overworked.

There is no need to put a hyphen between the two words "over" and "worked."

(24) The correct answer is: (A) Recommendation.

The correct spelling for (B) is temperature, for (C) is received and for (D) is convenience. Recommendation is a noun derived from the verb "recommend," whose meaning is endorsing something for its fitness or a person for being a good fit for what is required.

(25) The correct answer is: (C) Jane, Lucy and the rest of the team camped at the park for a whole week.

The problem with (A) is the comma that comes after Sasha, while (B) has a comma after the indirect object, "wife." As for putting a comma after the item just before the conjunction "and," it is an acceptable answer. In (D), neither of the two commas is necessary.

(26) The correct answer is: (A) Dr. Bernard was a well-respected surgeon. Nevertheless, his colleagues had no idea the good doctor was destined for fame.

"Dr. Bernard" is correct because the title should be capitalized.

(27) The correct answer is: (D) James watched TV on Sunday morning and he watched a movie in the afternoon.

(D) comprises two independent clauses that are connected by the word "and"— a conjunction—each of which is well understood on its own. (A) is not compound as only its second part is an independent clause. (C) is an example of a complex sentence whose grammatically independent clauses are still dependent on each other for meaning.

(28) The correct answer is: (C) The doctor followed up on the patient's progress until she recovered fully.

A sentence is said to be in the active voice when it describes how the subject carried out the action in the verb. When the sentence describes how the object of the sentence was affected by the action of the verb, it is said to be passive voice.

Practice Test 2: Questions

Reading Section – Test 2

Read the following passage and answer the two questions that follow.

Edna and Beatrice each bought a bike in preparation for college. Considering the price of gas was on the rise, they reasoned that their purchases were justified and considered that as they would be staying on campus, there would be no need for cars. However, their mother had a different opinion, feeling that they would be better off having a car to share, so she gave them one as a present. Subsequently, Edna and Beatrice decided to return one of their bikes so that they had one bike and one car to share between them. By keeping one bike, they reasoned they could still save some money.

(1) Which of the following is a synonym for "reasoned" as used in the above passage?

(A) Realized

(B) Dissuaded

(C) Worried

(D) Concluded

(2) This passage is _____.

(A) A nonfiction treatise

(B) A persuasive essay

(C) A new article

(D) A novel for young adults

(3) "Although the band had practiced for several months, the theatergoers were stunned by the cacophony of sounds that greeted them." The meaning of "cacophony" in this context is _____.

(A) Beautiful and unearthly

(B) Yelping sounds

(C) Loud but harmonious noises

(D) Massive, disharmonious sounds or noises

(4) After you have followed the instructions provided below, what word are you left with?

Begin with "limped" as a word. Extract the letter "d" from its position and place it at the start of the word. Next, extract the letter "l" from its position and place it immediately after the letter "p." Lastly, replace the letter "d" with the letter "s."

(A) Simpel

(B) Dimple

(C) Simple

(D) Slimed

(5) 'The sententious man ultimately relented, making room for John to slip away to the aisle with pharmaceutical products."

In the context of the given sentence, "sententious" means _____.

(A) Short-tempered

(B) Kind or courteous

(C) Self-conceited

(D) Ready to assist; accommodating

Read the following email and answer the five questions that follow.

Annabel,

Towards the end of this year, Mom and Dad will travel to the Seychelles for the Christmas holidays. Desmond and I thought we could still gather at the house so as to maintain tradition for the kids' sake. If you and Sue have no objection, we'd be willing to travel and be there three days prior to Christmas, as is our custom, and maintain our usual schedules. Since Mom and Dad will be absent, we'll need help preparing the Christmas dinner. We'll also need help where house decorations are concerned. Could you possibly bring lights and ornaments? We'll provide the Christmas tree.

Tell me what you think!

Sheila

(6)   The purpose of the email is _____.

(A)   To ask for Annabel's help in maintaining a family Christmas tradition

(B)   To tell Annabel that her parents will not be home for the Christmas festivities

(C)   To ask Annabel for help in taking care of Sue's children

(D)   To let Sheila know the plans for the family's Christmas celebration

(7)   Annabel's and Sheila's relationship is one of _____.

(A)   Cousins

(B)   Close friends

(C)   Sisters

(D)   Mother-daughter

(8)   Sheila's main goal in wishing to have Christmas at her parents' home is
_____.

(A)   To uphold the traditions her family has always kept

(B)   To travel during Christmas

(C)   To visit Hawaii alongside her mom and dad

(D)   To have her and Andrew spend Christmas together

(9)   One word that can be substituted for "maintain" and leave the original meaning of
the sentence unaltered is _____.

(A)   Correspond

(B)   Preserve

(C)   Neglect

(D)   Delay

(10)   Based on the Christmas traditions the family follows, one can conclude _____.

(A)   That those traditions are quite childish

(B)   That those traditions are lonely

(C)   That the celebrations are family friendly

(D)   That the celebrations can only be done in the presence of Annabel and Sheila

(11) A dictionary has the words "measly" and "melancholy" on the top left side of a page and on the top right side, respectively. From the list of answers provided below, identify the one you would expect to find on one of the pages.

(A)   Methane

(B)   Meadow

(C)   Meniscus

(D)   Megalomania

(12) Anthony wants to sell his vehicle, and so he makes a call to the local daily newspaper intending to place a "for sale" ad. The newspaper section that ad will go in is
_____.

(A)   Upcoming events

(B)   Classifieds

(C)   Local news

(D)   Sports

Read the passage below and then answer the three questions that follow.

When we are kids, adults teach us to read. Adults read to us at bedtime, the voice of a mother or father crooning to us. In due course, we learn how to read on our own. In kindergarten or earlier, we gain an understanding of what words mean when they appear on a page. As kids continue growing up, however, many of them fail to develop a liking for reading, instead finding it stressful, strictly academic and/or boring. For these children, reading is considered harrowing, tiresome and, thus, they may only read to receive a passing grade in a class. However, anyone who wishes to enhance his or her skills in communication may wish to review that attitude; constant reading has been proven to not just enhance one's skills in writing, but also help people communicate verbally and improve their understanding of verbal cues and facial ones. Hence, one should not regard reading as an unpleasant task, or some insurmountable challenge, but as an important activity that teaches individuals how to interact with other people and to express themselves.

(13) Which of the following is the best title for this reading passage?

(A)   Best Way to Read Well

(B)   The Reason it is Good to Read

(C)   Why it is Important to Learn to Read

(D)   Reading for Communication: A Crucial Skill

(14) The meaning of the word "harrowing" as it appears in the sentence, "For these children, reading is considered harrowing, tiresome ..." is _____.

(A)   Uncouth or foolhardy

(B)   Juvenile or troubled

(C)   Easy or simple

(D)   Distressing or very difficult

(15) The purpose of this passage is _____.

(A)   To admonish parents for their failure to teach their kids to read

(B)   To discourage students so they do not read

(C)   To encourage students to write

(D)   To communicate how important it is to read regularly

Read the sentence and then answer the question that follows.

"The obsequious mannerisms of Tammy's boyfriend frustrated her, and she started to dread his smarmy compliments and offers to help her."

(16) The meaning of "obsequious" is _____.

(A) Bored

(B) Sycophantic

(C) Attentive

(D) Uncaring

(17) The role of a footnote is to _____.

(A) Make a reference to some other point within the same text

(B) Make a reference to some other chapter within the text

(C) Add more commentary or references

(D) Provide needed space for the reader's own commentary

(18) A dictionary has the words "pelican" and "perambulate" on one page. One word from the list below that cannot be found on the same page is _____.

(A) Pepsin

(B) Perigee

(C) Pentathlon

(D) Penance

Read the excerpt below and then answer the question that follows.

Monologue: n. long speech by a single actor within a play or film, or as a part of a program being broadcast

(19) The above excerpt is most likely to appear in the _____.

(A) Table of contents

(B) Glossary

(C) Bibliography

(D) Introduction

(20) Which of the following does not exemplify a fact-based piece of work?

(A) An editorial

(B) A science journal

(C) An instruction manual

(D) Medical content for study

Read the text and then answer the five questions that follow.

When they are faced with anything difficult in academics, a good number of students seek the help of tutors. Tutors handle everything from reading to math and in between. There are different ways to find a tutor, one of them being to check with your own school. You can also search online for potential tutors. However, when seeking out a tutor, you need to appreciate that you may incur more charges by hiring tutors who specialize in certain areas. It's always a good idea to do a trial tutoring session so as to make sure your personalities mesh appropriately.

(21) Based upon context, what does "incur" mean?

(A) Sustain

(B) Establish

(C) Fool

(D) Remove

(22) The reason a trial tutoring session is recommended is _____.

(A) To confirm the tutor is not a scammer

(B) To confirm that the student and tutor are compatible

(C) To confirm the prospective tutor has credentials

(D) To ensure that the student is able to pass class tests

(23) What are ways that students can find tutors?

(A) By seeking a referral from a reliable friend or family member, or looking online

(B) By seeking assistance from the school that the student attends or online tutorial services

(C) Through local schools' tutorial programs

(D) By talking to a college

(24) Which of the following best summarizes the passage?

(A)   Tutoring services vary, and they ought to be employed as much as possible particularly if one is learning to read or needs help with science

(B)   Tutors are available at schools and online, and the availability of each depends on the amount of money you are prepared to pay

(C)   Many students resort to tutoring sessions whenever they require assistance in class, and the tutors are available in varying places, including schools and online.

(D)   While tutoring services vary greatly, you should always carefully vet any tutor you select

(25) The passage is an example of _____ writing.

(A)   Compare and contrast

(B)   Expository

(C)   Cause and effect

(D)   Narrative

Read the descriptions below and then answer the three questions that follow.

Blue Messenger Bag
Size of Purse: Large
Cost of Purse: $35
Durability of Purse: Very Durable

Mustard-Cream Cross-Body Purse
Size of Purse: Medium
Cost of Purse: $19.99
Durability of Purse: Medium Durability

Studded Clutch
Size of Purse: Mini
Cost of Purse: $70
Durability of Purse: Delicate

(26) Meghan, a student in college, is searching for a bag on sale. She requires something for college, which can serve her till the end of the semester. Considering she needs a bag that is durable and relatively cheap, which of the purses listed would be her preference?

(A) None of the bags

(B) The mustard-cream purse

(C) The blue bag

(D) The studded clutch

(27) Meghan is set to accompany her husband to a gala. Which of the following items would be best for her to store her tiny wallet in at the gala?

(A) None of the bags

(B) The mustard-cream purse

(C) The blue bag

(D) The studded clutch

(28) Esther is in search of a bag to give her favorite granddaughter, who is both bookish and very choosy. Which of the bags is best suited for that granddaughter?

(A) None of the bags

(B) The mustard-cream purse

(C) The blue bag

(D) The studded clutch

(29) Andrew is making his first trip to Florida, and he hopes to be able to visit places where he can learn something on local art and its history. Which of the following books would you consider best to serve Andrew's needs?

(A)   A complete guide to Florida's sights and attractions

(B)   *Florida: An Interesting Novel*

(C)   A complete atlas of Florida and its surroundings

(D)   *Florida: A Short History*

Read the following letter and then answer the question that follows.

Dear Applicant,

We appreciate your interest in joining Fresh Adventure Recruiting. Our recruiting agency is recognized nationwide, and we assist people who speak English to secure positions to teach ESL in South Korea. Every year, we are successful in placing thousands of ESL teachers within schools in different parts of the country.

We shall review your application and get in touch with you in fourteen working days if we would like to interview you for a position. Please refrain from contacting us during this period of review.

Meanwhile, we encourage all applicants to learn the map of South Korea that is enclosed, to prepare themselves for the anticipated interview. It is normal for us to ask all interviewees during the interview what their top two placement preferences are. We place applicants based on a first-come, first-served basis. However, you need to keep in mind that the demand for cities on the northern side of Andong is high. If you select a place outside this zone, your chances of being placed in your first choice are higher.

Once more, thank you for sending in an application.

Sincerely,

Fresh Adventure Recruiting

(30) Which of the following states the author's major purpose in writing the letter?

(A)   To let the applicant know that he/she should prepare to be interviewed in 14 days

(B)   To provide more instructions to the applicant regarding the hiring process

(C)   To let the applicant know that placement in the cities in the northern part of South Korea are in high demand; therefore, they are extremely competitive

(D)   To provide the applicant with an estimate of the waiting time during which his/her application will be reviewed

Read the two passages and then answer the four questions that follow.

First Passage

Obviously, it is imperative that the legal minimum age for driving in the US be changed. Though this minimum has remained sixteen years for a long time, studies indicate that children of that tender age cannot understand the heavy accountability that comes with operating a vehicle. Whereas sixteen-year-old teenagers are considered mature enough to watch R-rated films, they are essentially still kids in several ways. Psychologists are in agreement that people within this age category are not cognitively aware enough to be able to make any huge life decisions; yet, driving a vehicle inevitably puts them in such a position.

If the minimum driving age was raised to eighteen, American roads would have fewer accidents. People need to understand clearly that drivers who are sixteen years of age pose a danger not only to themselves but also to other people when they are permitted to drive without supervision.

Second Passage

The reason the minimum legal age at which one can drive in America has not been changed for several years is that it is reasonable. Although they are young, teenagers who are sixteen years old are mature enough to handle the responsibility that comes with driving on their own. Considering these are teenagers who are required to continue practicing for one year using a learner's permit and subsequently must pass a test, there is nothing to suggest they will not be fully capable of operating a motor vehicle. The people who believe sixteen-year-olds are too immature to drive should remember that these teenagers already handle a huge number of responsibilities daily. Consider tasks like doing homework, after-school activities, family-related responsibilities and social undertakings—they all require a variety of skills and time management. Since a teenager is capable of handling these day-to-day responsibilities, certainly teenagers are capable of driving a vehicle. The minimum driving age should not be changed.

(31) The writer of the first passage very likely would be in agreement with the statement that _____.

(A) Teenagers fail to practice sufficiently prior to receiving a license

(B) Teenagers are not concerned about other drivers' safety

(C) Teenagers are not good at handling personal responsibilities

(D) Teenagers are adept at planning social and academic matters

(32) Identify the statement in the second paragraph that provides the best assessment of the writer's viewpoint.

(A) Each teenage driver must be considered on an individual basis

(B) The legal driving age should be lowered

(C) The legal driving age should be raised

(D) Currently, the legal driving age is fine and should not be changed

(33) Which of the following arguments would the author of the second passage not have made?

(A) It must be mandatory for teenagers to pass a test prior to getting a driver's license

(B) Teenagers learn as they watch their own parents drive

(C) Teenagers practice driving for a year and need a learner's permit

(D) Teenagers' many activities indicate they are capable of handling driving

(34) Which of the following shows how the themes of the first and second passage relate to each other?

(A)   Both writers are very passionate on the issue of the minimum legal driving age, although their opinions differ

(B)   The writers have various concerns

(C)   Both writers are of the opinion that teenagers are entrusted with many responsibilities on a daily basis

(D)   Both writers are concerned with the minimum age at which one can drive, and they hold the same position on the issue

Study the table below and answer the question that follows.

Vehicle Accidents on Average Each Month in American Cities			
Month	Atlanta	New York City	Los Angeles
January	2,500	2,700	2,200
April	2,100	2,500	2,150
July	1,950	2,100	2,100
October	2,000	2,300	2,150

(35) The city with the fewest vehicle accidents in the months following January 2015 was _____.

(A)   Atlanta and New York had the same number of accidents

(B)   Los Angeles

(C)   New York

(D)   Atlanta

Read the following passage and answer the two questions that follow.

When I was a young kid, I adhered to a common routine all Saturday mornings. I made sure I was the first to wake up early in the morning, before anybody else in our family. The reason I did this was to have our living room to myself while I ate my cereal and watched cartoons. Once the shows I liked most were through, I proceeded to read the comics that appeared in the local newspaper for Saturday. I cut out the comics I liked most and pinned them on my bulletin board. The next thing I did was to dress for the day and to head outside. My friends and I often grabbed our bicycles and spent the entire afternoon in the neighborhood park. As we began getting tired of bike riding, dinnertime would invariably arrive. It was customary for my family and me to go out and enjoy a meal together every Saturday evening. Finally, when dinner ended, my entire family would enjoy a movie together, as we ate popcorn and ice cream. My favorite day of the week was Saturday.

(36) As per the passage, once the writer had finished reading the comics in the Saturday newspaper, he would _____.

(A)   Eat cereal

(B)   Get dressed

(C)   Go bike riding

(D)   Leave for dinner

(37) Which of the keywords listed below does the writer use as indication of the action that came last in the day?

(A)   Next

(B)   Lastly

(C)   By the time

(D)   Finally

(38) What is a thesaurus used for?

(A) Writing advice

(B) Locating synonyms

(C) Locating definition

(D) Finding rhymes

(39) Margaret does not consume red meat. Instead, she derives her protein from seafood as well as poultry. Which of the following would not be an acceptable meal for Margaret?

(A) Broiled tilapia with rice

(B) Baked salmon with pesto

(C) Veal parmigiana

(D) Baked halibut with fried potatoes

Read the passage and then answer the two questions that follow.

Technology is expanding the scope of what can be done both professionally and personally, such as in the case of smart phones. Professionals are now in possession of devices that they can use to access the internet, communicate by phone, schedule activities, create documents, etc. People in business who are mostly on the move can make maximum use of the functionalities available on smart phones.

People can also use these gadgets for frivolous matters like downloading ringtones and sending instant messages. Additionally, they can look up gossip, memes, etc.

The rising availability of these gadgets in the market may be a reflection of the fusion of work and people's personal lives.

(40) The word "frivolous," as used in the passage, means that the writer _____.

(A)   Is fascinated by the great scope of capabilities smart phones have

(B)   Is hopeful that technology will stop improving

(C)   Is of the opinion that the average person has no need for a smart phone

(D)   Would like smart-phone technology to improve further

(41) The sentence used at the end of the passage fulfills the purpose of _____.

(A)   Making a deduction regarding what is already known about the capabilities of the smart phone

(B)   Making an assumption regarding the direction technology is taking and the effect it is bound to have on society

(C)   Commenting on people's behavior as related to technology

(D)   Presenting a plausible explanation for why smart phones continue to grow in popularity

Read the following passage and answer the four questions that follow.

It is not man's destiny to simply vanish. It is possible for him to be murdered, but it is not possible to destroy him because he has a soul that is deathless as well as a spirit that is irrepressible. As such, even though the nations of the world are sometimes in conflict, spending immeasurable amounts of resources and energy in the production of dangerous weapons, it is certain that these weapons will never be used. Nations threaten one another, intimidate one another and even reach the brink of war, but they will never fully engage in an armed conflict.

(42) The author's viewpoint is that _____.

(A)   It is not possible for superpowers to destroy the soul and spirit of man

(B)   The destiny of man is not completely clear

(C)   The human community is bound to survive in spite of conflicts between nations

(D)   The safety of man is guaranteed by the existence of a delicate power balance among nations

(43) The phrase "reach the brink of war" as used in the passage means _____.

(A)   End a war

(B)   Proclaim war

(C)   Move towards war

(D)   Negotiate peace

(44) The opinion of the author is that _____.

(A)   The massive stocks of dangerous weaponry in existence have been responsible for saving the human race from devastation

(B)   The world's superpowers are starting to abandon their weapons

(C)   The human race is on its way to total devastation

(D)   The countries who have stocked up deadly weapons are making a great effort to refrain from real conflict

(45) The meaning of the word "irrepressible" as used in the passage is _____.

(A) Oppressive

(B) Not compatible

(C) Not possible to restrain

(D) Strong

Read the following passage and then answer the two questions that follow.

Greek mythology serves as a vehicle which makes use of mythological actors or characters, which can even be creatures, to educate people on various matters. Characters in myths are faced with dilemmas of a moral nature. Epics have protagonists who come face-to-face with creatures that challenge their values and courage. Scholars of Greek mythology note the common values that the stories convey. It is incumbent upon every reader to find his or her own personal truth and to take the teachings conveyed in Greek mythology to heart.

(46) Which of the following might be a message found in Greek mythology?

(A) Although love is hard, it is bound to last if the people involved are fated to be together

(B) To achieve success, it is important to resist temptation and instant gratification

(C) Always know your own history

(D) The fastest person in a race may not be the one who runs farthest

(47) Which of the following summarizes the writer's view of Greek myths?

(A) It is filled with pessimism

(B) It is critical

(C) It is idealistic

(D) It is dubious

Read the passage and then answer the two questions that follow.

When there is disequilibrium at that interface involving water as well as air, it becomes a factor that heat and water vapor transfers are based on as they leave the ocean and rise to fill the air. Water vapor almost saturates any air that is within around one millimeter of the mass of water, as the air temperature becomes almost the same as that of the water surface. Regardless of the small differences, they are important, and what maintains disequilibrium is the mixing of the air closest to the surface with the one that is a little higher, which ordinarily is evidently cooler and even lower in its water vapor concentration.

The turbulence, whose source of energy is the wind, ends up mixing with the air. Then, as the wind speed increases, the turbulence increases too, and ultimately the same happens to the heat and moisture transfer rate. If one studies this phenomenon further, he/she can attain a comprehensive understanding of it. The shifting of momentum to water from the wind, which happens the moment waves are effectively formed, is one phenomenon that is not only interactive but complicated. After the wind has constructed waves, there is transfer of crucial energy amounts; hence there is no longer energy available to create turbulence.

(48) The intention of the above passage is mainly to _____.

(A) Solve an argument

(B) Try to describe a phenomenon

(C) Outline a theory

(D) Tabulate research outcomes

(49) According to the passage, as wind blows across the ocean, it normally _____.

(A) Changes the temperature on the surface of the ocean

(B) Causes air that is cool and dry to rise to the surface of the ocean

(C) Ensures the rate of transfer of heat as well as moisture between ocean and air

(D) Causes uncontrollable turbulence in the ocean

Read the passage and then answer the four questions that follow.

Charles Johnson, or Abdi, as he was more commonly known, decided that he would make use of his talent as a modern playwright in order to broaden young people's horizons; specifically, gifted individuals from black communities. It was in the process of doing this that he noticed children milling about Hope Place's dangerous streets.

As the head of his community center, Abdi tried to win every available grant in order to bring the young people puppet shows that warned against drug use and which encouraged education. He also brought outdoor showings of *A Midsummer Night's Dream*. It was Abdi's belief that it was possible to find something for every person in Shakespeare, even the youth of Hope Place. He believed that if he could only broaden their own horizons, it would change their lives.

The children who often hung out in the vicinity of the local community center were fond of Abdi, and the reason was that he hardly preached to them, and it was evident that whenever they talked, he would listen. He excelled at zeroing in on a child with a real difficulty. Whether it was by way of an offhand quip as a pool game went on or a face-to-face chat on the basketball court, Abdi somehow managed to make kids feel extra special just by saying a couple of words.

Abdi wished that his family had remained together. He and his three siblings had all landed in foster care. He understood the reason, but still he kept wondering if a better way existed.

As a child, Abdi was assigned to a home which already had two foster care boys. The Watsons had a tiny bungalow right outside Minden Hills. Yet, Mother Watson insisted they inform anyone asking that they lived within Minden Hills, which was an address with more prestige than Hope Place. The Watsons' home was immaculately maintained. However, the memories Abdi had of the place revolved around hardly having enough to eat. Mother Watson would give them a sandwich and a half, made out of white bread, with butter and margarine. Each kid would also get half an apple. Whenever Abdi dreamed of running away, he visualized living in an apartment of his own that had a refrigerator, with food he could eat to his heart's content.

Abdi stayed with the Watsons for nine long years. When he won a scholarship to a college in the neighborhood, he left the Watsons' home and became self-sufficient as he pursued his studies by doing some work at a doughnut shop.

By this point, Abdi's mother was finally able to take back her children, but he decided to remain where he was since he had already become independent. After all, it would be one less mouth for his mother to feed. After graduating from college with a degree in social work, he could then help her out with a little money.

One important thing for which Abdi thanked the Watsons was ensuring he kept away from gangs. They enforced a strict curfew and required the kids to attend church. "When you leave and become independent," Father Watson would say, "you will have the freedom to do as you wish, but as long as you are at my own home, I expect you to adhere to my rules." The Watsons were not cruel, but they were stingy with food and affection. Spending so many years on the margins of hunger and kindness made Abdi appreciative of life lived to the fullest: take up whatever work pleases you, irrespective of how much it pays, and make your home a sea of love. Well, the community center became home for him, and it was very close to Hope Place.

The children who spent their time hanging around at the community center had not reached the end of the road. Abdi believed there was still hope for them. Abdi had a motto: do not lose any child to street life. On the few occasions that it happened, he would go home and cry, yet he avoided showing his real emotions at the workplace. To the children, he remained just one big, rather quiet dude, who never went out looking for problems, yet would not run away to escape them.

He was continually challenged by new sets of boys who kept showing up at the center at various times, but he let them know in no uncertain terms that the community center was his own territory and his rules prevailed. Abdi repeatedly demonstrated that being kind did not mean he was feeble. Rules were necessary, and in these boys' world some discipline was needed. If they could understand this, he would work with any of them, seriously and devotedly, to make them realize there was an opportunity for them.

(50) The best way to describe the perspective of the author is _____.

(A)   A person reminiscing on his happiest years while working as a community center director within a neighborhood ridden with strife

(B)   An anonymous narrator describing a man whose life was devoted to helping children in his neighborhood after having a difficult childhood

(C)   The admiration of a man by a relative who witnessed his generosity towards children who in turn respected him as he helped turn a failing community center around

(D)   A person narrating his personal experiences as they unfold, beginning with his childhood to adulthood when he served as an advocate for troubled children

(51) Which of the following was Abdi's dream?

(A) To have the community center's kids use sports and theater as a means of escape

(B) To guide children to a better future

(C) To become rich so he could reunite with his family

(D) To use his experience at the community center to establish similar centers across the state

(52) Which of the following can you infer that Abdi and the Watsons would agree upon?

(A) Children are fulfilled only when they are exposed to famous artwork and literature

(B) Children can only attain greatness if they value community over themselves

(C) Children thrive and become respectable members of the community when they develop discipline

(D) Children are happy only when they develop a strong religious foundation when still very young

(53) Which of the following people lived a full life as per Abdi's definition of it?

(A) Father Watson

(B) Abdi's mother

(C) Mother Watson

(D) Abdi in his adulthood

Math Section – Test 2

(1) Calculate the area of a square whose side measures 2.5 cm.

(A) 39 cm²

(B) 10 cm²

(C) 5 cm²

(D) 6.25 cm²

(2) A rectangular sheet of paper measures 52 cm in length and 38 cm in width. If Naomi cut the sheet into several squares measuring 5 cm on each side, how many whole squares did she cut?

(A) 25

(B) 79

(C) 70

(D) 79.04

(3) Calculate the sum of the lengths of a cube's edges if one of its faces has an area of 49 cm².

(A) 98 cm

(B) 112 cm

(C) 84 cm

(D) 48 cm

(4) What is (x + 2z) (y + 2z) if x = 4, y = -6 and z = 8?

(A) -200

(B) 200

(C) 20

(D) -104

(5) Solve this inequality: 17 − 2b < 10

(A) b > 3.5

(B) b < 3.5

(C) b < 2.3

(D) b > 5

(6) Find y in (y + 3)/4 = (2y − 3)/5

(A) 12

(B) 9

(C) 15

(D) -9

(7) Express 3/(2y − 1) − 4/ (5y + 2) as a fraction in simplest form.

(A) (7y + 10) / ((2y − 1)(5y + 2))

(B) 7y + 10/10y − 2

(C) -1/10y − 2

(D) 7y − 10/(2y − 1)(5y + 2)

(8)   Find x in the following equation: $6x/5 - 2x/2 = 1/2$

(A)   5

(B)   2/5

(C)   5/2

(D)   20/4

(9)   Anna's age is given as $10y - 24$ and her cousin Jon is y years old. Calculate Anna's age if she is two times older than Jon.

(A)   6

(B)   8

(C)   10

(D)   24

(10) If Kendra is y years old and her twin cousins are 6 years younger than she is, what is their mean age?

(A) $y - 4$

(B) $y - 2y - 2$

(C) $y - 3y - 3$

(D) $y - 4y - 4$

(11) If x = 8 and y = 22, express x in terms of y.

(A) x = 144/(y − 4)

(B) x = 144y − 4

(C) x = 32(y − 2)

(D) y = 72/x − 4

(12) Three teams—x, y and z—scored 150 points in total, with team x scoring 40% of that total and team y scoring four times more points than team z. How many points did team y score?

(A) 60

(B) 18

(C) 72

(D) 90

(13) Stacy, Kelly and Tommy shared some money amongst themselves in a ratio of 14:16:18. How much did Tommy get if Stacy received $2,100?

(A) $2,000

(B) $2,400

(C) $2,700

(D) $5,100

(14) Calculate the number of seats in a hall if there are 2,000 more red seats than white seats and the white seats are 30% in total.

(A) 4,000

(B) 5,000

(C) 6,000

(D) 3,000

(15) Calculate the actual area of a plot if 4 cm on a map represents 1 km and the area of that plot is given as 60 cm².

(A) 3.75 cm²

(B) 0.26 km²

(C) 15 km²

(D) 3.75 km²

(16) How many sides does a polygon have if each interior angle is 156°?

(A) 8

(B) 15

(C) 6

(D) 14

(17) Calculate the present ages of Ken and Stephen if Ken is five times as old as Stephen and the product of both their ages four years ago was 52.

(A) Ken is 15 and Stephen is 2

(B) Ken is 60 and Stephen is 30

(C) Ken is 5 and Stephen is 30

(D) Ken is 30 and Stephen is 6

(18) Find x in the following equation: $12/(4x - 10) - 8/(2x - 6) = 0$.

(A) 1

(B) 4

(C) 8

(D) -1

(19) When you subtract a certain number from 125, you get a value that is twice that initial number after dividing it by 12. What is the number?

(A) 41

(B) 5

(C) 10

(D) 25

(20) Arrange the following numbers from smallest to largest: 5, 4.26, 9/4, 13/3, 8/2.

(A) 13/3, 8/2, 4.26, 5, 9/4

(B) 9/4, 8/2, 13/3, 4.26, 5

(C) 9/4, 8/2, 4.26, 13/3, 5

(D) 4.26, 9/4, 13/3, 8/2, 5

(21) Arrange the following numbers from smallest to largest: 0.09, 0.9, 0.099, 0.009, 0.091.

(A) 0.009, 0.09, 0.091, 0.099, 0.9

(B) 0.009, 0.9, 0.09, 0.099, 0.091

(C) 0.9, 0.09, 0.099, 0.091, 0.009

(D) 0.09, 0.009, 0.9, 0.099, 0.091

(22) What is $9+(-41) - (-3) + 11$?

(A) 64

(B) 24

(C) -24

(D) -18

(23) What do you get from $(3) (-4) (-3) (5) (-2)$?

(A) 17

(B) 360

(C) -360

(D) -1

(24) Which of the following fractions is equal to 0.032?

(A) 8/125

(B) 4/250

(C) 4/125

(D) 32/100

(25) What percentage listed below is equal to 0.0067?

(A) 67%

(B) 6.7%

(C) 0.067%

(D) 0.67%

(26) What is 85% written as a fraction in the simplest form?

(A) 17/200

(B) 8/5

(C) 17/20

(D) 5/8

(27) What is 0.33% written as a decimal?

(A) 0.33

(B) 33.0

(C) 0.0033

(D) 0.033

(28) What value does 6 have when expressed as a percentage of 15?

(A) 90%

(B) 32%

(C) 20%

(D) 40%

(29) Five friends travelled for four days and covered 1/4, 1/6 and 4/9 of their total distance on the first three days respectively. How much distance did they cover in those three days?

(A) 31/36

(B) 12/49

(C) 6/9

(D) 21/36

(30) Three men needed to dig one two-foot deep tunnel, and each was to dig one-third of that tunnel. If the first man dug a 1/9 distance, how much further did he have to dig?

(A) 2/9

(B) 8/9

(C) 3/9

(D) 2/3

(31) What is 7/8 ÷ 1/16?

(A) 13

(B) 14

(C) 7/128

(D) 3

(32) In a weather station, the rainfall received in January, February, March and April was 10.8, 5, 3.47 and 0.9 inches respectively. What was that station's total rainfall in those four months?

(A) 20.17

(B) 14.92

(C) 40.17

(D) 4.69

(33) If an athlete trained for a total of 6.25 hours and covered 114.75 miles of rough road, what was the average speed that the athlete was running at?

(A) 21 miles/hr

(B) 19.61 miles/hr

(C) 18.36 miles/hr

(D) 18.22 miles/hr

(34) Solve the following expression: $2(5 - 8 \cdot 10) + 5$

(A) -15

(B) -145

(C) -55

(D) -50

(35) Solve the following expression: $3 + 2(3 + 4)^2 - 6$

(A) 19

(B) 38

(C) 239

(D) 95

(36) Which expression below is equivalent to $2(4y - 2)(y - 5)/4(y - 5)$?

(A) $13y - 7$

(B) $7y + 38$

(C) $2y - 1$

(D) $8y + 34$

Science Section – Test 2

(1) What is the appropriate conclusion Mendel could have drawn out of the results he got from his experiment involving green and yellow pea plants?

(A) Green is a recessive trait in peas

(B) When pea plants are inbred, mutation occurs

(C) Pea plants contain carbohydrates, such as starch

(D) All the traits in pea plants are paired, and one trait is always dominant while another is recessive

(2) Carbohydrates are macromolecules which can be categorized into three major types. Those types are _____.

(A) Monosaccharides, disaccharides, polysaccharides

(B) Monosaccharides, polysaccharides, glycosidic bonds

(C) Lipids, proteins, nucleic acids

(D) Sugar, starch, proteins

(3) The autonomic nervous system is divided into _____.

(A) Sympathetic and nervous

(B) Central and peripheral

(C) Central and somatic

(D) Sympathetic and parasympathetic

(4)   The body's vagus nerve is in charge of conveying which of the following signals?

(A)   Signals emanating from a person's jaw

(B)   Signals emanating from a person's inner ear

(C)   Signals emanating from a person's eye

(D)   Signals emanating from the person's abdomen

(5)   The space that exists in between a neuron's axon and dendrite is called the _____.

(A)   Nerve impulse

(B)   Synapse

(C)   Band gap

(D)   Neurotransmitter

(6)   Which of the following is not regulated by the body's parasympathetic nervous system?

(A)   Slowed heart rate

(B)   Constricted blood vessels

(C)   Increased glandular activity

(D)   Increased intestinal activity

(7)   Which of the following valves is/are responsible for a person's heartbeat sounds?

(A)   Hydraulic valves and solenoid valves

(B)   Systole valves

(C)   Hypertension valves

(D)   Atrioventricular valves and semilunar valves

(8)   Which bodily function is controlled by the sympathetic part of the autonomic nervous system?

(A)   Breathing

(B)   Shivering

(C)   Fight or flight response

(D)   Swallowing

(9)   Which of the following is a carbohydrate?

(A)   Myosin

(B)   ATP

(C)   Cellulose

(D)   Collagen

(10) A person's eye color gene has three alleles, which are E^B, E^{Bl} and E^G. These correspond to brown eyes, blue eyes and green eyes, respectively. If someone is E^B/E^G, can that person be said to be homozygous or just heterozygous with regard to the color of the eyes?

(A)   Neither, considering the genotype is not complete

(B)   Homozygous

(C)   Heterozygous

(D)   Neither; if there are two probable alleles for one gene, heterozygous and homozygous cannot be significant

(11)   Which of the following is not a function of the body's pancreatic juice?

(A)   Increase in acidity of the stomach's contents

(B)   Chemical digestion of carbohydrates

(C)   Chemical digestion of proteins

(D)   Neutralizing chime's pH

(12)   Which of the following happens when a person is stressed?

(A)   High levels of glucose leave the liver and enter the person's bloodstream

(B)   Blood vessels dilate within the person's digestive system

(C)   Glucose is taken up by the person's liver and muscles as well as the adipose tissues

(D)   Blood vessels constrict within the person's skeletal muscles

(13) Which of the organelles listed below is responsible for the digestion of cellular structures that have been damaged, as well as the macromolecules alongside bacteria that the cell has ingested?

(A) Golgi apparatus

(B) Mitochondria

(C) Lysosomes

(D) Endoplasmic reticulum

(14) Which of the following is a chronic joint inflammation caused by the autoimmune damage of articular cartilage?

(A) Osteoporosis

(B) Osteoarthritis

(C) Brittle bone disease

(D) Rheumatoid arthritis

(15) The statements listed below are about pH. Identify the one that is true.

(A) When pH values are higher, it means [H+] is higher

(B) If you add some acid to a given solution, the pH rises

(C) When pH is 7, it is more acidic than pH 8

(D) The pH of blood is acidic

(16) Identify the statement that is true about protons.

(A) There are atoms that do not have protons

(B) Protons beat neutrons in mass

(C) Protons have a negative charge

(D) A nucleus' proton number is the property that defines a given element

(17) Plant X and Plant Y were growing side by side in an outdoor field. The former produced vegetables while the latter had flowers, and these had the effect of attracting pollinators. An observation was made that when X and Y grew a good distance apart, there were no vegetables on X, but Y still had flowers. From the answers below, choose the one that correctly explains the reason for X's failing to produce vegetables when far from Y.

(A) Y produced hormones that enhanced the growth of X

(B) Y shielded X from the heat of the sun

(C) Those insects responsible for pollinating Y also pollinated X

(D) Y had the effect of repelling insects that were harmful from X

(18) In the options listed below, there is an attempt to match neurons with their respective functions. Identify the answer whose pairing is correct.

(A) Axon; to send stimulus to the axon terminal

(B) Cell body; to release neurotransmitters

(C) Dendrites; to serve as the metabolic activity site

(D) Axon terminal; to receive stimulus from the cell body

(19) Which of the following is correct?

(A) Gas neither has a definite volume nor a definite shape

(B) Solids do not have a constant volume or shape

(C) The volume of gas is constant, and its shape is definite

(D) Liquids neither have a definite volume nor a constant shape

(20) Which of the following is not a function of mitosis?

(A) Asexual reproduction

(B) An organism growing

(C) Production of gametes

(D) Repairing damaged tissue

(21) Different foods produce varying levels of urea. Which of the following foods produces the most urea that would need to be cleared from the blood by the kidneys?

(A) Fruits like apples and tangerines

(B) Grains like pasta or rice

(C) Protein like meats or eggs

(D) Oil like olive oil or corn oil

(22) Which of the following characteristics applies to those bonds that hold together non-polar covalent molecules?

(A)   They are created as two distinct atoms, sharing metal ions

(B)   They are created as two distinct atoms and share electrons that come as a pair

(C)   They are formed between two dissimilar atoms

(D)   It is only possible for them to be formed between identical atoms

(23) Which of the layers of a person's skin has stores of subcutaneous fat?

(A)   The dermis

(B)   The sebaceous layer

(C)   The epidermis

(D)   The hypodermis

(24) Which of the following shows the sequence in which inhalation takes place?

(A)   The pharynx, the nasal cavity, the larynx, the trachea, the bronchi, the bronchioles

(B)   The nasal cavity, the trachea, the pharynx, the larynx, bronchioles, the bronchi

(C)   The nasal cavity, the bronchi, the bronchioles, the trachea, the pharynx, the larynx

(D)   The nasal cavity, the pharynx, the larynx, the trachea, the bronchi, the bronchioles

(25) One vessel carries blood that has been depleted of oxygen out of the heart, and another carries blood that is rich in oxygen as it approaches the heart. Choose the answer that has those two vessels in their respective order.

(A)   The pulmonary artery, the pulmonary vein

(B)   The aorta, the pulmonary artery

(C)   The pulmonary vein, the pulmonary artery

(D)   The vena cava, the pulmonary artery

(26) The cholera-causing bacterium is known as vibrio cholera. A disease-causing agent is generally known as _____.

(A)   A pathogen

(B)   A commensal microorganism

(C)   An interferon

(D)   A vaccine

(27) Researchers carried out an experiment that was well-controlled, and they observed that a new antibiotic had the capacity to eliminate sinus infections caused by bacteria. From that observation, one can infer _____.

(A)   That this medication assisted in the elimination of the allergies the patient had

(B)   That this medication managed to kill the particular bacteria that caused sinus infections

(C)   That this medication changed the DNA of the patient to assist him/her in fighting infection

(D)   That this medication served as an antihistamine and cured the patient's runny nose

(28) Which of the following is another term for "kneecap"?

(A)   The pisiform

(B)   The popliteal bursa

(C)   The meniscus

(D)   The patella

(29) Which of the following refers to a person's shoulder joint?

(A)   The ball and socket joint

(B)   The hinge joint

(C)   The saddle joint

(D)   The pivot joint

(30) The human body has one organ known as "corti," and it is located within _____,

(A)   The mouth

(B)   The nose

(C)   The ear

(D)   The lungs

(31) Rickets is linked to a deficiency of _____.

(A)   Vitamin A

(B)   Vitamin D

(C)   Vitamin C

(D)   Vitamin Z

(32) Steroids are _____.

(A) Lipids

(B) Enzymes

(C) Proteins

(D) Weak acids

(33) The X-cranial nerve is also _____.

(A) The abducens nerve

(B) The facial nerve

(C) The hypoglossal

(D) The vagus

(34) The answers listed below have varying ranges of pH. Identify the one that represents a strong base.

(A) 1.3 to 2.0

(B) 7.1 to 9.0

(C) 4.5 to 5.2

(D) 11.2 to 12.0

(35) Which heart chamber is responsible for pumping blood from a person's heart to the person's systemic circulation?

(A)   The left atrium

(B)   The left ventricle

(C)   The right atrium

(D)   The right ventricle

(36) Which of the following represents Newton's second law of motion?

(A) $F = ma$

(B) $v = d/t$

(C) $F = mva$

(D) $p = mv$

(37) DNA has an important part to play during the cell cycle phase known as the S-phase. Identify the answer that reflects that role.

(A)   To condense and become the smallest possible size so as to replicate

(B)   To remain unaltered

(C)   To uncoil and be ready to be copied

(D)   To be converted into RNA

(38) Which of the following best describes what is measured by a pH test?

(A) How strong a base is

(B) How concentrated hydrogen ions are

(C) How strong an acid is

(D) How concentrated anions are

(39) Which body system's role is it to ensure nutrients reach all organs of the body, including the tissues?

(A) The circulatory system

(B) The digestive system

(C) The respiratory system

(D) The nervous system

(40) A controlled experiment is only used to test _____.

(A) A single hypothesis at a time

(B) A single variable at a time

(C) A single theory at a time

(D) A single control at a time

(41) Which passage is used both for swallowing and breathing?

(A) The esophagus

(B) The larynx

(C) The trachea

(D) The pharynx

(42) The answers listed below represent pairs of organs within the central nervous system, apart from one. Which is that exception?

(A)   The spinal cord and brain

(B)   The spinal cord and frontal lobe

(C)   The brain and the frontal lobe

(D)   The spinal cord and arm nerve

(43) Which of the following constitutes the basis of the food chain within the ocean?

(A)   The fish

(B)   The phytoplankton

(C)   The algae

(D)   The coral

(44) The size of any animal is several times that of any bacterial cells. By how many times, on estimate, are animal cells larger?

(A)   Ten times

(B)   A thousand times

(C)   A hundred times

(D)   Ten thousand times

(45) Which of the following organelles carries out autophagy?

(A) Proteasome

(B) Ribosome

(C) Cytoskeleton

(D) Lysosome

(46) Consider the reaction process shown next, and then answer the question that follows.

$Fe + O_2 \rightarrow Fe_2O_3$

Which of the following shows the right molarity for the above reaction?

(A) $Fe + O_2 \rightarrow 2Fe_2O_3$

(B) $Fe + 3O_2 \rightarrow Fe_2O_3$

(C) $Fe + 3O_2 \rightarrow 2Fe_2O_3$

(D) $4Fe + 3O_2 \rightarrow 2Fe_2O_3$

(47) Which of the following is performed by the luteinizing hormone?

(A) Pregnancy protection

(B) Menstruation

(C) Ovulation

(D) Labor

(48) Which of the following words is correctly spelled?

(A) Kneumonia

(B) Numonia

(C) Neumy

(D) Pneumonia

(49) Which of the following has a correct atomic number if the element under consideration has 45 protons and 64 as its atomic mass?

(A) It is not possible to tell

(B) 45

(C) 19

(D) 64

(50) Which of the following is true regarding a person's blood pressure?

(A) It is normally greater within the arteries than within the veins

(B) It is normally lower within the arteries than within the veins

(C) It is normally the same within the arteries and within the veins

(D) None of the above

(51) The instrument used to measure a person's blood pressure is ____.

(A) The thermometer

(B) The anapesticmeter

(C) The sphygmomanometer

(D) The anemometer

(52) The human body has nerve cell projections that are long and slender, and they are responsible for conducting impulses of an electrical nature, meaning that they carry information to different parts of the body, including the glands and muscles. These nerve cell projections are referred to as _____.

(A) Axons

(B) Schwann

(C) Myelin

(D) None of the above

(53) _____ are known to tap information from the environment and convey it to the brain.

(A) Axons

(B) Nerve endings

(C) Nuclei

(D) Dendrites

English and Language Use Section – Test 2

(1)   Which of the following best explains the meaning of "draft" as used in the sentence: "There is a draft in the hallway as a result of the broken duct system"?

(A)   Unit of liquid measure

(B)   First copy of something written

(C)   Cash amount withdrawn from a fund

(D)   Air current

(2)   What part of speech is the word "in" within the sentence? "The police officers waited in an unmarked car to see if anyone would come under the dark of night to pick up the hidden parcel."

(A)   Subject

(B)   Object

(C)   Preposition

(D)   Verb

(3)   Choose the best word to complete the sentence. "Betty was eager to receive her college ____ letter."

(A)   Exception

(B)   Acceptance

(C)   Exceptance

(D)   Axeptance

(4)   Which of the following words has an irregular plural?

(A)   Monkey

(B)   Crisis

(C)   Horse

(D)   Baby

(5)   Consider the antecedent and identify the appropriate pronoun to complete the sentence. "The plastic chairs were put one on top of another to form a high irregular tower against the wall. Soon, ____ all came tumbling down."

(A)   He

(B)   It

(C)   She

(D)   They

(6)   Identify the answer that best corrects the errors in the sentence. "Jane's two dog consume plenty of food. It eats a whole bag every week."

(A)   Jane's two dogs consume plenty of food. It eat a whole bag every week.

(B)   Jane's two dogs consume plenty of food. They eat a whole bag every week.

(C)   Jane's two dog consumed plenty of food. It eats a whole bag every week.

(D)   Jane's two dogs consumes plenty of food. They eats a whole bag every week.

(7) "As she devoured the food with her bare hands, it was clear she enjoyed every morsel of it." What part of speech is "bare"?

(A) Noun

(B) Verb

(C) Adjective

(D) Object

(8) Identify the correct verb-tense used in the sentence. "Patel had given his younger brother loans several times before."

(A) Future tense

(B) Simple past

(C) Present perfect

(D) Past perfect

(9) Identify the meaning of the word "tacit" from the context of the sentence. "When Susan was unable to contact John to seek confirmation on the plans they had discussed before, she translated his silence to be tacit compliance; hence, she proceeded with the plans."

(A) Expressed nonverbally

(B) Wholeheartedly

(C) Snobbishly

(D) Disinterestedly

(10) Identify the most probable meaning of the word "firm" as used in the sentence. "She was filled with trepidation as she eyed the large firm, and she opted not to seek a job interview there.'"

(A) A massive structure built of strong material

(B) Tight and solid

(C) Emotion-causing situation

(D) Group of people who made up the business

(11) Which of the following words is misspelled?

(A) Desparate

(B) Laboratories

(C) Conceivable

(D) Separation

(12) Which of the following words need to be separated with a hyphen to make a compound word?

(A) World, wide

(B) Life, like

(C) Grand, mother

(D) First, rate

(13) Choose the correct set of punctuation marks to complete the sentence.

"James was prepared to drive the whole night ___ however ___ he knew he'd be out of gas after just fifty kilometers."

(A)   Semicolon/period

(B)   Colon/semicolon

(C)   Comma/comma

(D)   Semicolon/comma

(14) What kind of sentence is this: "After Singh completed his degree in engineering studies, he found it difficult to secure a job in the rural country"?

(A)   Compound sentence

(B)   Complex sentence

(C)   Dependent clause

(D)   Simple sentence

(15) Which of the following is correctly capitalized?

(A)   All the Senators were expected to leave their phones behind during the meeting.

(B)   Trees are notorious for shedding their leaves in Autumn.

(C)   Joginder's family, living in the South, often pays visits to their kin who live in the Southwest.

(D)   Dr. Cornell and his sister, who has a Doctorate in Philosophy, are the most learned members of their family.

(16) Identify the answer that represents the sentence in active voice. "The piano was magnificently played by John."

(A) John's piano was played magnificently.

(B) The piano that belonged to John was magnificently played.

(C) John played the piano magnificently.

(D) Because John had practiced well, he played the piano notes well.

(17) Identify the answer that rectifies the run-on sentence. "James wanted to invest in stocks he had just enough money to educate his children."

(A) James wanted to invest in stocks, he had just enough money to educate his children.

(B) James wanted to invest in stocks: he had just enough money to educate his children.

(C) Although James wanted to invest in stocks he had just enough money to educate his children.

(D) Although James wanted to invest in stocks, he had just enough money to educate his children.

(18) Identify the answer that clarifies the sentence's structure. "Mary and Michelle were very eager to attend the party, and their sisters and colleagues."

(A) Sisters Mary and Michelle and colleagues were very eager to attend the party.

(B) Colleagues and their sisters were Mary and Michelle, very eager to attend the party.

(C) Mary and Michelle, their sisters and colleagues, were very eager to attend the party.

(D) Very eager to attend the party, were colleagues Mary and Michelle and sisters.

(19) What are the two pronouns in this sentence? "The blue car in the parking lot is his, but the red one on the roadside is hers."

(A)   Blue, red

(B)   Parking, roadside

(C)   His, hers

(D)   Road, side

(20) Which of the following is a compound sentence?

(A)   Susan applied for the position of human resources manager because of her training in personnel management.

(B)   Susan is trained in personnel management, so she felt comfortable applying for the position of human resources manager.

(C)   Because of her training in personnel management, Susan applied for the position of human resources manager.

(D)   Because of her training in personnel management, Susan applied for the position of human resources manager, and she is optimistic she will be hired.

(21) Which of the following sentences is not compound-complex?

(A)   The headmaster initiated an after-school program for young children because he realized the local community did not have such a program.

(B)   The local community lacked child-friendly programs, so the headmaster initiated one because he wanted to help.

(C)   Because the local community lacked child-friendly after-school programs, the headmaster initiated one, and he was impressed with the massive attendance.

(D)   The headmaster initiated after-school programs for young children because he wanted to assist, and he noticed the local community lacked this kind of program.

(22) Which of the following exemplifies a third-person narrative?

(A)   You applied here for a job, and you worked hard the first and the second day. However, you began to slow down on your third day, and now you don't seem to care if you meet our standards or not.

(B)   I applied for a job and waited for the response. I received the invitation on the second day, and from then on I've been working diligently.

(C)   I looked at the waving crowd and waved back at them. It was finally my moment.

(D)   Tom and Francis sang impressively. Jane, Tom's wife, was teary as she watched him walk to the dais to receive his prize.

(23) Which of the following sentences is properly punctuated?

(A)   "Jane encouraged us all to take to the dance floor, saying, Come on, now. Let's have a good time!

(B)   Jane encouraged us all to take to the dance floor, saying, "Come on, now. Let's have a good time!"

(C)   Jane encouraged us all to take to the dance floor, saying, Come on, now. "Let's have a "good time"!

(D)   Jane encouraged us all to take to the dance floor, saying, "Come on, now. Let's have a 'good time'!

(24) After reading the paragraph, identify where you are likely to find such a passage.

I have previously held the position of administrative assistant in a busy real estate company, and in my two most recent jobs I was an administrative assistant in companies within the manufacturing sector. My experience has prepared me for the position of executive assistant. I can type reasonably fast, and I'm adept at multitasking. I have also taken a course in Microsoft Office, and so, I can carry out computer-based tasks such as creating worksheets, designing letters, and others.

(A)   In a big firm's newsletter

(B)   In an article within a business magazine

(C)   In a newspaper advertisement

(D)   In a job applicant's cover letter

(25) Identify the subject and object in the sentence. "The rugby team devoured the barbecue meat as though they had not eaten in three days."

(A)   Rugby team, devoured

(B)   Rugby team, barbecue meat

(C)   Devoured, not eaten

(D)   Devoured, barbecue meat

(26) Choose the option that correctly explains how to identify a second-person narrative.

(A)   When the pronoun "you" is used

(B)   When the writer uses the present tense

(C)   When the pronoun "I" is used

(D)   When the simple past tense is used

(27) If you add a dependent clause to each of the answers listed below, which of them will not turn into a complex sentence?

(A) James' relatives and their pets were exhausted by midday.

(B) The cheetah raced quickly across the plains.

(C) Mr. Tom loved coaching the students, but driving to his new home was too strenuous for him to continue.

(D) Susan, Mary, Purity and Ann spent hours in the line.

(28) Each of the answers below, apart from one, has two independent clauses. Identify the exception.

(A) She was about to be late for school, but she remained very calm.

(B) Mary always does more than expected, so the firm has given her a promotion.

(C) He looked forward to hearing from his relatives, but everyone forgot his birthday.

(D) The butterflies flew over the flowery garden, occasionally perching on the plants, because they wanted to get some nectar.

Practice Test 2: Answers

Reading Section – Test 2 Answers

(1)   The correct answer is: (D) Concluded.

The reason (D) is the correct answer is that the word "concluded" can be used as a substitute for "reasoned" in the passage and the meaning of the sentence will still remain intact.

(2)   The correct answer is: (D) A novel for young adults.

The reason (D) is correct is that the passage concentrates on two young adults, Edna and Beatrice, and some of the decisions they need to make as they prepare to leave home for college.

(3)   The correct answer is: (D) Massive disharmonious sounds or noises.

The reason (D) is correct is that the experience the audience are said to have had was in contrast to what would have been expected from a band that had apparently thoroughly practiced.

(4)   The correct answer is: (C) Simple.

The best way to get to the right answer is to note how the word looks at every stage of following the instructions. After the first part, you get the word "dlimped," and after the second, you get "dimple." After implementing the last instruction you end up with the word "simple."

(5)   The correct answer is: (C) Self-conceited.

The reason (C) is the correct answer is that a conceited person thinks so highly of himself that in such a case he may think he reserves the right to use the space as he wishes, without consideration for other customers.

(6)   The correct answer is: (A) To ask for Annabel's help in maintaining a family Christmas tradition.

The reason (A) is the correct answer is that Sheila has explicitly requested Annabel's help in maintaining their family's Christmas tradition. The fact that their parents will be away on Christmas day is a 'by-the-way' and not the core purpose of writing the email.

(7)   The correct answer is: (C) Sisters.

It is evident that (C) is correct because Sheila speaks of "Mom and Dad." She doesn't say "my" mom and dad, so the inference is that the two women share the parents. Hence, they are sisters.

(8)   The correct answer is: (A) To uphold the traditions her family has always kept.

The email opens with Sheila expressing her hope that they, including Annabel, might congregate in one place and spend Christmas together so as to maintain their tradition. Travel is mentioned in the email, but it is not Sheila's main point of focus. She also does not give any indication of taking her family to Hawaii.

(9)   The correct answer is: (B) Preserve.

To preserve is to ensure something lasts for long, and it is fitting as a substitute for "maintain" as used in the email because what Sheila wants is to have the family Christmas tradition preserved.

(10) The correct answer is: (C) That the celebrations are family friendly.

The reason (C) is the correct answer is that the activities mentioned in the email are all family-oriented as opposed to being childish or adult-oriented. A good example of the family friendly activities is decorating, which can be done by children and adults together.

(11) The correct word is: (D) Megalomania

(D) is correct because "megalomania" can be found on the open page. When considering the range from "measly" to "melancholy," take the first three letters of both words. The correct word should begin with "me-" with its third letter being anything from "a" to "l." "t" and "n" in (A) and (C) come after, while "meadow" is before.

(12) The correct answer is: (B) Classifieds.

The reason (B) is the correct answer is that the classifieds section also accepts personal advertisements.

(13) The correct answer is: (D) Reading for Communication: A Crucial Skill.

The reason (D) is the correct answer is that it covers the important points highlighted in the passage, among them, the capacity to read and how that affects one's ability to communicate. The other choices are either generic or fail to specify communication.

(14) The correct answer is: (D) Distressing or very difficult.

Based on the passage context, the word "harrowing" means "distressing" or "very difficult." In fact, it is explained that many students only engage in reading for the purpose of attaining a passing grade in a class.

(15) The correct answer is: (D) To communicate how important it is to read regularly.

(D) encompasses the core message of the passage; writing is only mentioned in regard to writing skills development. The importance of regular reading is the main message, indicating the impact it has on communication and social interaction. The passage does not mention parents' reprimands and it does not discourage reading.

(16) The correct answer is: (B) Sycophantic.

The word "obsequious" as used in the given sentence means "sycophantic," which also means being excessively attentive. The words that provide the clue are "smarmy compliments." There is nothing to indicate the boyfriend was either bored or uncaring, and "attentive" does not convey the negative connotation "obsequious" and "sycophantic" have.

(17) The correct answer is: (C) Add more commentary or references.

The reason (C) is the correct answer is that a footnote adds to any existing commentary, and other times it provides a reference or source data in case the reader wishes to learn more. All the other suggestions are erroneous.

(18) The correct answer is: (B) Perigee.

Consider "pelican" and "perambulate" and you realize the commonness of spelling ends at the first syllable, "pe." From then on you need to look for words whose third letter falls from "l" up to "r," and you find "pentathlon," "penance" and "pepsin." If the word has "r" in third place, it needs to have "a" after it, unlike "perigee."

(19) The correct answer is: (B) Glossary.

(B) is correct because a glossary is the place where definitions of words from the text are found. A table of contents shows book chapters or sections. A bibliography comprises a reference list.

(20) The correct answer is: (A) An editorial.

The reason (A) is the correct answer is that an editorial only expresses the opinion of the editor, which may not be based on any facts. All the other three options are factual and normally use data to back up their content.

(21) The correct answer is: (A) Sustain.

Based on the context, it is understood that some specialties may be subjected to higher fees; or they may be the subject of higher fees than other specialties. None of the other three options have a similar meaning to "incur."

(22) The correct answer is: (B) To confirm that the student and tutor are compatible.

(B) is the correct answer because it reflects the text's suggestion that determining compatibility between a student and tutor is vital.

(23) The correct answer is: (B) By seeking assistance from the school that the student attends or online tutorial services.

The reason (B) is correct is that the text outlines reliable ways to find a good tutor. These include consulting the student's own school or searching online.

(24) The correct answer is: (D) While tutoring services vary greatly, you should always carefully vet any tutor you select.

(D) is the correct answer because all the points it highlights are discussed in the text. The text says tutorial services are available and cover a wide range of specialties. It is also emphasized in the text that there is a need to thoroughly check tutors before hiring anybody.

(25) The correct answer is: (B) Expository.

The reason (B) is the correct answer is that the text is informative to readers, explaining the advantages of engaging a tutor and giving advice on optimizing a student's experience with the tutor. The text does not compare or contrast tutors. It also does not deal with cause and subsequent effect.

(26) The correct answer is: (C) The blue bag.

(C) is correct because though the blue messenger bag is pricier, it is more likely to serve a student better in college as she transports large, heavy books, and probably a laptop.

(27) The correct answer is: (D) The studded clutch.

(D) is the correct answer because a clutch is classic enough for a gala, yet it has enough space to accommodate a wallet.

(28) The correct answer is: (C) The blue bag.

The reason (C) is the correct answer is that the messenger bag is most functional for someone who is "bookish," meaning she is probably academically oriented.

(29) The correct answer is: (A) A complete guide to Florida's sights and attractions.

The reason (A) is the correct answer is that a complete guide is bound to contain helpful information pertaining to the local art and its history.

(30) The correct answer is: (A) To let the applicant know that he/she should prepare to be interviewed in 14 days.

(A) is the correct answer because the writer has clarified the agency has received the application and is in the process of reviewing it, then proceeds to detail how the applicant should carry out certain requirements. Such instructions include refraining from contacting the agency during the 14-day waiting period.

(31) The correct answer is: (C) Teenagers are not good at handling personal responsibilities.

It is clear that the author of the first passage believes that teenagers are not capable of handling everyday responsibilities. Although there are other sections of the passage that indicate the author's position, it is most explicit in the sentence: "Whereas sixteen-year-old teenagers are considered mature enough to watch R-rated films, they are essentially still kids in several ways."

(32) The correct answer is: (D) Currently, the legal driving age is fine and should not be changed.

(D) is backed up by several arguments that the writer of the second passage makes for retaining the minimum legal age for driving at sixteen years. The statement at the very end of the passage is also significant, where the author clearly states his position.

(33) The correct answer is: (B) Teenagers learn as they watch their own parents drive.

(B) is correct because nowhere in the passage does the author try to justify his position for allowing sixteen-year-olds to drive by indicating they will have learned by watching their parents. He cites the many other responsibilities teenagers are entrusted with as an indication they can be safely entrusted with driving.

(34) The correct answer is: (A) Both writers are very passionate on the issue of the minimum legal driving age, although their opinions differ.

The main topic both writers concentrate on is the minimum legal age at which one can drive. (A) is also correct because it highlights that the writers have divergent views on their common issue of interest.

(35) The correct answer is: (D) Atlanta.

The reason (D) is the correct answer is that if you add the number of accidents in the months that come after January, as per the given table, the total comes to 6,050 for Atlanta (2,100 + 1,950 + 2,000), whereas New York totals 6,900 and LA 6,400. Hence, Atlanta has the fewest accidents.

(36) The correct answer is: (B) Get dressed.

The reason (B) is the correct answer is that the passage explicitly states that as soon as the author completed reading the newspaper, he got dressed and went outside with his friends. The other three answers are, therefore, incorrect.

(37) The correct answer is: (D) Finally.

(D) is the correct answer because it has been used in the sentence that introduces the day's last activity as a family. The sentence is "Finally, when dinner ended, my entire family ..."

(38) The correct answer is: (B) Locating synonyms.

A thesaurus serves as a resource to find synonyms in order to avoid overusing any one word.

(39) The correct answer is: (C) Veal parmigiana.

The reason (C) is the correct answer is that veal is red meat. Margaret doesn't consume red meat.

(40) The correct answer is: (C) Is of the opinion that the average person has no need for a smart phone.

The reason (C) is correct is that, from the context of the passage, it is clear that some people, according to the author, use their smart phones for frivolous matters.

(41) The correct answer is: (D) Presenting a plausible explanation for why smart phones continue to grow in popularity.

The reason (D) is correct is that it portrays the writer's position as far as reasons for smart phones' growth. Whereas people are using smart-phone technology for serious work, they may also be taking advantage of that available connectivity for leisure.

(42) The correct answer is: (C) The human community is bound to survive in spite of conflicts between nations.

The reason (C) is correct is that the passage states that the human race faces the danger of decimation from superpowers engaging in conflict. However, the passage also states that weapons will never be used and thus a full-on armed conflict is unlikely to occur, implying humanity's survival.

(43) The correct answer is: (C) Move towards war.

(C) is the correct answer and supports the author's statement that even countries that have massive stocks of dangerous weapons are doing their best to avoid using them.

Moving to the brink has the connotation of moving to the edge or very near the cliff, meaning reaching a dangerous position.

(44) The correct answer is: (D) The countries who have stocked up deadly weapons are making a great effort to refrain from real conflict.

(D) is the best answer because it notes exactly what the writer's opinion is regarding the fact that some countries have massive stocks of deadly weapons. Refraining from war does not mean that countries, including superpowers, agree on all important issues. They argue and are tempted to go to war, but they refrain from it.

(45) The correct answer is: (C) Not possible to restrain.

(C) is correct because it supports the position that it is not possible to vanquish a person completely, for the soul lives on even after physical death; no human being can fully control or suppress another's spirit.

(46) The correct answer is: (B) To achieve success, it is important to resist temptation and instant gratification.

In (B), the author directly refers to the dangers and temptations that people encounter, but also alludes to life outcomes that depend on how well a person handles these.

(47) The correct answer is: (C) It is idealistic.

(C) is supported by the fact that the writer has described Greek mythology as instilling important values in a reader. Considering the author has selectively highlighted only the positive features of Greek mythology, the term "idealistic" is fitting.

(48) The correct answer is: (B) Try to describe a phenomenon.

(B) is the correct answer as the passage is dominated by an elaborate description of a particular natural phenomenon. The passage describes how water and air are affected by heat, and how they are involved in a reduction of turbulence often created by the wind.

(49) The correct answer is: (B) Causes air that is cool and dry to rise to the surface of the ocean.

(B) is the correct answer because it conveys facts explicitly stated in the passage. For example, the passage states, "Water vapor almost saturates any air that is within around one millimeter of the mass of water, as the air temperature becomes almost the same as that of the water surface."

(50) The correct answer is: (B) An anonymous narrator describing a man whose life was devoted to helping children in his neighborhood after having a difficult childhood.

(B) is correct because the narrator is not identified in the passage, but it is a person who has ample information regarding the man known on the streets as Abdi, who was committed to helping young people. The narrator is conversant with Abdi's difficult childhood and describes it in detail, from hunger to very strict rules at home.

(51) The correct answer is: (B) To guide children to a better future.

(B) is supported by the opening sentence in the passage, "Charles Johnson, or Abdi, as he was more commonly known, decided that he would make use of his talent as a modern playwright in order to broaden young people's horizons; specifically, gifted individuals from black communities."

(52) The correct answer is: (C) Children thrive and become respectable members of the community when they develop discipline.

(C) is correct because the Watsons believed in discipline, as reflected in the manner they handled Abdi and the other children they fostered—curfews and mandatory church attendance—and Abdi used discipline to ensure no boy messed up at the community center.

(53) The correct answer is: (D) Abdi in his adulthood.

(D) is correct because after recalling the difficulties of his childhood, Abdi says a life lived in full entails doing the work you like, not worrying about the pay, and making your home a sea of love—exactly what Abdi did as an adult.

Math Section – Test 2 Answers

(1) The correct answer is: (D) 6.25.

The formula for getting the area of a square is $L \cdot W$. Since a square's sides are all equal, it means that if one side measures 2.5 cm, then all sides measure 2.5 cm. As such, $L \cdot W$ = 2.5 · 2.5, which is 6.25 cm².

(2) The correct answer is: (C) 70.

Naomi cut x number of 5-cm squares along the 52-cm length. To get this number, divide 52 by 5 and get 10.4 squares. Only whole squares were needed, so she had 10. Similarly, 38 cm width produces 38/5, which is 7.6. So she had 7 whole squares along the width. Now get the total squares by multiplying 10 · 7 = 70 squares.

(3) The correct answer is: (C) 84 cm.

If the area of one face is 49, then the length of one edge will be the square root of 49 since area = $L \cdot W$ and each edge of a cube has the same measurement. $\sqrt{49}$ = 7, so each side is 7 cm. Cubes have 12 edges, so if each edge is 7 cm then 12 edges will be 12 · 7 = 84 cm.

(4) The correct answer is: (B) 200.

Substitute the given values into the equation to get (4 + 2(8)) (-6 + 2(8)). First, solve the parentheses, so (4 + 2(8)) will be (4 + 16) and (-6 + 2(8)) will be (-6 + 16). Next, add (4 + 16) to get 20 and (-6 + 16) to get 10. Your final parentheses will be (20) (10), which can also be written as 20 · 10 = 200.

(5) The correct answer is: (A) b > 3.5.

If $17 - 2b$ is less than 10, then the value of b must be half the value of a number that when subtracted from 17 gives a value that is less than 10. To get the value of b, subtract 17 from both sides of the equation to get $17 - 17 - 2b < 10 - 17$ as $-2b < -7$. Divide both sides by -2 to get b > 3.5

(6)   The correct answer is: (B) 9.

When given (y + 3)/4 = (2y + 3)/5, start by eliminating the denominators on both sides. Do this by cross-multiplying both sides of the equation with the denominators, so 5(y + 3) = 4(2y − 3) will give you 5y + 15 = 8y − 12. Next, put like terms together, so 5y −8y = -12 - 15 will be -3y = -27. When you divide both sides by -3, you get y = 9

(7)   The correct answer is: (A) (7y + 10) / ((2y − 1) (5y + 2)).

Give the two fractions a common denominator by getting the LCD of both fractions, which is (2y − 1) (5y + 2). Solve parentheses first to get 3(5y + 2) − 4(2y − 1) / (2y − 1) (5y + 2) as (15y + 6) (-8y + 4) / (2y − 1)(5y + 2). Put the like terms together and solve 15y − 8y + 6 + 4 / (2y − 1) (5y + 2) = (7y + 10) / (2y − 1) (5y + 2). (Retain the denominator as it is.)

(8)   The correct answer is: (C) 5/2.

Get a common denominator for the two fractions by getting the LCD of 5 and 2, which is 10. Multiply both fractions by 10 to get 10(6x/5) − 10(2x/2) = 1/2 (10) as (12x − 10x)/10 = 1/2 (10). When you solve the parentheses, you get 2x/10 = 1/2(10). This will give you (12x − 10x) = 1/2(10). Simplified, you get 2x = 10/2 or 2x = 5, so x = 5/2.

(9)   The correct answer is: (A) 6.

Create an equation to solve this problem. If Anna is 10y − 24 and Jon is half the age of Anna, then Jon is half of 10y − 24, so 10y − 24/2 = 5y − 12. Put the like terms together and solve to get 5y − y = 12, which is 4y = 12. So y = 3. If Jon is 3 and Anna is twice his age, then Anna is 3 * 2 = 6

(10) The correct answer is: (A) y − 4.

Mean is calculated by dividing the sum of values by the number of given values. Here we are given Kendra's age as y years and the two cousins are (y + 6). The proportion should then be: y + (y − 6) + (y − 6) /3, which when solved, gives us 3 (y − 4)/3 = y − 4.

(11) The correct answer is: (A) $x = 144/(y - 4)$.

When a value is inversely proportional to another, it means that when one value increases, the other decreases. Here, x is inversely proportional to y, so your equation will be: $x = k/(y - 4)$, where k represents the constant of proportionality. Substitute the provided values, so $8 = k/(22 - 4)$. Solve this to get $8(22 - 4) = k$. $k = 144$, so $x = 144/(y - 4)$

(12) The correct answer is: (C) 72.

Team x scored 40% of the 150 points, so they scored $40/100 \times 150 = 60$ points. Team y scored four times what team z scored, so they scored $a \times 4$ points. And team z scored "a" points. In an equation, this will be: $60 + 4a + a = 150$. So $60 + 5a = 150$. Solve this and get $a = 18$. If team z scored 18 points, then team y scored $18 \times 4 = 72$.

(13) The correct answer is: (C) $2,700.

First, make this ratio a fraction. To do this, find a common denominator for the three ratio portions by getting the sum of the 3 portions. So $14 + 16 + 18 = 48$. The result is $14/48$, $16/48$ and $18/48$. If $14/48$ is $21,000, then $1/48$ should be $21,000 \div 14 = 150$. Now multiply 150 by 18 to get $2,700.

(14) The correct answer is: (B) 5,000.

Let "a" represent white seats, then create a proportion so $a + (a + 2,000) =$ total number of chairs. If "a" is given as 30%, then $30\% + (30\% + 2,000) = 100\%$. When you solve this, you get $60\% + 2,000 = 100\%$. This means that $40\% = 2,000$ and to get the value of 1% you divide 2,000 by 40 to get 50. If $1\% = 50$, then $100\% = 50 \times 100 = 5,000$.

(15) The correct answer is: (D) 3.75 km².

4 cm in the map represents 1 km of the actual distance. Since the area is given in cm², first convert the ratio to square measurements. 4 cm² is $4 \times 4 = 16$ cm², so 16 cm² = 1 km². If the area is represented as 60 cm² on the map and every 4 cm represent 1 km, then divide 60 cm² by 16 cm² to get 3.75 km².

(16) The correct answer is: (B) 15.

The formula for determining the angles of a polygon is $180(n-2)/n = x$, where x represents the interior angles' measurement and n represents the total number of sides. When you substitute the information that is already given, your equation will be $180(n-2)/n = 156$. When you solve this, you get $n = 15$.

(17) The correct answer is: (D) Ken is 30 and Stephen is 6.

Create an expression and let "a" represent Stephen's age. So Ken and Stephen are now 5a and "a" years old and the product of their ages four years ago was $(a-4)(5a-4) = 52$. When you solve this, you get $a = 6$ and $5a = 30$.

(18) The correct answer is: (A) 1.

First, cross-multiply the two fractions to get rid of the denominators. So $12/(4x-10) - 8/(2x-6)$ will be $12(2x-6) = 8(4x-10)$. Then solve this to get $24x - 72 = 32x - 80$. Simplified further, this is $-72 + 80 = 32x - 24x$, which is $8 = 8x$. To get the value of x, divide both sides by 8 to get $x = 1$.

(19) The correct answer is: (B) 5.

You are to identify a number which, when subtracted from 125, then divided by 12, gives you twice its initial value. So let x represent that number, then formulate an equation as follows: $(125 - x)/12 = 2x$. Next, cross-multiply to get $125 - x = 12(2x)$. Then simplify to get $125 = 25x$. To get x, divide both sides by 25 and get $x = 5$.

(20) The correct answer is: (C) 9/4, 8/2, 4.26, 13/3, 5.

First, convert the figures into decimals. To achieve this, divide the numerators by the denominators. So 9/4 will be 2.25, 8/2 will be 4 and 13/3 will be 4.33. All the figures in decimals will be 5, 4.26, 2.25, 4, 4.33, 5 which, when arranged from the smallest, are 9/4, 8/2, 4.26, 13/3, 5.

(21) The correct answer is: (A) 0.009, 0.09, 0.091, 0.099, 0.9.

The easiest way to determine this is to add zeros to each value in order to have equal decimal places in all of them. That gives you 0.090, 0.900, 0.099, 0.091 and 0.009. Now, compare the thousandths place value in each figure to get the correct order.

(22) The correct answer is: (D) -18.

Whenever you have two negative signs together, they become positive; so the equation 9+(-41) − (-3) +11 can be written as 9+ (-41) + 3 + 11. When you solve the addition first, you get 23 + (-41). To add a positive number to a negative number, use its absolute value and subtract the lesser number from the greater number and don't forget to add the negative sign to the end answer. So 23 +(-41) will be 41 − 23 = 18. Hence, -18.

(23) The correct answer is: (C) -360.

To get the product of (3) (-4) (-3) (5) (-2), first ignore the negative and positive signs and get the product of all the numbers. $3 \cdot 4 \cdot 3 \cdot 5 \cdot 2$ will give you 360. In the initial values there were three negative numbers. Since 3 is an odd number, the product will have a negative sign. So 360 will become -360.

(24) The correct answer is: (C) 4/125.

First, convert the decimal to a fraction. Since 0.032 has three decimal places, when converted into a fraction it becomes 32/1000. To simplify this fraction, divide the numerator and the denominator by the GCF of 32 and 1000, which is 8. That will give you 4/125.

(25) The correct answer is: (D) 0.67%.

To get the percentage that is equivalent to 0.0067, first convert 0.0067 to a fraction: 67/10,000. Next, multiply that by 100 to get $67/10,000 \cdot 100 = 67/100$. This fraction, when converted to a decimal, will be 0.67.

(26) The correct answer is: (C) 17/20.

First write 85% as a fraction. 85/100. Then simplify by dividing the numerator and denominator by the GCF of 85 and 100, which is 5. This will give you 17/20.

(27) The correct answer is: (C) 0.0033.

To write 0.33% as a decimal, start by converting it into a fraction; 0.33/100. When dividing 0.33 by 100, move your decimal point two places to the left and this will give you 0.0033.

(28) The correct answer is: (D) 40%.

6 expressed as a percentage of 15 simply means dividing 6 by 15. Then, to get the percentage, you multiply the result by 100. So 6/15= 2/5. When you multiply that by 100, you get $2/5 \cdot 100 = 40\%$.

(29) The correct answer is: (A) 31/36.

Start by adding the three distances together. 1/4 + 4/9 + 1/6 = x. Get a common denominator for the three fractions by finding the LCM of those three denominators. The LCM of 4, 9 and 6 is 36, so the distances will be 9/36 + 6/36 + 16/36 = 31/36.

(30) The correct answer is: (A) 2/9.

Each man pledged to dig one-third of the tunnel and one man had only completed 1/9. So, 1/3 − 1/9 will give us the remaining work he had. First get the LCM of 3 and 9, which is 9. Then divide both denominators by 9 and add the two values. 3/9 − 1/9 = 2/9.

(31) The correct answer is: (B) 14.

To divide 7/8 by 1/16, first get the LCM of both denominators. The LCM of 8 and 16 is 16. Next, multiply both sides by 16 to get 7/8 × 16 = 14 and 1/16 × 16 = 1. When you divide 16 by 1, you get 14.

(32) The correct answer is: (A) 20.17.

To get the total rainfall amount, add the four measurements together. First give each number the same number of decimal places, which in this problem will be two decimal places for each value. So 10.80 + 5.00 + 3.47 + 0.90 = 20.17 inches.

(33) The correct answer is: (C) 18.36 miles/hr.

Average speed = total distance/total time. Here, distance is given as 114.75 and time as 6.25 hrs. Since the decimal places are the same in the two values, ignore the decimals first and divide 11,475 by 625 to get 1,836. Now return the two decimal places by placing the decimal point two places to the left to get 18.36.

(34) The correct answer is: (B) -145.

When using BEDMAS, we start with the parentheses first. So in $2(5 - 8 \cdot 10) + 5$, we solve $(5 - 8 \cdot 10)$ first to get $5 - 80$, which is -75. Next, work on the multiplication to get $2 \cdot -75 = -150$. Then end with the addition. $-150 + 5 = -145$.

(35) The correct answer is: (D) 95.

Using BEDMAS, the first thing to do in $3 + 2(3 + 4)^2 -6$ is to solve the parentheses. So $(3 + 4)^2$ will be $3 + 4 = 7$. So $7^2 = 49$. Next, work on the multiplication to get $2(49) = 98$. Then do the addition to get $3 + 98 = 101$. Finally, do the subtraction. $101 - 6 = 95$.

(36) The correct answer is: (C) 2y - 1.

To solve $2(4y - 2) (y - 5)/4(y - 5)$, eliminate y-5 from the top and bottom to get $2(4y-2)/4$. Then simplify to get $(4y-2)/2$, which then simplifies further to $2y - 1$.

Science Section – Test 2 Answers

(1)   The correct answer is: (A) Green is a recessive trait in peas.

(A) is correct because the only thing Mendel could tell was that when the sperm and eggs were from the same yellow pea plant, the green peas produced constituted a mere quarter of the offspring. The plant's yellow peas were a dominant trait owing to the fact that the first offspring of cross-pollination between yellow and green peas was yellow.

(2)   The correct answer is: (A) Monosaccharides, disaccharides, polysaccharides.

The three types of carbohydrates are monosaccharides, disaccharides and polysaccharides. Monosaccharides are simple sugars, and disaccharides are comprised of two monosaccharides bound together by a covalent bond. As for polysaccharides, they are comprised of monosaccharides bound together in lengthy chains by glycosidic bonds. (C) and (D) are outright incorrect.

(3)   The correct answer is: (D) Sympathetic and parasympathetic.

(D) is correct because it is possible to split the autonomic nervous system into the sympathetic and parasympathetic system. Each of these divisions works in opposition to the other, and the systems dictate the way a person's body responds to any perceived threat.

(4)   The correct answer is: (D) Signals emanating from the person's abdomen.

The reason (D) is the correct answer is that the vagus nerve plays the role of conveying signals that emanate from the organs within the abdomen and delivering them to the person's brain. This has the effect of controlling digestion and a person's heart rate as well as different parasympathetic kinds of responses.

(5)   The correct answer is: (B) Synapse.

(B) is correct because for two neurons next to each another, there is some space, known as the synapse, which exists between one neuron's axon and the other's dendrite. It is possible for signals to be transmitted across that space. The neuromuscular junction is a type of synapse, existing between one motor neuron and one muscle fiber.

(6)   The correct answer is: (B) Constricted blood vessels.

(B) is correct because constricted blood vessels are linked to a person's sympathetic nervous system as opposed to the parasympathetic nervous system, whose responsibility it is to return the body to normalcy following any fight or flight threat.

(7)   The correct answer is: (D) Atrioventricular valves and semilunar valves.

(D) is correct because, as the heart pumps, the atrioventricular and semi-lunar valves continue opening and closing in alternate order, causing the heart sound. The heart's upper chambers and lower chambers are separated by the atrioventricular valves, while the semi-lunar valves are located within those arteries exiting the heart.

(8)   The correct answer is: (C) Fight or flight response.

(C) is correct because the sympathetic section of the body's autonomic nervous system is responsible for controlling a person's response when faced with a fight or flight situation. The parasympathetic system returns the body to a normal state following the cessation of the perceived threat.

(9)   The correct answer is: (C) Cellulose.

The reason (C) is correct is that cellulose is a sugar, specifically a polysaccharide, which comprises a chain of many hundreds or thousands of β-linked molecules of D-glucose, all in a linear structure. Incidentally, the composition of carbohydrates is simple sugars. ATP is an organic chemical that is complex, and collagen is a structural protein. Myosins are motor proteins.

(10) The correct answer is: (C) Heterozygous.

(C) is correct because the person indicated has two distinct alleles, these being gene pairs within a chromosome with the capacity to determine a person's hereditary traits; a good example is eye color. A human being, and every other organism that replicates via sexual reproduction, inherits a single allele for the two genes—one from each parent.

(11) The correct answer is: (A) Increase in acidity of the stomach's contents.

(A) is correct because pancreatic juice is not at all acidic, meaning it has a high pH; and for that reason it is not easy for it to raise the level of acidity in the stomach. Pancreatic juice is comprised of a number of enzymes used in digestion, along with massive amounts of bicarbonate ions; the reason it is alkaline.

(12) The correct answer is: (A) High levels of glucose leave the liver and enter the person's bloodstream.

(A) is correct because as the body attempts to respond to a stressful situation, it mobilizes glucose so that it leaves the person's liver and enters his/her bloodstream. This mobilization is meant to provide energy in abundance to the different cells that have heeded the prompt to respond to stress.

(13) The correct answer is: (C) Lysosomes.

(C) is correct because it is the lysosomes' function to carry out the intercellular digesting of structures that have been damaged, as well as macromolecules and bacteria. The Golgi apparatus transports proteins within and beyond the cell, while the mitochondria converts nutrients to create energy like ATP. The rough endoplasmic reticulum facilitates processing and sorting of synthesized protein.

(14) The correct answer is: (D) Rheumatoid arthritis.

The reason (D) is correct is that rheumatoid arthritis is a chronic joint inflammation that results from a person's articular cartilage suffering autoimmune destruction. Meanwhile, osteoporosis results from a bone remodeling imbalance that leads to fragile bones. Osteoarthritis is also joint inflammation, but its cause is cartilage wear and tear along articular bone edges.

(15) The correct answer is: (C) When pH is 7, it is more acidic than pH 8.

The reason (C) is correct is that the higher the pH level, the higher a solution's alkalinity. In this case, since 7 is lower than 8, it means a pH of 7 is an indication of greater acidity than a pH of 8. Acids raise a solution's [H+], and that in turn reduces the solution's pH level.

(16) The correct answer is: (D) A nucleus' proton number is the property that defines a given element.

(D) is correct not only because a proton is a subatomic particle with a charge of +1, but all atoms have a minimum of a single proton within the nucleus, and the amount of protons a nucleus has defines an element.

(17) The correct answer is: (C) Those insects responsible for pollinating Y also pollinated X.

(C) is correct because it is the only one that is logical as it pertains to the conditions under which the plants grew. Normally, for the production of vegetables and fruits to take place, there must be pollination, and this is what must have happened in the first instance.

(18) The correct answer is: (A) Axon; to send stimulus to the axon terminal

A neuron is mainly made up of the axon, the dendrites and the cell body, and the cell body has organelles within which activity of a metabolic nature takes place. The axon is responsible for carrying signals to other neurons via an axon terminal, which are first received by dendrites and then transmitted to the cell body.

(19) The correct answer is: (A) Gas neither has a definite volume nor a definite shape.

(A) is correct because a gas does not have a definite volume or a definite shape, unlike liquids or solids, whose volumes do not easily vary. The shape and volume of solids is definite, though solids fall under two categories, some crystalline and others amorphous.

(20) The correct answer is: (C) Production of gametes.

(C) is the correct answer because where the organism is unicellular, mitosis, an asexual type of reproduction, makes identical copies of one cell, which are referred to as daughter cells. Meanwhile, haploid gametes, which are either ova or sperm, are produced via meiosis; these have a 23-chromosome set.

(21) The correct answer is: (C) Protein like meats or eggs.

(C) is correct because urea is the main form of waste derived from protein. Formation of urea happens after a sequence of reactions that break down the protein's amino acids. Other foods on the list do not have amino acids as their primary composition, and so, they do not produce significant amounts of urea.

(22) The correct answer is: (B) They are created as two distinct atoms and share electrons that come as a pair.

(B) is correct because nonpolar covalent bonds are bound chemically between two individual atoms, bond formation happening as electrons are shared in equal proportions between these atoms. This type of bond formation can occur both between identical atoms, and also those that are entirely different. An example of this is the bond between two atoms of hydrogen.

(23) The correct answer is: (D) The hypodermis.

(D) is correct because the hypodermis layer, which is also referred to as subcutaneous, is the deepest of all the skin layers, and it is the one that holds all the fat associated with the skin.

(24) The correct answer is: (D) The nasal cavity, the pharynx, the larynx, the trachea, the bronchi, the bronchioles.

When a person inhales, he/she takes in air via the nose and mouth, which proceeds via the larynx and pharynx; all these passages warm the air and prepare it for the gas exchange. This warm air proceeds via the trachea or windpipe, then some enters the right and the left bronchi; this finally enters the bronchioles.

(25) The correct answer is: (A) The pulmonary artery, the pulmonary vein

(A) is correct because the pulmonary artery is responsible for carrying blood leaving the heart's right ventricle to a person's lungs to collect oxygen. The pulmonary artery is unique because it carries deoxygenated blood while other arteries carry oxygenated blood. After blood oxygenation, the pulmonary vein carries the blood back to the person's heart via its left atrium.

(26) The correct answer is: (A) A pathogen

(A) is correct because a bacterium or any other microorganism that brings about disease is referred to as a pathogen. An interferon is a molecule discharged for the purpose of signaling an antiviral immune response. Commensal is ordinary flora existing harmlessly within its host. A vaccine is something made to enhance people's immunity against a specific disease.

(27) The correct answer is: (B) That this medication managed to kill the particular bacteria that caused sinus infections.

(B) is correct as it is the most logical explanation for the sinus infection treatment, killing the relevant bacteria. Antibiotics are known to kill bacteria or to interfere with their growth. They are not known to treat allergies or to have an impact on DNA, and they are not antihistamines; that makes (A), (C) and (D) incorrect.

(28) The correct answer is: (D) The patella.

(D) is correct because the term "patella" is used in reference to the human kneecap, a bone that covers the knee joint. This bone works in league with a person's femur.

(29) The correct answer is: (A) The ball and socket joint.

(A) is correct because the ball and socket enable a person to move in different directions; a joint being a structure with two different bones attached to each other. In a ball and socket, there is a bone that has a well-rounded ball-like ending, and that ending is held within a different bone.

(30) The correct answer is: (C) The ear.

The reason (C) is correct is that the corti is one of the organs of a person's body, and it is situated within the part of the ear known as cochlea, an area that is central to a person's hearing. The corti has three rows of hair cells on its outside and a single row of hair cells on its inside.

(31) The correct answer is: (B) Vitamin D.

(B) is correct because rickets is a disorder resulting from a lack of vitamin D, and often, also a lack of calcium or phosphate. These are nutrients that help to develop bones that are strong and healthy. A person who has rickets often has weak, soft bones and there is a chance of suffering stunted growth or developing physical deformities.

(32) The correct answer is: (A) Lipids.

(A) is correct because steroids are hydrophobic and not water soluble. Nevertheless, steroids do not resemble lipids as they possess a structure that comprises four well-fused rings. Cholesterol is the most common steroid in a human body, and it serves as a vitamin D precursor; it's also a precursor to testosterone and other hormones.

(33) The correct answer is: (D) The vagus.

(D) is correct because a person's vagus nerve is the tenth cranial nerve or the "CN X," and traditionally, it is considered the body's pneumogastric nerve. Between the parasympathetic control done by a person's heart plus lungs as well as the digestive tract on one hand, and the vagus on the other, there is an interface.

(34) The correct answer is: (D) 11.2 to 12.0.

The reason (D) is correct is that bases are considered strong if their level of pH is 12 or higher. Some liquids are neither acid nor base, and thus they are considered neutral; a liquid such as water, whose pH is 7, is taken to be neutral.

(35) The correct answer is: (B) The left ventricle.

(B) is correct because blood that has been oxygenated leaves the heart's left ventricle and joins the systemic circulation via the various arteries that ultimately arrives in the myriad capillaries within the body's tissues. That blood becomes deoxygenated once in the tissues, and the vein system then returns it to the heart via its right atrium. The process repeats.

(36) The correct answer is: (A) F = ma.

(A) is correct because the second of Newton's laws of motions spells out the relationship that exists between the mass and force of an object, represented by the formula, F = ma. F stands for force, m for mass and a for acceleration.

(37) The correct answer is: (C) To uncoil and be ready to be copied.

(C) is correct because DNA is replicated during the S phase, in the form of chromosomes. The S phase is the cell's period of synthesis. It is a crucial phase because it enables cells made out of cell division to adopt a similar genetic make-up as all the other cells.

(38) The correct answer is: (B) How concentrated hydrogen ions are.

(B) is correct because the pH test is used in measuring the quantity of hydrogen ions within a particular solution. If their concentration is high, the pH is low, which means that particular substance is acidic. On the contrary, where the concentration of hydrogen ions is low, it means the pH is high; hence the substance is a base.

(39) The correct answer is: (A) The circulatory system.

(A) is correct because the circulatory system has arteries that transport nutrient-rich blood throughout the body, alongside the oxygen and hormones cells require. After nutrients have been absorbed, blood-bearing waste material such as carbon dioxide is carried away by the veins.

(40) The correct answer is: (B) A single variable at a time.

(B) is correct because in a controlled experiment, every one of the factors remains constant apart from the independent variable. This basically means that all changes that may involve different variables are minimized, saved for the single variable under testing.

(41) The correct answer is: (D) The pharynx.

(D) is correct because the pharynx has a connection between the nasal and oral cavity, which are linked to the larynx and the esophagus. The pharynx is basically the throat. Air has to pass through the throat, whether inhaled via the nose or mouth, and the throat also facilitates the passage of food from the mouth to the esophagus.

(42) The correct answer is: (D) The spinal cord and arm nerve.

(D) is correct because of the arm nerve. The spinal cord is certainly part of the body's central nervous system, the reason it does not interfere with (A) and (B). The central nervous system's major parts are the brain, which includes the frontal lobe, and the spinal cord.

(43) The correct answer is: (B) The phytoplankton.

(B) is correct because phytoplankton, which is marine algae of microscopic size, is the basis of many food webs for aquatic living things. Phytoplankton ensures there is food to sustain many creatures of the sea, big and small, inclusive of snails, jellyfish and even whales.

(44) The correct answer is: (A) Ten times.

(A) is correct because the cells of bacteria are ten times tinier than those of either animals or plants. The size of a bacterium ranges from 0.2 microns to 10 microns. The reason for this small size is that bacteria need a big surface area in order to take in nutrients.

(45) The correct answer is: (D) Lysosome.

(D) is correct because the lysosome is an acidic organelle involved in autophagy, which is essentially self-digestion. It has enzymes that digest those organelles that are worn out and release their various components for reuse within the cell's cytoplasm. Proteasome degrades proteins that are malfunctioning, turning them into peptides. Ribosome turns mRNA into protein.

(46) The correct answer is (D) $4Fe + 3O_2 \rightarrow 2Fe_2O_3$

This reaction shows iron oxidation. First, note how many oxygen moles are in the respective products. Having 3 moles of oxygen means it is imperative that the moles of oxygen on the left, which are the reactants, are multiplied by 3. The right-side oxygen moles are multiplied by 2.

(47) The correct answer is: (C) Ovulation.

(C) is correct because, in the case of females, whenever there is a great rise in the level of the hormone LH, ovulation is triggered. This hormone is generated in the body's gonadotropic cells, which are found within the anterior part of the pituitary gland. Menstruation occurs when the progesterone hormone decreases; such a decrease in pregnancy causes labor.

(48) The correct answer is: (D) Pneumonia.

The reason (D) is the correct answer is that it is the only answer spelled right. Pneumonia is a disease that manifests as an infection of the lungs, caused by bacteria or a virus.

(49) The correct answer is: (B) 45.

(B) is correct because it is normal that within the nucleus of any atom, whatever the number or quantity of protons, is also the correct atomic number; in this case, that number is 45.

(50) The correct answer is: (A) It is normally greater within the arteries than within the veins.

Blood pressure within the arteries is greater than within the veins because the arterial walls are thicker and can handle such elevated blood pressure as well as the velocity at which blood is ejected from the heart. The vein walls are comparatively thinner and better suited to carry the blood back to the heart at lower pressure.

(51) The correct answer is: (C) The sphygmomanometer.

(C) is correct because blood pressure is measured using a sphygmomanometer, which is an inflatable rubber cuff. It exerts pressure on a person's arm, connected to a mercury column that is set against a graduated scale to enable readings of the systolic and diastolic levels of blood pressure.

(52) The correct answer is: (A) Axons.

The reason (A) is correct is that axons are nerve fibers responsible for conducting electrical body impulses emanating from the soma or the body of the nerve cell. These long projections are essentially the transmitters of impulses within a person's nervous system.

(53) The correct answer is: (B) Nerve endings.

The reason (B) is correct is that a person's nerve endings send signals to his/her sensory neurons. This essentially means they tap information and convey it to the person's brain. They contribute significantly to the manner in which a vertebrate detects pain.

English and Language Use Section – Test 2 Answers

(1)   The correct answer is: (D) Air current.

The word "draft" in this sentence refers to the air that one can feel piping in from outside when the duct system is damaged. The word could have different meanings in other contexts; for example, a draft can also be the first version of a writing assignment.

(2)   The correct answer is: (C) Preposition.

"In" is a preposition of place because it provides information as to the location of something or someone. It is in the same category as "at" and "on." If something is within something else, "in" is used; if something is along a horizontal or vertical plane, "on" is used, and if the location is specific, "at" is used.

(3)   The correct answer is: (B) Acceptance.

A university acceptance letter is a document that shows that the applicant has been admitted to study at the institution. (A) is incorrect as "exception" means something that is not like the others to which it is being compared. There are no such English words as in (C) and (D).

(4)   The correct answer is: (B) Crisis.

The reason (B) is correct is that the noun "crisis" becomes "crises" in plural form. The other words have regular plural forms, where "monkey" becomes "monkeys," "horse" becomes "horses" and "baby" becomes "babies" when "y" is substituted with "-ies" as is conventional.

(5)   The correct answer is: (D) They.

Considering the word "chairs" is the antecedent, the pronoun should be "they," which is in the third-person plural. Among the reasons that the other options are incorrect is the fact that "he," "it" and "she" are pronouns in their singular form.

(6) The correct answer is: (B) Jane's two dogs consume plenty of food. They eat a whole bag every week.

(B) is correct because it has subject-verb agreement in both its sentences; "two dogs consume" and "they eat." Also, the pronoun matches its antecedent. The second part of (A) is incorrect on account of the wrong pronoun, (C) on account of the subject count—two dog—and wrong pronoun, and (D) for not having subject-verb agreement.

(7) The correct answer is: (C) Adjective.

An adjective describes a noun so that it can be better understood. In this case, 'bare hands" means using just one's hands, as opposed to using a spoon, fork or any other piece of cutlery. An example of a noun in the sentence is "food," while "devoured" is an example of a verb. "Food" exemplifies an object.

(8) The correct answer is: (D) Past perfect.

You can tell the tense is past perfect from the use of the word "had," a helping verb in the past tense, and "given," a verb in the participle form. In the future tense, the helping verb "will" is used, while in the present perfect, the auxiliaries "has" and "have" are used depending on the suitability of the subject-verb agreement.

(9) The correct answer is: (A) Expressed nonverbally.

Although the dictionary meaning of the word "tacit" is "implicit," in this context, the best definition is "expressed nonverbally." After all, the sentence indicates that Susan could not reach John for confirmation, yet she found it fit to proceed with the plans that both John and Susan were privy to.

(10) The correct answer is: (D) Group of people who made up the business.

In the context of the sentence, (D) is the most probable meaning for the word "firm." If there were no options provided, you might have given the word "company," "enterprise" or "business" as your answer.

(11)   The correct answer is: (A) Desparate.

(A) has the incorrectly spelled word, whose spelling should be "desperate." The word describes a state of despair. It is an adjective that describes someone who is on the verge of hopelessness. The other three words are correctly spelled.

(12)   The correct answer is: (D) First, rate.

If you combine the words "first" and "rate" to create a compound word, the word will need a hyphen to become "first-rate." None of the other pairs of words require a hyphen. Hence, you will have "worldwide," "lifelike" and "grandmother."

(13)   The correct answer is: (D) Semicolon/comma.

The reason (D) is the best answer is that it is acceptable to have a semicolon separating two independent clauses. Also, the fact that the word "however" begins with a lowercase letter means the first punctuation mark cannot be a period. The word "however" is normally followed by a comma.

(14)   The correct answer is: (B) Complex sentence.

The reason (B) is the correct answer is that the sentence has two parts that are unequal in importance. The first one is dependent on the second to convey logical meaning, while the second clause is independent. All the clauses that make up a compound sentence are normally independent.

(15)   The correct answer is: (C) Joginder's family, living in the South, often pays visits to their kin who live in the Southwest.

The reason (C) is the correct answer is that "South" and "Southwest" highlight specific locations and thus it is appropriate to capitalize them. "Senators" in (A) and "Autumn" in (B) should be lowercased. In (D), "Doctorate in Philosophy" is descriptive and should not be capitalized.

(16)   The correct answer is: (C) John played the piano magnificently.

The reason (C) is correct is that it starts with the originator of the action or the doer—the subject. So the sentence follows what is described as the SVO format—Subject-Verb-Object. In the passive voice, it is the object that begins the sentence.

(17)   The correct answer is: (D) Although James wanted to invest in stocks, he had just enough money to educate his children.

A run-on sentence is a poorly punctuated complex sentence. If you use a comma to divide the two continuous sentences, as in (A), you create a comma splice. The colon in (B) is incorrect. In (C), "although" is correctly added at the beginning, but the sentence remains a run-on sentence because there is no comma separating the constituent sentences.

(18)   The correct answer is: (C) Mary and Michelle, their sisters and colleagues, were very eager to attend the party.

Although (C) is correct, avoid putting a comma immediately after the subject unless the subject is compound or very long. When the subject is made up of different things or people, it is important to have them assembled all together so that the verb or verb phrase comes after that compound or long subject.

(19)   The correct answer is: (C) His, hers.

A pronoun is a word that is used in place of a noun. (C) is the correct answer notwithstanding the fact that the sentence does not have any antecedents, which are normally nouns, with which to match the pronouns. It is obvious "his" represents a male while "hers" represents a female in the possessive sense.

(20)   The correct answer is: (B) Susan is trained in personnel management, so she felt comfortable applying for the position of human resources manager.

(B) is a compound sentence, and this is clear from the fact that it comprises two independent sentences, "Susan is trained in personnel management," and "She felt comfortable applying for the position of human resources manager." The word "so" in between them is a conjunction, a word used to connect clauses or sentences.

(21) The correct answer is: (A) The headmaster initiated an after-school program for young children because he realized the local community did not have such a program.

(A) is correct on account of being a complex sentence. It has two clauses, one of them dependent. The other answers are incorrect because they are compound-complex, meaning that each of them contains two independent clauses and one dependent clause.

(22) The correct answer is: (D) Tom and Francis sang impressively. Jane, Tom's wife, was teary as she watched him walk to the dais to receive his prize.

(D) is correct because the narration is not first or second-person. The narration used in (D) is third-person.

(23) The correct answer is: (B) Jane encouraged us all to take to the dance floor, saying, "Come on, now. Let's have a good time!"

(B) is correct because the actual spoken words are enclosed in quotation marks.

(24) The correct answer is: (D) In a job applicant's cover letter.

In such a question, you are expected to rely on clues within the text. The letter indicates the applicant served as an administrative assistant in different types of companies. This shows the writer is intent on portraying experience. The writer also indicates there is an open executive assistant position.

(25) The correct answer is: (B) Rugby team, barbecue meat.

As indicated in (B), "rugby team" is the subject of the sentence, since it is the noun that carries out the main action of the sentence, which is "devoured." "Barbecue meat" is the object of the sentence, because it is the recipient of the action or verb—the devouring happened to the barbecue meat.

(26) The correct answer is: (A) When the pronoun "you" is used.

Whenever the pronoun "you" is used, it is an indication the writer is writing in second-person. In contrast, the use of "I" indicates the first-person. (B) and (D) are incorrect. This is because tenses do not influence the first-, second- or third-person points of view.

(27) The correct answer is: (C) Mr. Tom loved coaching the students, but driving to his new home was too strenuous for him to continue.

The reason (C) is correct is that if you add a dependent clause to it, the sentence will become a compound-complex sentence. The other answers would each have a complex sentence, which means each would have an independent and dependent clause.

(28) The correct answer is: (D) The butterflies flew over the flowery garden, occasionally perching on the plants, because they wanted to get some nectar.

(D) is correct because it only has one independent clause, "The butterflies flew over the flowery garden." The other answers have two independent clauses that are connected with the conjunctions "but" and "so." An independent clause not only has a subject and a verb, but it also expresses a complete idea.

Practice Test 3: Questions

Reading Section – Test 3

Read the next passage and then answer the two questions that follow.

Swimming is no longer a primitive way to move but has evolved into an advanced, competitive sport. It makes you exercise every group of muscles, as it is rigorous and calls for extreme training. During competitions, swimming participants try to swim as fast as possible using a particular type of swimming stroke. At the same time, swimmers put effort into developing endurance to swim for long stretches. Since swimming has evolved into a cutthroat competition, where a mistake in technique can get you disqualified, it's interesting to consider the future of the sport. The sport will either progress significantly or regress to the point where swimming is as primitive as it once was.

(1) The best way to describe the way the above passage is structured is ____.

(A) A narrow purpose that is specified, but broadened to accommodate future needs

(B) A narrow purpose that is specified, but broadened to accommodate future variations

(C) A hypothesis that has been tested within particular conditions and developed to become a bigger thesis

(D) A single activity whose different roles are clearly explained

(2) Which of the following fulfills the prophecy the author makes pertaining to swimming?

(A)   Human beings occupy the moon and make use of swimming strokes to navigate through space

(B) Swimming remains one of the Olympics' competitive sports

(C) People are able to swim at home and in various communal pools

(D) Fish can swim at incredible speeds

Read the following passage and then answer the seven questions that follow. It is about a Mexican-American historian describing a research technique she used.

I accepted another strong cup of the black coffee that Doña Teodora generously gave me. The small kitchen was filled with the fragrance of Sonoran tortillas that were as thin as paper, and considering I had coffee, I was certain I was going to receive some buttered tortillas. It would come directly from the round comal that sat on the gas stove. A comal is a flat earthen pan that is used for cooking. I had sat through three full days that started at 10 a.m. and lasted until early in the evening, on the very same wooden chair that was, nevertheless, comfortable, and I had drunk many cups of black coffee in succession, accompanied by nicely hot tortillas.

Doña Teodora was ninety years old, and even though once in a while she took breaks from turning the tortillas over, it seemed as if I was always the only exhausted person by evening. However, once I stood and scanned over what I had written, filed the notes and arranged the recordings in order, I was exhilarated.

Doña Teodora did not have her personal thoughts written somewhere, yet her recollections were invaluable to anyone interested in knowing things regarding the lives of the Mexicans who lived in the towns on either side of the US-Mexico border during the beginning years of the twentieth century. Doña Teodora had vivid memories of her family's genealogy. She shared detailed information of the marriages, births and deaths of several families that comprised her local community. Evidently, I had found a rich oral history pertaining to the Mexicans' history, on which to base my research.

I started my search in various libraries and archives, which are repositories for the conventional kind of history. Whatever I could find was in the form of census reports, records from churches and directories and statistics-based information. However, these sources of information, though important, lack one crucial historical dimension; the complete narrative about people's actual experience, which is not possible to quantify and classify. Within particular social setups, such a gap could be bridged using diaries and memoirs, as well as letters and reports.

Preservation and transfer of culture is normally done through the documentation of past events. However, such records are typically lost when a culture is conquered, as the Aztecs were by the Spaniards in the sixteenth century. Invariably, there is a gap between where records ceased after conquest and then began again. Any historian attempting a reconstruction of past happenings will experience frequent frustration because documentation is incomplete.

Though my preparation had led me to the kitchen of Doña Teodora, at first I was uncertain of where I stood. Would I consider myself among insiders, or did the experiences from my interviewees' lives put me in a position where, though I was a Mexicana who was able to speak Spanish, I still remained an outsider? Nonetheless, I came to the realization that the spoken word's richness and depth pose a challenge to the accepted theories and models that give comfort within social sciences.

The history of the Mexicans poses a challenge to models of social sciences that are derived strictly from the successful experiences of the imperialists. It is not possible to write our history without including fresh sources. These are the sources that will inform which ideas are required for the illumination and interpretation of the past, and these ideas need to originate from the people in question. This then makes it possible to describe events and structures from a perspective that is culturally appropriate, emphasizing the Mexican people's viewpoint.

(3)   The part of the research the author did which most resembled a conventional project was _____.

(A)   Paying attention to details of daily life within particular communities

(B)   Looking into the lives of previous tribes

(C)   Studying local families' memories of past events

(D)   Looking up census records, statistics, church records, etc.

(4)   The sense in which census reports, church-related records, etc. are insufficient is _____.

(A)   They rely too much on politics

(B)   They don't differentiate between politics and religion

(C)   They are not accurate enough to be helpful to a historian

(D)   They fail to show the human aspect of the narrative

(5)   The "gap" indicated in the passage should be understood as that distance that exists between _____.

(A)   The politically biased view of the state of affairs and personal bias

(B)   When a people were conquered, and their record-keeping was forever altered to the point when record-keeping eventually resumed in a different fashion

(C)   Personal stories and a nation's history

(D)   Depictions by traditional sources of history and personal narrations that are subjective

(6)   The closest meaning of the phrase "where I stood" as used in the passage is _____.

(A)   Where I resided

(B)   Where I was working

(C)   What my role was

(D)   Where my original home was

Consider the question below and then answer the question that follows.

"Would I consider myself among insiders, or did the experiences from my interviewees' lives put me in a position where, though I was a Mexicana who was able to speak Spanish, I still remained an outsider?"

(7)   What effect does the above question have?

(A)   It clarifies the difference between an insider and an outsider

(B)   It hints that to share ethnicity and language does not necessarily make a person an insider

(C)   It negates the assertion that it is crucial to be an outsider to be able to do research

(D)   It hints that the sympathy people have is of more importance than their ethnicity or language

(8)   Which of the following statements is an accurate representation of what the author feels regarding the relationship that exists between "spoken word" and "accepted theories and models that give comfort within social sciences"?

(A)   The theories and models ought to be first used if one is to understand the spoken word

(B)   The theories and models are rendered irrelevant by the spoken word

(C)   There is greater likelihood of there being errors where spoken word is used in research as you're relying on a person's memories

(D)   Spoken word is likely to bring better insight than accepted theories and models

Consider these sentences quoted next and answer the question that follows.

"It is not possible to write our history without including fresh sources. These are the sources that will inform which ideas are required for the illumination and interpretation of the past, and these ideas need to originate from the people in question."

(9)   According to the author, the ideas noted in the above sentences have their origin in _____.

(A)   Records kept informally and information sourced from the people in question

(B)   Remarks made by senior community members pertaining to the manner a particular community functions

(C)   Patterns of social mannerisms previously exhibited during cultural study

(D)   Historians' own experiences as they conduct interviews

Read the paragraph and then answer the two questions that follow.

Cities all over the globe are basically conglomerations of tinier cultural setups that result in a wide range of cultural differences. Every city has a wide range of dining options and different institutions of art, such as museums and theaters. Still, even when all the art and dining and forms of nightlife are considered, what single characteristic of a city distinguishes it from others? It is history. There is a bond that exists among the locals that underscores any of the other cities' mélange of institutions of food and art.

(10) The word 'mélange' in the context of the given paragraph means _____.

(A) Cheap

(B) Custom

(C) Assortment

(D) Chance

(11) According to the author, _____ can be said to be a city's greatest attraction or trait.

(A) A government that is democratic

(B) A luxurious French hotel within a European locality

(C) A famous ruin

(D) A museum

Read the two passages and then answer the four questions that follow.

First Passage

Performance is the realm of stage fright. The actor knows that making an appearance before an audience can be scary. Retaining the authenticity of a character is on its own a fragile undertaking; it calls for the person acting to transform himself/herself in complex ways. The person acting faces a unique challenge in that he/she has to hide and show simultaneously.

The actor does not consciously worry about making an error, but rather about letting his/her audience observe something they are not required to see: specifically, the fear the performer has.

Second Passage

That term "stage fright" has become almost obsolete, because people are now aware that any time you dwell on a weakness, that is tantamount to according it power. If I ask you to stop being afraid, chances are you are going to concentrate on that fear. If I ask you not to imagine a delicious burger, what happens? Immediately, you start thinking of it.

The solution to the greatest proportion of fears is substitution. You replace a monster with something less threatening to occupy your consciousness. If you concentrate more on your audience's comfort as opposed to their judgment, everything else is bound to fall in place.

(12) One can best describe the role of the two passages as _____.

(A)   First passage analyzing a phenomenon; second passage suggesting a way of solving a problem

(B)   First passage tracing the repercussions of an incident; second passage narrating a process

(C)   First passage interpreting a string of examples; second passage presenting a common case

(D)   The two passages presenting commonly known examples to counter a misconception

(13) In the passage, "retaining the authenticity of a character" is said in reference to ____.

(A)   The actor having the belief he/she is actually the character

(B)   The actor using the Method Acting system

(C)   The actor showing his/her audience strictly the behavior that pertains to the particular character

(D)   The actor refraining from being imaginative

(14) In the two passages, stage fright with respect to people's behavior is viewed as indicated in an option below. Which option correctly encompasses this phenomenon?

(A) The first passage says stage fright is the problem of the individual, but the second passage says it is a social problem

(B) The first passage says stage fright is normal and even healthy, but the second passage says it is an excessive reaction

(C) The first passage stresses that it is the uniqueness of the theater realm that causes stage fright, but the second passage says stage fright is similar to various other fears

(D) The two passages consider stage fright a normal phenomenon experienced by people on a daily basis

(15) Which of the following provides a description of an actor trying to manage stage fright as per the advice suggested in the second passage?

(A) The performer trying to impress his/her audience

(B) The performer thinking of his/her audience as his/her friends

(C) The performer following a ritual prior to his/her performance

(D) The performer blocking out any thoughts of his/her audience

Read the passage. Then answer the eight questions that follow.

There are different ways one can classify the world, and these ways depend on an individual's interests and the principles used in the classification. These classifications, also termed taxonomies, are responsible for determining both natural and unnatural comparisons as well as literal and anagogical comparisons. For instance, living things have normally been classified into three different groups; human beings, animals and plants.

Based on this particular classification, humans are not considered a special type of animal, and animals are not considered a special type of plant. As such, any comparison made among these three classes is merely analogical.

A different method to classify living things is mostly considered to have originated from Aristotle. Every living thing has a soul that can be described as vegetative, which gives it the capacity to grow. Among these living things, some possess a sensory soul, which gives them the capacity to sense the environment they are in and to move within it. There is also a species with a soul that is rational, and it has the capacity to truly understand. Hence, humans are a special kind of animal, whereas animals happen to be a special kind of plant. As per both of those classifications, the human species is unique. For one, it alone owns an entire kingdom; secondly, it remains at the apex of the hierarchy of taxonomy.

Homo sapiens are distinct. Every species is. However, this kind of distinction is not sufficient for many (maybe most) people, and that includes philosophers. Somehow, it is crucial that the genus we fit in be distinct. It is of great importance that the human genus be segregated from every other species as far as the manner of explaining particular qualities is concerned. Humans obviously have the capacity to develop and learn languages. Somehow, it is of great importance that the bees' waggle dancing not be categorized as a real language. It has never become clear to me why. In my thinking, the bees' waggle dance is different from the language used by human beings to the extent that there would be minimal gain in categorizing both of them as "languages," although if "language" is defined in such a manner that it is easy for the waggle dance to fit the definition, it is a fact that bees would still remain bees.

Similarly, some people find it important that there is not another species that can make use of tools. Irrespective of the ingeniousness of other genera in manipulating objects within their environment, it is of absolute significance that whatever they do does not count as "use of tools." Every one of these species will always be species that are biologically distinct, irrespective of any label.

(16)   From the author's perspective, _____ is responsible for shaping the perception we have when comparing different species.

(A)   How organisms behave within their natural habitat

(B)   The organizational plan that researchers and philosophers have imposed on the world of living things

(C)   The language style scientists use to present their respective research findings

(D)   Communication complexity among organisms

(17) Where the Aristotelian way of classification is concerned, which of the following answers does not apply?

(A)   Two species being similar because each has a sensory soul but differing because one of them does not have a soul that is rational

(B)   Two species being alike because either of them possesses a vegetative soul but differing because just one of them possesses a sensory soul

(C)   One species possessing a vegetative soul yet not having a sensory or rational soul

(D)   One species possessing a vegetative soul and a rational soul yet not having a sensory one

(18) Which of the following can pass as "legitimate" for every living thing, going by Aristotle's beliefs?

(A)   Comparisons made on the basis of a vegetative soul

(B)   Comparisons made on the basis of a sensory soul

(C)   Comparisons made on the basis of a rational soul

(D)   Comparisons made on the basis of sensory and rational souls

(19) When the writer states "maybe most" when expressing how various people feel in the passage, very likely the use of "most" is referring to _____.

(A)   The practicality of different biological genera

(B)   Research of a biological nature

(C)   The part language plays in technological development

(D)   Not being objective in the manner homo sapiens are classified

(20) The writer makes use of the word "somehow" in the passage to indicate ____.

(A)   Disapproval

(B)   Uncertainty

(C)   Rage

(D)   Despair

(21) Which of the following summarizes the concept of being "distinct"?

(A)   We, humans, are just as unique as every other species

(B)   We, humans, are entirely defined by the qualities we possess that no other species possesses

(C)   Because we know we are unique, this makes humans a rational species

(D)   What appears to be our distinct status happens to be a non-planned by-product of classification systems

(22) In the phrase "the human genus can be segregated from every other species," the word "segregated" means _____.

(A)   Warmed

(B)   Covered

(C)   Insulated

(D)   Barred

(23) The author expresses criticism for people who hold the belief that ____.

(A)   Homo sapiens and other living beings have more similarities than differences

(B)   Homo sapiens and other species of animals differ only in degrees

(C)   Homo sapiens and other animals are categorized entirely differently in the world of living things

(D)   Homo sapiens, like other animals, are able to control the environment to which they belong.

Read the following passage and then answer the five questions that follow.

Monarch Butterflies

For a minute, visualize a butterfly—any type. There is a good chance that what will come to mind is a monarch butterfly with a distinct color like orange, yellow or black. This species of butterfly is probably the most attractive of all butterflies. In short, to the human eye, its color is beautiful in a way that is different from any other animal. The butterfly's color seems like a red light being flashed to possible predators, alerting them that here is an insect that is not only foul in taste but also poisonous. However, predators may not be the greatest threat to the monarch, but human activity.

At the larval stage, the monarch, in caterpillar form, feeds almost strictly on milkweed plants. These plants are crucial for the survival of these monarch caterpillars, and in their adult stage they return to places where there is milkweed in abundance for the sake of laying eggs specifically on those plants. This milkweed plant that the butterflies consume has a toxin that is poisonous, which is stored inside the body. It is the reason monarch butterflies have a taste too foul for predators. Animals feeding on a monarch will not die, but they are bound to feel sufficiently ill to want to avoid a similar meal in the future.

Probably what is most remarkable about this species of butterfly is the three-thousand-mile migration it undertakes annually. Every single year, when winter is approaching, the insects depart from their homes within the US and Canada, and they head to the southern parts of California and Mexico. Their travel each day ranges from fifty to a hundred miles, a journey that takes around two whole months to finish. Each year, the monarch butterflies go back to the very same forests, some of them ending up on the very same trees their own ancestors landed on many years earlier. The number of these fragile creatures that reach the Mexican mountains every year can reach a billion. As winter season nears the end, the butterflies mate. Soon, the males among them die and the females go back north, leaving deposits of eggs on milkweed while in transit. They also ultimately die while on that journey. Their eggs will end up hatching and soon all larvae will turn into butterflies. These are the insects that will end up continuing the journey to the north.

Unfortunately, this majestic insect has several threats to its existence. First, scientists foresee winters becoming wetter and colder due to climate change. Monarchs can survive dry temperatures as low as sub-freezing, but they will freeze in similarly cold wet temperatures. Moreover, as it becomes warm during summer, the habitats considered appropriate for the monarchs will start to push farther to the north. This leads to migration journeys becoming longer. Soon, the lengthy distances might become simply too great for these insects to withstand. Lastly, this butterfly is faced with an extreme loss of habitat within Mexico. There is illegal logging taking place there, whose result is a great reduction in the forests that are home to the butterflies during winter. This problematic issue has become so grave that the International Union of Conservation of Nature has identified the monarch butterfly as a "phenomenon under threat." Does the monarch have a chance of survival? It appears that this depends on how human beings behave.

(24) Which of the following paraphrases the main topic in the fourth paragraph?

(A)   The monarch lays eggs in the warm Mexican climate

(B)   The monarch is doomed to slowly become extinct owing to climate change effects

(C)   The monarch can survive in temperatures that are sub-freezing

(D)   The monarch can only survive if people modify their activities

(25) The purpose of the third paragraph in the passage is _____.

(A)   To add details regarding the struggles the monarch butterfly goes through in order to survive

(B)   To provide an explanation for why the monarch butterflies' journey is not only difficult but also admirable

(C)   To suggest that if only it was possible for the monarch butterflies to make their migration journey shorter, they would manage to survive.

(D)   To offer an explanation of how negative the effect of people's actions is

(26) The word "distinct" as used in the first paragraph means _____.

(A) Confusing

(B) Very thick

(C) Easy to distinguish

(D) Extraordinary

(27) Which of the following is a detail meant to support the notion that the monarch species has several threats to its existence?

(A) Soon, the males among them die and the females go back north, leaving deposits of eggs on milkweed while in transit

(B) Animals feeding on a monarch will not die, but they are bound to feel sufficiently ill to want to avoid a similar meal in the future.

(C) They (the females) also ultimately die while on that journey

(D) Soon, the lengthy distances might become simply too great for these insects to withstand

(28) Which of the following statements rephrases the writer's major argument regarding the monarch butterflies' fate?

(A) The female of the monarch species lays eggs on milkweed's leaves

(B) The outstanding coloration of the monarch is meant as a warning to predators

(C) The monarch butterfly can withstand dry, sub-freezing temperatures

(D) People must adjust their own activities for the monarch butterfly to continue existing as a species

Read the passage and then answer the two questions.

An old woman and a wealthy man sat next to one another as they traveled by air from San Francisco to Denver. The man inquired if the woman would like to play a game: "Let me ask something, and if you fail to answer, you pay me five dollars. And vice versa." The woman turned down the proposal and attempted to sleep. Upset, the man suggested, "All right. If your answer is wrong, you will just owe me five bucks. However, if I fail to get the right answer, I'll be obliged to pay you five hundred dollars." The proposal was too good to turn down, and so the woman accepted. The man, who was a lawyer, was the first to ask a question. "What is the earth's circumference?" No answer came to mind, and so she had no choice but to pay the man five dollars. It was the woman's turn to ask a question. "What makes a u and walks on three legs?" No answer came to the man's mind. He retrieved his laptop and searched unsuccessfully for the correct answer; unfortunately, he was out of luck. An entire hour lapsed, and he finally gave up and handed the woman the five hundred dollars. After the woman thanked the man, she tried to get some sleep. Very upset, the man inquired about the answer to her question. She just smiled without uttering a word and handed the lawyer one five-dollar bill.

(29) Which of the following is a logical deduction on the basis of the passage?

(A)   The lawyer had no interest in playing the game

(B)   The woman had no idea what the correct answer to her question was

(C)   The two people had previously met

(D)   The lawyer had cheated by using a laptop to search for an answer

(30) The purpose of the passage was _____.

(A)   Entertainment

(B)   Information

(C)   Persuasion

(D)   Description

Read the next paragraph and then answer the question that follows.

Abdi tells Meshack, "I'll stop at your place for a game of chess, but before then, I'll take some time to grab a quick lunch. After that, I'll get my car cleaned. As soon as I'm through with these things, I'll meet up with you."

(31) When should Meshack anticipate Abdi at his place?

(A) After his car has been cleaned

(B) After he has played chess

(C) As soon as the phone conversation ends

(D) Before he has had lunch

(32) Read the numbers and instructions given and then answer the question that follows.

1 2 3 4 1 3 2 3 4 1

Substitute the above numbers with A for 1; E for 2; I for 3 and T for 4. If a particular letter appears more than two times, get rid of the one that appears the first time. Next, get rid of the letter at the beginning and the one at the end of the series. Finally, replace every consonant in the series with "Q." The answer that represents the final lineup of letters is _____.

(A) Q I Q E A E

(B) Q Q I A I E

(C) Q A I E I Q

(D) Q I A E E Q

Read the passage and then answer the question that follows.

Superhero movies are among the hottest movie genres today. And why shouldn't they be? They're very entertaining. A good number of top cinematic productions have been superhero movies.

Still, how is it that a genre whose main target used to be children is now so popular? One of the reasons is the fact that superheroes are good individuals. They exhibit a level of humanity and virtue that is astonishing, and one can easily identify with it. A superhero is the type of person we, ourselves, dream of being.

In addition, the origin of superhero stories is usually death and loss, which has the potential to evoke from audiences a response of sympathy. Taking Batman as an example, his struggles throughout life are clear, starting with his memories of having watched his parents dying. Is there any one of us who has not felt a similar loss? Therefore, in a world with misfortunes, people would love to watch their own superheroes symbolize virtuous behavior as they subjugate villains—alongside their personal weaknesses.

(33) Which of the following lists one assertion the author makes as the reason superhero-based movies are so popular?

(A) Computer-based animations now account for over 95% of all forms of movie special effects

(B) More than half of moviegoers like to watch sequels and prequels better than other kinds of films

(C) Over 80% of women polled stated that they could identify with the struggles of Wonder Woman

(D) 75% of movie watchers stated during a survey that they would rather identify with villains than superheroes

Read the advertisement below and then answer the two questions that follow.

Welcome to AllCare Insurance

You will enjoy AllCare's high level of protection, flexible coverage, variety of policy lengths, friendly premiums and excellent customer service.

Autos: AllCare accords you comprehensive motor vehicle insurance that includes drivers that our competitors may be hesitant to cover. We specialize in providing insurance to drivers, many of whom have either never been insured or have found themselves excluded from different insurance packages or plans. We have policies that offer drivers reduced rates whenever they show an improved driving record and any time they have not made a claim for a specified time period.

Motorcycles: We have popular insurance plans for motorcycles that include the kind of protection not easy to find under most conventional policies, like collision coverage whose insurance includes the entire towing cost and on-the-road service, up to $2,500. You can buy additional coverage for any accessories whose value exceeds $2,500. We also offer a special discount to members who belong to riding clubs that are approved, riders who complete a certified training course and those who have gone five years without making any claims.

Make sure to ask about the $200 discount we have for our new customers!

Call our uptown location at (555)-555-4539

Call our downtown location at (555)-555-9587

Alternatively, submit your online application and get a discount of 10% for simply downloading our new app!

*Note that discounts vary, and you may find them applicable only in some states.

(34) Based on the above advertisement, AllCare insurance can cover ____.

(A) Any driver whose insurance policy has been canceled

(B) Any driver who has been involved in different accidents

(C) Elderly drivers denied coverage by other insurers

(D) Any driver who has had his/her license revoked in the past

(35) Which of the following shows information found within the advertisement?

(A) Addresses of the company's two local offices

(B) Information on the safe drivers' discount of $2,500

(C) Information on AllCare's new clients' special discount

(D) The company headquarters' telephone number

(36) Look at the line of numbers below and then read the guidelines provided.

3 4 5 6 12 14

Organize the above numbers to form a pyramid. The lowest row of the pyramid should have three numbers, and all should be even numbers; the middle row should have two numbers and the difference between the two should be 1; and the top row should have just one number and it should be a factor of 15. Identify the correct pyramid from the list below.

(A)
```
      5
    6   3
  4  12  14
```

(B)
```
       5
     3    4
   6   12   14
```

(C)
```
      6
    12   3
  4   5   14
```

(D)
```
      6
    5   3
  4  12  14
```

Read through the text provided next that includes a table of contents and then answer the question that follows.

Magazine for Global Communications

Summer Edition

Table of Contents

(37) Which of the following has a great likelihood of being addressed in the summer edition of the *Magazine for Global Communications*?

(A) The country with the most efficient policy on public relations

(B) The effect journalism has had on society over time

(C) The members likely to be enrolled in the foreseeable future

(D) Changes that have taken place in the way companies utilize public relations

(38) "Solanum tuberosum," commonly known as the potato, is a crop consumed in almost all the countries of the world. The reason the words "solanum tuberosum" are enclosed in quotation marks is that _____.

(A) They are the botanical name of the potato

(B) They are meant to emphasize the importance of the potato

(C) They are difficult words

(D) They are the title of a book on farming

(39) Jane is preparing to write a paper on astronomy, and she requires statistical data from the period covering 1986. Where can she find that information?

(A) An almanac

(B) A magazine

(C) A dictionary

(D) A newspaper

(40) "I informed my counterparts that it would be foolhardy to accept to be part of the ill-conceived plan." Which of the following words' meanings is closest to "foolhardy"?

(A) Odd

(B) Creative

(C) Reckless

(D) Prestigious

(41) When you are writing an essay and are weighing which two words to use in a sentence, and there is no clear reason why one of the words is more appropriate, you should select ____.

(A) The word that sounds nicest

(B) The word that is simplest

(C) The word that is more complex

(D) The word that is more positive

(42) What does the word "transition" mean in a piece of writing?

(A) An opinion that is properly defended

(B) A scheme within an organization

(C) A word or phrase used for connection

(D) Evidence for a citation

(43) Which of the following is a transition that can complete the sentence?

"Tegla Loroupe was determined to continue her campaign to have communities coexist in peace. _____, she knew from the very start she was going to face challenges."

(A) Previously

(B) For instance

(C) Similarly

(D) Nevertheless

Read the passage and then answer the three questions that follow.

Each time I go to the bookstore, there is a fresh title on science fiction about the survivors of the apocalypse seeking refuge in the tunnels of the New York City subways. Some of these stories of survival make for an interesting read. They also make you reflect on reality.

New York's city engineering crews work all throughout the day pumping 13 million gallons of water from the subway network; if there is heavy rain, the number rises fast. Suppose you remove the engineers from the operation and with them, the electricity that works the pumps to the sump. The next major flood would fill those subway tunnels. Once this happens, any people underground, as in the apocalyptic novels I like to read, would have to develop gills or emerge from the tunnels.

(44) The most suitable title for the passage is _____.

(A) *A Stopover at the Bookstore*

(B) *Science behind Growth of Gills*

(C) *Refuge within Fiction; Not Factual*

(D) *The Most Popular Fiction of the Decade*

(45) Which of the following could be used to further illustrate the author's point?

(A)   A blueprint that shows how deep the subways in New York City are

(B)   A graph that compares New York City's subway ridership to ridership in big US cities

(C)   A table that shows the volume of water running through the subway system of New York City under varying conditions

(D)   A map that shows any emergency exit within New York City's subway system, alongside procedures to be taken in times of floods

(46) Which of the following is likely to be found on a sidebar together with this text?

(A)   An illustration of people with gills behind their ears

(B)   A description of an electrified subway rail with some explanation of how it functions when powering a train

(C)   A list of novels about people's lives in the subway tunnels

(D)   A description of a subway engineer's work qualifications

(47) If you have a map with no compass, which side should you consider north?

(A)   Down

(B)   Right

(C)   Up

(D)   Left

(48) Which of the following is not a function of text-related features?

(A) Introducing a topic

(B) Emphasizing a particular concept

(C) Expounding on a theme

(D) Providing superfluous information

(49) Identify the revision which eliminates gender-related bias in the following sentence:

"A hospital nurse is expected to keep her patients' personal information confidential."

(A) A hospital nurse is expected to keep his patients' personal information confidential

(B) Hospital nurses are expected to keep their patients' personal information confidential

(C) No patients' personal information should ever be disclosed by a hospital nurse

(D) A hospital nurse is expected to keep any patients' personal information confidential, gender notwithstanding

(50) Which of the following is not a kind of erroneous reasoning?

(A) The fallacy of either/or

(B) Overgeneralization

(C) A statement expressing an opinion

(D) Circular reasoning

Read the paragraph and then answer the three questions that follow.

Fiona sighed as she watched the elderly woman cooing at the beautiful baby and talking about her own children's childhood. Five kids! Every one of them could walk and talk at a very early age! Every one of them was a tiny genius! Blah blah blah! Fiona had spent all day taking care of a tiny, drooling, incontinent person, and the reward she was getting was listening to endless stories about other tiny, incontinent, drooling people. She felt like taking a page out of the kid's book and screaming.

(51) Which of the following is the paragraph's topic sentence?

(A) She felt like taking a page out of the kid's book and screaming.

(B) Fiona had spent all day taking care of a tiny, drooling, incontinent person, and the reward she was getting was listening to endless stories about other tiny, incontinent, drooling people.

(C) Fiona sighed as she watched the elderly woman cooing at the beautiful baby and talking about her own children's childhood.

(D) All of the above are incorrect; the paragraph's topic is implied.

(52) Which of the following states the paragraph's main idea?

(A) Fiona greatly regrets having become a mother and may even be contemplating giving up her baby for adoption

(B) Fiona detests having to clean up her baby's drool just as she hates having to change her diapers; she believes the elderly woman is lying about her own children

(C) Fiona gets frustrated listening to people nostalgically reminisce about taking care of little children

(D) Fiona is an unlikeable person who lacks empathy for elderly women who are lonely and looking for someone to share their past experiences with

(53) The meaning of "cooing" as used in the passage is _____.

(A) Gazing

(B) Speaking softly and gently

(C) Smiling

(D) Snuggling next to

Math Section – Test 3

(1) Which expression below is equivalent to $4(4y - 10)(y + 5)/4(y - 5)$?

(A) $4y - 5$

(B) $(4y - 10)(y + 5)(y - 5)$

(C) $9y + 1/4y - 20$

(D) $5y + 3/2(y - 5)$

(2) Alice bought a truck for \$35,000 and after one year the truck's value was about \$23,850. The year after, it was estimated to be worth \$20,400. What was the approximate truck value's percentage decrease between the year of purchase and the two years after?

(A) 14%

(B) 86%

(C) 24%

(D) 42%

(3) A broker has been directed to sell his client's shares if there is a stock value increase of over 10% but to buy more shares if there is a 10% decrease in value. If each share is currently going for \$73.50, which expression would correctly represent an interval, p, during which this broker should not sell or buy any shares?

(A) $73.60 < p < 73.60$

(B) $69.83 < p < 77.18$

(C) $63.50 < p < 83.50$

(D) $66.15 < p < 80.85$

(4) Joshua is a part-time employee in three different companies. In company x, he works for 15 hours a week and gets $20 per hour; in company y, he works for two hours every day from Monday to Friday and is paid $18.25 per hour and in company z he receives $15 for every hour worked. How much does Joshua make in a week if he works for 37 hours per week in total?

(A) $662.50

(B) $632.50

(C) $266.25

(D) $497.50

(5) Kendra bought six two-liter cases of wine for her birthday party and by the end of the party the guests had consumed 7,264 cm³ of the wine. How much wine was left over after the party, to the nearest liter?

(A) 2 liters

(B) 5 liters

(C) 3 liters

(D) 7 liters

(6) Last year, Patrick was to receive $65,000 as his base salary, not inclusive of his end-of-year bonus. He eventually learned that his total compensation was $77,500, and this included his bonus and his health benefits, which were 15% of his base salary. What percentage was Patrick's bonus?

(A) 23.6%

(B) 4.2%

(C) 3.5%

(D) 3.9%

(7)   If a certain foreign currency was trading at 1.32075 on Monday and by Friday the same currency had dropped to 1.29620, what was the decrease in value during that week? Round your answer to the nearest thousandth.

(A)   0.025

(B)   0.024

(C)   0.02455

(D)   0

(8)   Mike has been hired to paint Jackie's living room area. If the wall surface of the room is 66 m² and a one-liter tin of paint can only cover 9 m² of the wall, how much paint will Mike need to paint the entire wall?

(A)   73 liters

(B)   73 kilometers

(C)   594 milliliters

(D)   73 deciliters

(9)   According to data from 20 different studies, when people drink more coffee, type 2 diabetes cases are reduced. Based on these results, what conclusion can we draw about the link between the reduced cases of diabetes and the increased intake of coffee?

(A)   There is a negative covariance noted between the intake of coffee and the risk of diabetes

(B)   There is a positive covariance noted between the intake of coffee and the risk of diabetes

(C)   There is no correlation between coffee intake and the risk of diabetes

(D)   There is a random covariance noted between the intake of coffee and the risk of diabetes

(10) What is 30 divided by 0.049 rounded to one significant figure?

(A) 610

(B) 600

(C) 612

(D) 612.2

(11) If three numbers—m, n and 27—collectively have an average of 30, what should the sum of m and n be?

(A) 28

(B) 67

(C) 31

(D) 63

(12) If three numbers a, b and 27 have an average of 30, while a, b, 27, m and n have a mean of 45, what should the mean of m and n be?

(A) 70

(B) 25

(C) 69

(D) 67.5

(13) Identify the median in this set of numbers: 9, 1, 8, 4, 7, 8, 2, 4, 9, 10, 4.

(A) 7

(B) 6

(C) 10

(D) 8

(14) Identify the modal score in this series of numbers: 1, 0, 2, 0, 2, 0, 2, 1, 3, 2, 1.

(A) 1

(B) 3

(C) 2

(D) 0

(15) An object was weighed by two different scientists on a scale and each of them got different measurements. Scientist x recorded his weights as 103, 104, 106, 105 and 107 while scientist y recorded his weights as 101, 103, 107, 105 and 109. Which statement below accurately describes the variation and the average of their results?

(A)   The variability and the average for both measurements was the same

(B)   Scientist y got an average and a range that was higher than that of scientist x

(C)   Scientist y got an average that was higher than that of scientist x but they both had a similar range

(D)   Both scientists got a similar average weight and scientist y got a higher variability and range than scientist x

(16) An office is renting some office equipment to small businesses around the city. If there are 25 computers, 14 printers, 18 photocopiers, 12 staplers and 19 desks in that office, and 25% of this inventory is being rented out, how many items can a small business use?

(A) 44

(B) 66

(C) 20

(D) 22

(17) If a doctor sees his patients from 1400 hrs to 2100 hrs, what hours of the day does the doctor work in standard time?

(A) 2 a.m. to 9 a.m.

(B) 2 p.m. to 9 p.m.

(C) 1:40 p.m. to 2:10 a.m.

(D) 10 p.m. to 3 a.m.

(18) If a farmer has 8 cows, 5 goats, 2 sheep and 5 pigs, what is the percentage representation of his pigs?

(A) 25%

(B) 40%

(C) 33.3%

(D) 5%

(19) Convert 98.6°F to Celsius.

(A) 37°C

(B) 119.88°C

(C) 86.77°C

(D) 72.55°C

(20) How is the Roman numeral MCMLXVII written in Arabic numbers?

(A) 2,167

(B) 1,967

(C) 14,167

(D) 2,267

(21) What do you get from the sum of 8.65 and 0.056?

(A) 0.921

(B) 9.21

(C) 865.056

(D) 8.706

(22) How many cm are in 1 mm?

(A) 1000

(B) 100

(C) 1/10

(D) 10

(23) You are required to dilute powdered paint in three quarts of clean water, but your container is in liters. How many liters will you need to dilute that powder?

(A) 0.96 liters

(B) 5.76 liters

(C) 2.88 liters

(D) 1.44 liters

(24) A patient who is on a clear liquid diet consumes the following liquids in a day: 2 pints of warm water, one 8 oz bowl of soup and one 8 oz mug of coffee. The nurse in charge of the patient notes that the patient's drainage bag indicates 1,000 ml of urine for the previous day. How much is the patient's deficit in milliliters?

(A) 40 ml

(B) 400 ml

(C) 560 ml

(D) 440 ml

(25) The consumption of a vehicle on average is 27 m/gal, where "m" stands for miles and "gal" for gallon. If the cost of gas is $4.04 for every gallon, which of the following answers is nearest to the probable cost of gas if the vehicle travels 2,727 miles?

(A) $109

(B) $408.04

(C) $44.40

(D) 109.08

(26) If you have x = 3 and then y = 5, find the precise value by which 3x² – 2y surpasses that of 2x² – 3y.

(A) 20

(B) 16

(C) 4

(D) 14

(27) Calculate x, given the equation 2x + 3 = 3x – 4

(A) 7

(B) 1/5

(C) -7

(D) 1

(28) Which of the following has the largest common factor for 42, 126 and 210?

(A) 14

(B) 42

(C) 21

(D) 6

(29) A company's sales in its third year totaled $38 million and they were double in its second year of operation. In the second year, the sales had exceeded the first year's sales by $3 million. Find the value of the company's first year's sales.

(A) $20.5 million

(B) $16 million

(C) $22 million

(D) $17.5 million

(30) A mine often fills up with water that must be drained in order for work to continue. The ideal pump to use depends on how deep the mine is. When the depth of the mine is x, the rate of pumping out the water is $x^2/25 + 4x - 250$ gallons every minute. A mine whose depth is 150 ft should use a pump capable of extracting ___gallons/minute

(A) 1,750

(B) 362

(C) 1,250

(D) 500

(31) There is a box whose measurements are length that is less than double its width by 3 inches. Which of the following equations represents the length "l"?

(A) $l = w - 3$

(B) $l = 2w - 3$

(C) $l = w + 3$

(D) $l = 2w + 3$

(32) Find the number of irrational numbers within the range of 1 to 6.

(A) 5

(B) 3

(C) 7

(D) Infinite

(33) On average, a student in high school consumes 67.5 pounds of sugar annually. Now, members of a sports team went to reduce their sugar intake by 20% at the minimum, and each of them has been consuming sugar at the rate of an average high school student. What should be the maximum consumption by one team member for the next year?

(A) 66 pounds

(B) 14 pounds

(C) 54 pounds

(D) 44 pounds

(34) The term "lead" as pertains to a screw is used to denote the distance the screw creates as a straight stretch when turned one full turn. If a screw has a length of 2.5 inches and a lead of 1/8 inch, find the number of turns the screw would have to make to fully penetrate a wooden surface.

(A) 1.5 turns

(B) 5 turns

(C) 20 turns

(D) 16 turns

(35) xy = 144; x + y = 30; & x >y. Find x – y.

(A) 6

(B) 20

(C) 18

(D) 24

(36) Which of the following is a factor of the polynomial $2x^2 - 3x - 5$?

(A) x – 1

(B) 2x – 5

(C) 3x + 5

(D) 2x + 5

Science Section – Test 3

(1) The spleen is part of what system?

(A) The digestive system

(B) The endocrine system

(C) The lymphatic system

(D) The circulatory system

(2) Which of the following exemplifies deductive reasoning?

(A) 21% of a town's population wants all vehicles banned. As such, the new proposal to have all vehicles banned is unlikely to go through.

(B) Every professional soccer player can kick the ball well. As such, all future professional soccer players will kick the ball well.

(C) Anyone who brushes their teeth on a regular basis has fewer cases of heart problems. As such, proper dentistry has the capacity to preempt heart attacks.

(D) Every secretary is a great typist. Catherine is a secretary. Hence, Catherine is a great typist.

(3) Which of the following indicates a possible reason for disc herniation?

(A) Hepatitis

(B) Plantar fasciitis

(C) Whiplash

(D) Ulcer

(4)   Which of the following is a characteristic associated with the autonomic nervous system?

(A)   It makes use of skeletal muscles to regulate voluntary control affecting body movements

(B)   It regulates the heart's, stomach's, lungs' and intestines' involuntary activity

(C)   It is the part of the nervous system that has the brain and spinal cord

(D)   It is considered the intelligence center

(5)   As photosynthesis takes place, what two compounds combine to produce glucose and oxygen?

(A)   Water combines with carbon dioxide

(B)   Water combines with bicarbonate

(C)   Bicarbonate combines with carbon dioxide

(D)   Carbon dioxide combines with several alkaline substances

(6)   Which of the following is subatomic particles found within the nucleus of an atom?

(A)   Electrons and neutrons as well as protons

(B)   Electrons and protons

(C)   Neutrons and protons

(D)   Electrons

(7)   Which of the following is a true statement with regards to trophic levels?

(A)   Consumers at the tertiary level receive more energy than consumers at the secondary level

(B)   Consumers at the secondary level receive more energy than consumers at the primary level

(C)   Producers receive less energy than consumers at the primary level

(D)   Consumers at the tertiary level receive less energy than consumers at the primary level

(8)   A person's eye perceives a red dress as red. Which of the following reasons explains why?

(A)   A dress has molecules with no capacity to absorb the wavelengths of red light

(B)   A dress that is red primarily absorbs wavelengths of red light

(C)   The dress has molecules with the capacity to absorb wavelengths of green and blue light

(D)   A dress does not have the capacity to absorb wavelengths of light from colors that are not red

(9)   What is the light variable used when plants are being grown in artificial light within a laboratory setup, for the purpose of observing the plants' growth rate?

(A)   Dependent variable

(B)   Random variable

(C)   Independent variable

(D)   Responding variable

(10) Which of the organ systems listed below is primarily responsible for regulation of metabolism, mood and growth?

(A) The respiratory system

(B) The endocrine system

(C) The digestive system

(D) The lymphatic system

(11) An observation can be made that within a vacuum, a big animal like an elephant cannot accelerate faster than a penny as it drops to the ground. Identify the reason from the answers provided.

(A) A big animal has vector components that are of greater complexity than a penny

(B) The acceleration of both the big animal and the penny is 9.8 m/s^2

(C) A big animal is not a projectile, unlike a penny

(D) The mass of a big animal is greater, but air resistance does not slow it

(12) Which of the trains below has the highest momentum?

(A) A train that is 9,500 kg and traveling at 200 mph

(B) A train that is 9,300 kg and traveling at 190 mph

(C) A train that is 8,000 kg and traveling at 215 mph

(D) A train that is 8,600 kg and traveling at 195 mph

(13) A research scientist observed that any time an invasive species was brought to a river, the population of native salmon dropped. The correlation that exists between the newly introduced species and the native salmon can be said to be _____.

(A) A direct relationship

(B) A relation that is indecisive

(C) An inverse relationship

(D) A relation that is both direct and indirect

(14) When a catalyst is added to a chemical reaction, the effect produced is ____.

(A) An increase in the amount of energy needed to fuel the reaction

(B) A rise in the chemical reaction rate

(C) An increase in the duration needed for the chemical reaction to be accomplished

(D) A reduction in the quantity of products involved in the chemical reaction

(15) The pharynx belongs to a person's _____ system.

(A) Respiratory

(B) Lymphatic

(C) Muscular

(D) Skeletal

(16) Which of the following is true regarding eukaryotic cells?

(A) They have no lysosomes

(B) They have no nucleus

(C) They have a single chromosome

(D) They have mitochondria

(17) Which of the following characteristics of an element can determine its particular isotope?

(A) The element's proton count

(B) The element's electron count

(C) The element's neutron count

(D) The element's quark count

(18) Which of the following statements pertaining to RNA is false?

(A) It has ribose, which is a form of sugar

(B) Under alkaline conditions, it becomes unstable

(C) Its base pairings do not include thymine

(D) The sugar it has is much less than that of DNA

(19) Which of the following is a scenario that cannot produce any normal distribution?

(A)   US families' annual income distribution

(B)   Toxic waste plus the pollution percentage in the air versus an organism's life span in that location

(C)   Height distribution within a massive people sample

(D)   A curve that has 97% of its population in the initial two standard deviations

(20) Which of the following holds the Golgi apparatus?

(A)   The cell nucleus

(B)   The cell wall

(C)   The cell mitochondria

(D)   The cytoplasm

(21) From "Order," the taxonomic rank that is next in smallness is _____.

(A)   Phylum

(B)   Species

(C)   Family

(D)   Genus

(22) Complete the sentence with the correct words.

"There are two related things in any plant, the first being _____, which involves the formation of _____."

(A) Cytokinesis, the cleavage furrow

(B) Cytokinesis, the cell plate

(C) Telophase, the cell plate

(D) Prophase, DNA

(23) Which of the following has a base not present in DNA?

(A) Guanine

(B) Uracil

(C) Cytosine

(D) Adenine

(24) Which of these atmospheric layers is nearest to outer space?

(A) The troposphere

(B) The mesosphere

(C) The stratosphere

(D) The thermosphere

(25) Tissue can be categorized into four major types. Which of the answers listed is not one of them?

(A) Parenchyma

(B) Connective

(C) Epithelial

(D) Nervous

(26) Choose the words that best complete the sentence.

"The stomach's position is _____ to the small bowel or intestine."

(A) Lateral

(B) Posterior

(C) Superior

(D) Proximal

(27) An atom has 42 protons, a similar number of electrons and 37 neutrons. What is the atom's atomic mass?

(A) 42

(B) 84

(C) 79

(D) 121

(28) James sustained trauma to the head, so he failed to recognize any person he had met within one hour, yet he could recognize people whom he knew or had met prior to the injury. Very likely, the injury affected his _____.

(A) Medulla oblongata

(B) Hippocampus

(C) Corpus callosum

(D) Pituitary gland

(29) Which of the following is not a kind of chemical bond?

(A) Ionic bond

(B) Polar bond

(C) Magnetic bond

(D) Covalent bond

(30) The quantity of hydrogen inside a balloon whose size is fixed is doubled. Which of the following indicates how the balloon's mass and density are affected?

(A) Both mass and density decrease

(B) Mass drops while density rises

(C) Mass rises while density decreases

(D) Mass and density increase

(31) On the table is 200 milliliters of a solution that is 60% sodium chloride. What is the amount of NaCl that has been dissolved in that solution?

(A) 20 grams

(B) 80 grams

(C) 50 grams

(D) 120 grams

(32) Answer the question about the following reaction:

$4C_6H_{12}O_6 + 24O_2 \rightarrow \_CO_2 + 24H_2O + Energy$

What is the number of molecules of carbon dioxide required to balance the equation?

(A) 4

(B) 24

(C) 8

(D) 16

(33) A research scientist is preparing an equation that will use a, b and c as variables. Considering "a" stands for time, "b" for energy and "c" for power, the relationship among those three variables should be _____.

(A) 2ab = c

(B) ac = 2b

(C) c = a/b

(D) c = b/a

(34) What type of cell is produced through mitosis?

(A) 4 haploid cells

(B) 2 haploid cells

(C) 2 diploid cells

(D) 1 diploid cell

(35) The cheetah, the rainbow trout and even inchworms are animals of the same ____.

(A) Kingdom

(B) Class

(C) Phylum

(D) Order

(36) Which hormone does not cause water retention?

(A) ADH

(B) ANP

(C) Aldosterone

(D) Renin

(37) Oxygenated blood leaves the heart via _____.

(A) The right ventricle

(B) The right atrium

(C) The left ventricle

(D) The left atrium

(38) Which of the hormones listed is secreted by the hypothalamus?

(A) Melatonin

(B) Dopamine

(C) Hepsidine

(D) Calcitonin

(39) Which of the following answers has the capacity to store oxygen?

(A) Myoglobin

(B) Anaphase I

(C) Prophase II

(D) Metaphase II

(40) The _____ controls the movement of a person's tongue muscle.

(A) Facial nerve

(B) Hypoglossal nerve

(C) Trigeminal nerve

(D) Vagus nerve

(41) Which of the following is a mammal that has a true placenta?

(A) Kangaroo

(B) Platypus

(C) Echidna

(D) Mongoose

(42) Many endangered species have been victims of _____.

(A) Acid rain

(B) Habitat destruction

(C) Excessive hunting

(D) Stiff competition from new species

(43) Prions within a _____ are responsible for causing a disease known as bovine spongiform.

(A) Cow

(B) Sheep

(C) Human being

(D) Potato

(44) Suppose forensic experts collect bloodstain samples at a crime scene, which of the following is best to use in order to identify the criminal using DNA profiling?

(A) Erythrocytes

(B) Platelets

(C) Leukocytes

(D) Serum

(45) Transgenic crops can be exemplified by BT brinjal. "BT" stands for _____.

(A)   Bacillus tuberculosis

(B)   Beta-carotene

(C)   Biotechnology

(D)   Bacillus thuringiensis

(46) Silkworms sometimes develop pebrine caused by nosema bombycis, which is a ____.

(A)   Virus

(B)   Protozoa

(C)   Bacterium

(D)   Fungus

(47) Human beings have receptors that facilitate detection of taste. They are known as _____.

(A)   Gustatory receptors

(B)   Nerve-ending receptors

(C)   Olfactory receptions

(D)   None of the above

(48) The disease pyorrhea affects the _____.

(A) Liver

(B) Digestive system

(C) Pancreas

(D) Gums

(49) Which of the following is often used for food preservation?

(A) Citric acid

(B) Sodium chloride

(C) Potassium chloride

(D) Sodium benzoate

(50) LASER is an acronym for _____.

(A) Light Amplification by Stimulated Emission of Rays

(B) Light Amplification by Stimulated Emission of Radiation

(C) Light Amplification by Stimulated Energy of Radiation

(D) Light Amplification by Spontaneous Emission of Radiation

(51) Which of the following diseases is not transmitted by mosquitoes?

(A) Filariasis

(B) Dengue fever

(C) Goiter

(D) Malaria

(52) Smallpox is a disease caused by _____.

(A) Algae

(B) Bacteria

(C) Virus

(D) Fungus

(53) Thalassemia is a health condition that affects a person's _____.

(A) Heart

(B) Blood

(C) Kidneys

(D) Lungs

English and Language Use Section – Test 3

(1)   Identify the answer that is most likely to appear in an academic journal.

(A)   An eyewitness reported that the driver had run a red light, and that when he crashed into the old station building, he almost hit some bystanders. Police are on the hunt for the vehicle and hope to catch the driver as well. The department requests anyone with helpful information regarding this incident provide it at any police station.

(B)   As the researchers' control group continued as normal, with no change in behavior, the test group reported several significant changes. This observation led the scientists to assume they were dealing with a viable hypothesis.

(C)   Soap Purest is the kind of soap that gives your skin a glow and a feeling of freshness. It does not cause irritation or excessive dryness. You should try it.

(D)   Jane lay on a mat outside her beautiful house and watched the planes fly past. She imagined how it would have been if she had become a pilot as she had once dreamed.

(2)   Which of the following answers is the third-person version of this sentence? "I let out a sigh of relief and allowed my entire upper body to fall back onto the sofa."

(A)   You let out a sigh of relief, and allowed your entire upper body to fall back onto the sofa.

(B)   She let out a sigh of relief and allowed her entire upper body to fall back onto the sofa.

(C)   I let out a sigh of relief, and that made her entire upper body fall back onto the sofa.

(D)   She let out a sigh of relief as your entire upper body fell back onto the sofa.

(3)   One answer in the list is a modifier from the given sentence. Identify it. "James hastily moved the books from the table to the bookshelf."

(A)   James

(B)   Hastily

(C)   Books

(D)   Moved

(4)   From the answers listed below, identify the one with the set of direct and indirect objects from the sentence in respective order. "Susan and Sam bought the children some snacks."

(A)   Susan, Sam

(B)   Snacks, children

(C)   Snacks, Susan and Sam

(D)   Children, snacks

(5)   Choose the answer where the sentence is restated in a formal manner. "I guess I'll have to bite the bullet and start the project right away."

(A)   There is no way the project is going to get itself done!

(B)   I better knock off dillydallying and do the project.

(C)   I need to do the work without further ado.

(D)   I should begin working on the project now, without further procrastination.

(6) After reading the paragraph, identify the best word to fill in the gap in the sentence.

Jane works as a receptionist at the cotton factory, ___ she believes there is room for her to be hired by the HR department. In order to improve her chances, she has enrolled in an evening course in administration.

(A) So

(B) Nevertheless

(C) But

(D) Also

(7) After reading the paragraph, identify the answer choice that is most considered informal.

Jane always wanted to be a nurse, even when she was a young girl. She would assemble her friends and talk to them about health-related issues. She would, for example, highlight the importance of handwashing. Her friends were good sports and always listened to her without interruption.

(A) Wanted to be a nurse

(B) Health-related issues

(C) When she was a young girl

(D) Were good sports

(8) One of the choices listed cannot be used to complete the sentence. Identify it. "She has always disliked the smell of raw onions, but _____."

(A) She eats them in salads for health

(B) She never eats them

(C) Her friend Mary doesn't mind it

(D) These days she is trying to withstand it

(9)   Which of the following comes closest to defining "circumnavigate"?

(A)   To find your way around something as you sail

(B)   To ensure you avoid sailing

(C)   To offer instructions on how to navigate different waters

(D)   To alter the circumstances you find yourself in

(10) Which transitional word best completes the sentence?

"____ I don't like politics, my commentaries on political issues do not betray me."

(A)   So

(B)   Since

(C)   Although

(D)   Because

(11) From the list of answers provided, choose the one with an article and complement from the sentence in respective order.

"As I watched the zoo animals, I found the chimpanzee most fascinating."

(A)   I; chimpanzee

(B)   The (before "zoo"); found

(C)   The (before "chimpanzee"); fascinating

(D)   Zoo animals; fascinating

(12) Which of the following answers has correct structure, grammar and spelling?

(A) The sheriff explained that the suspect had not broken any criminal law, although there were myriad unsettled traffic tickets in his file.

(B) In spite of not having any criminal record on his file, it were apparent the suspect had committed many traffic offenses before.

(C) As per the suspect's file records, secured in the police department, the traffic offenses he had committed in California were more than in other different states.

(D) Following a search through the records the police had kept over the years, which showed the suspect's offenses recorded under different aliases.

(13) Identify the pair of words that best completes the following sentence:

"Tergat halted for a short ____ in order to tighten his shoelaces. He had felt them slide and become ___ as he covered the initial three kilometers of the long-distance race."

(A) Brake; loose

(B) Break; loose

(C) Break; lose

(D) Brake; lose

(14) The variety of animals kept in the laboratory was virtually a/an ____ that comprised seals, rodents, apes and dogs.

(A) Arboretum

(B) Milieu

(C) Menagerie

(D) Sanctuary

(15) About a third of the student community flew to Haiti to help the communities there rebuild their lives after the storm; the rest of the students remained behind and helped with the restoration of ____ houses within the neighboring suburb.

(A) Mediocre

(B) Dilapidated

(C) Demolished

(D) Effervescent

(16) Identify the answer that best corrects the following sentence:

"Preachers all over the country need to refrain from making Political Statements."

(A) Put a comma immediately after the word "country"

(B) Remove the capitalization from "Political Statements"

(C) Put an apostrophe at the end of the word "Preachers"

(D) Change "Political Statements" to "Political Statement"

(17) Choose the best answer to complete the sentence.

"The ex-convict has been scared of _____ to his hometown."

(A) To return

(B) Returning

(C) Have returned

(D) Return

(18) Complete the sentence using the best answer from those listed below.

"The teacher observed that the anticipated exam would be ____ than the one the students had taken the previous month."

(A) Challenge-most

(B) Challenge charged

(C) More challenging

(D) More challenge

(19) Identify the pair of words that best complete the given sentence.

"Experienced pet owners prefer to obtain their purebred puppies from a breeder who is ___, one whom customers and fellow breeders ____ and respect."

(A) Shy, like

(B) Reputable, admire

(C) Discerning, fear

(D) Demanding, charm

(20) Identify the answer that best modifies the sentence.

"The behavior of the Nobel Prize recipient shows that he is a man of integrity, intelligence and he is courageous."

(A) Integrity, intelligence and courageous

(B) Integrity, intelligence and is courageous

(C) Integrity, has intelligence and is courageous

(D)   Integrity, intelligence and courage

(21) Identify the pair of words that best completes the sentence.

"The Spanish sailors had ____ sailed across the seas using their well-illustrated maps, and they had made provisions for any problems; nevertheless, as the storm became stronger and the tide _____ shifted the direction of their ship, there was no way they could have reached their destination in time."

(A) Rashly, moderately

(B) Hastily, sharply

(C) Carefully, drastically

(D) Resignedly, slowly

(22) Read the underlined word in the sentence and choose the answer that indicates its part of speech.

"She had done her research so <u>extensively</u> that she had no difficulty impressing the interviewing panel."

(A) Pronoun

(B) Adverb

(C) Verb

(D) Adjective

(23) Identify the answer whose capitalization is correct.

"Everyone who watched ____ felt like they personally knew the contestants."

(A) American Idol

(B) american idol

(C) American idol

(D) AmeriCan Idol

(24) Note the underlined word in the sentence and identify the part of speech it belongs to.

"She has been sending out job applications <u>since</u> losing her previous job last month."

(A)   Adverb

(B)   Preposition

(C)   Verb

(D)   Conjunction

(25) Read the following sentence, then identify which of the following words has more than one meaning.

"Unless a species of animal has a very strong constitution, it cannot survive the climate in the Arctic."

(A)   Strong

(B)   Survive

(C)   The

(D)   Constitution

(26) The word that is underlined in the sentence has more than one meaning. From the list of answers provided, identify the contextual meaning of the word.

"The team members were asked by the project manager to submit the final <u>draft</u> of their report before the weekend."

(A)   A special system used by project managers to choose team members

(B)   Cool air that circulates within a confined area

(C)   One version of a written document, such as an assignment or research findings

(D)   Instructions issued for one party to issue payment to another

(27) Identify the word that means the same thing as the underlined word.

"As they walked across the desert, they could feel the temperatures <u>fluctuate</u>, and they were glad they had carried different kinds of clothes."

(A) Increase

(B) Fall

(C) Change

(D) Stagnate

(28) Identify the situation where the use of formal language would be most appropriate.

(A) At a school dance

(B) When speaking to your son

(C) When speaking to a new coworker

(D) When speaking to your neighbor at home

Practice Test 3: Answers

Reading Section – Test 3 Answers

(1)   The correct answer is: (B) A narrow purpose that is specified, but broadened to accommodate future variations.

(B) is correct because the passage is about one activity, swimming, which is seen to have a single purpose as a competitive sport, yet it is also portrayed as having the potential to serve different purposes in the future.

(2)   The correct answer is: (A) Human beings occupy the moon and make use of swimming strokes to navigate through space.

The author's prophecy is that sometime in the future, swimming might serve some more advanced purpose; or alternatively, the sport will regress. None of the choices show a regressed role, but (A) shows a much more advanced role of people using swimming strokes to move around space.

(3)   The correct answer is: (D) Looking up census records, statistics, church records, etc.

The reason (D) is correct is that conventional research involves looking up exactly this kind of documentation, whereas the additional research the author does involves something slightly more unconventiona—putting herself in the shoes of Mexicans living on the border.

(4)   The correct answer is: (D) They fail to show the human aspect of the narrative.

The reason (D) is the correct answer is that census reports and many of those other conventional sources, though providing credible data and information, do not help the researcher understand the people's actual experiences.

(5)   The correct answer is: (D) Depictions by traditional sources of history and personal narratives that are subjective.

(D) is correct because although conventional sources like libraries have facts, they do not depict the human side of the narrative. Other materials written by individuals, such as diaries, may have some personal biases, but they do provide the human aspect of the narrative. If the two sources are well utilized, the "gap" can be filled.

(6) The correct answer is: (C) What my role was.

The reason (C) is the correct answer is that the author wondered what the true meaning of her research was and where she stood in the eyes of people like Teodora.

(7) The correct answer is: (B) It hints that to share ethnicity and language does not necessarily make a person an insider.

The author appreciates that there is a lot she does not know about the experiences of the Mexicans after interviewing Teodora and others, even though, like them, the author is Mexican by birth and can speak Spanish. Her question is a hint that birth and language on their own are not sufficient to make a person an insider.

(8) The correct answer is: (D) Spoken word is likely to bring better insight than accepted theories and models.

(D) is confirmed correct by the statement "The history of the Mexicans poses a challenge to models of social sciences that are derived strictly from the successful experiences of the imperialists. It is not possible to write our history without including fresh sources."

(9) The correct answer is: (A) Records kept informally and information sourced from the people in question.

(A) is the correct answer as it represents the information the writer indicates would come from "fresh sources," providing a well-rounded perspective on past events.

(10) The correct answer is: (C) Assortment.

From the context of the paragraph, it is easy to deduce that the word "mélange" refers to a mixture (assortment) of establishments such as restaurants, museums, etc.

(11) The correct answer is: (C) A famous ruin.

(C) is the correct answer because it exemplifies what the author contends is a city's most important asset in terms of making it unique. A famous ruin is unique to a city and will not be replicated anywhere else.

(12) The correct answer is: (A) First passage analyzing a phenomenon; second passage suggesting a way of solving a problem.

The reason (A) is correct is that the first passage explains how an actor is sometimes gripped by stage fright, and the reason that happens; hence, the passage provides an analysis. In the second passage, the author explains how an actor can prevent stage fright, providing a solution to the problem.

(13) The correct answer is: (C) The actor showing his/her audience strictly the behavior that pertains to the particular character.

(C) is the correct answer because it indicates the need to highlight the character's traits, yet the actor is not the character per se. In the passage, this explanation is encompassed in the clause "he/she has to hide and show simultaneously."

(14) The correct answer is: (C) The first passage stresses that it is the uniqueness of the theater realm that causes stage fright, but the second passage says stage fright is similar to various other fears.

(C) is correct because it is clear that in the first passage the author considers the individual performance as the cause of stage fright, whereas in the second passage the author offers a general solution to stage fright—substitution.

(15) The correct answer is: (B) The performer thinking of his/her audience as his/her friends.

(B) is correct because the advice provided in the second passage pertains to the performer thinking of the comfort of his/her audience as opposed to any judgment they may be making. A performer thinking of the audience as friends would certainly be thinking of how best to make them comfortable, and that would preempt stage fright.

(16) The correct answer is: (B) The organizational plan that researchers and philosophers have imposed on the world of living things.

The reason (B) is correct is that the author provides an explanation on the various ways of categorizing the world, and also states that it is on the basis of these classifications that some comparisons appear natural and others unnatural.

(17) The correct answer is: (D) One species possessing a vegetative soul and a rational soul yet not having a sensory one.

(D) is correct because the scheme of classification referred to as Aristotelian is hierarchical, and the three possibilities are solely vegetative; vegetative and sensory; and vegetative, sensory and rational. Hence, if a given group has a rational soul, it will automatically have a sensory one too.

(18) The correct answer is: (A) Comparisons made on the basis of a vegetative soul.

The reason (A) is the correct answer is that the concerned scheme has its classifications done as per some hierarchy that contains every species, even those within the utmost bottom of all layers; with a vegetative soul; those at the bottom-most layer are also within the mid-layer that additionally has a sensory soul.

(19) The correct answer is: (D) Not being objective in the manner homo sapiens are classified.

(D) is correct because it is clear the author is questioning people's obsession with being recognized as a distinct species. The writer suggests that this need emanates from insecurity and a sense of defensiveness.

(20) The correct answer is: (A) Disapproval.

(A) is correct because, according to the author, there is no logic in considering homo sapiens distinctly unique just to make them more special than other species are in their own right. The author is ridiculing human beings for their need for special recognition and classification.

(21) The correct answer is: (B) We humans are entirely defined by the qualities we possess that no other species possesses.

(B) is correct because the author explains that every species is unique as per its classification. However, per conventional classification of species, homo sapiens are given a special place.

(22) The correct answer is: (C) Insulated.

(C) is correct because being "segregated" means to be insulated; being put in a position where the species cannot have its unique qualities shared by other species. Some examples are given to show how eager human beings are to be classified as species, including refusing to acknowledge the bees' dance as a language.

(23) The correct answer is: (C) Homo sapiens and other animals are categorized entirely differently in the world of living things.

(C) is correct because the author explains how distinctly human beings are categorized by different experts, portraying them as having little in common with other animals; which, according to the author, is not the case. The author is sarcastic about this subjective attempt at portraying homo sapiens as entirely distinct, and believes this attempt to be of no benefit.

(24) The correct answer is: (D) The monarch can only survive if people modify their activities.

(D) is correct because the authors state that, in order for monarchs to survive, climate change must be addressed, as must illegal logging. These are both modifications of human activities.

(25) The correct answer is: (B) To provide an explanation for why the monarch butterflies' journey is not only difficult but also admirable

(B) is correct because the author explains in detail the degree of difficulty the butterflies face, yet, despite the long, exhausting journey they still reach their destination.

(26) The correct answer is: (C) Easy to distinguish

(C) is correct because, as used to describe the color of the butterflies, it means the monarchs' color stands out from all other species' color. It deliberately stands out so as to warn predators away.

(27) The correct answer is: (D) Soon, the lengthy distances might become simply too great for these insects to withstand.

(D) is correct because it describes the negative impact climate change is likely to have on the monarch butterfly. If the distance the butterflies have to travel during migration proves too long, so many of the butterflies will die that the species might be decimated.

(28) The correct answer is: (D) People must adjust their own activities for the monarch butterfly to continue existing as a species.

(D) is correct as it spells out what needs to be done for the monarch butterfly to survive, including reducing climate change.

(29) The correct answer is: (B) The woman had no idea what the correct answer to her question was.

The fact that the woman handed the man $5 leads one to logically conclude she was adhering to the rules of the game already agreed upon; it means she did not know the answer. The way the passage introduces the two suggests they are strangers.

(30) The correct answer is: (A) Entertainment.

(A) is correct because the passage is a fictitious, entertaining story. An informative text has facts or educational points, while a persuasive one requires the writer to take a stance and opine on something.

(31) The correct answer is: (A) After his car has been cleaned.

(A) is the correct answer because according to the passage, having his car cleaned was the other thing Abdi needed to do, besides having lunch, before going to Meshack's place to play chess.

(32) The correct answer is: (C) Q A I E I Q.

The letters begin as "1 2 3 4 1 3 2 3." The first step, substitution, produces AEITAIEITA. The second step, removing excessive letters, produces ETAIEITA. The third step, removing the beginning and end letters, produces TAIEIT, and the final step of constant substitution produces QAIEIQ.

(33) The correct answer is: (C) Over 80% of women polled stated that they could identify with the struggles of Wonder Woman.

(C) mirrors the assertion of the author that the reason people like superhero movies is that they can identify with the superheroes' struggles.

(34) The correct answer is: (A) Any driver whose insurance policy has been canceled.

(A) is correct because AllCare insures drivers who have found themselves excluded from plans offered by other insurance companies.

(35) The correct answer is: (C) Information on AllCare's new clients' special discount.

The advertisement states the company's readiness to offer any new client a $200 discount. The other options contain information that is not found within the advertisement.

(36) The correct answer is: (B)

$$
\begin{array}{ccc}
 & 5 & \\
3 & & 4 \\
6 & 12 & 14
\end{array}
$$

.

Lay out all the even numbers: 4, 6, 12, 14. You are left with 3 and 5, and only 5 can be a factor of 15; hence, 5 will be at the apex. This means 3 must fall in the middle row. The only even number fit to join 3, as per the difference stipulation, is 4.

(37) The correct answer is: (D) Changes that have taken place in the way companies utilize public relations.

(D) is the most suitable answer because when you consider changes that have taken place, updates inevitably come to mind, and these include newly acquired information. As such, the content included in the pages on "Updated Policy on Public Relations" would, very likely, include changes in the manner companies conduct public relations.

(38) The correct answer is: (A) They are the botanical name of the potato.

The reason (A) is correct is that the potato is also scientifically known as "solanum tuberosum," and the scientific branch that deals with crops is botany, as opposed to the branch that deals with animals, known as zoology. Those scientific words are put in quotations but are often italicized, an indication they are not common English words.

(39) The correct answer is: (A) An almanac.

An almanac is an annual calendar, and it shows dates that are considered important as well as data on astronomy, tide-related tables and data as such. It would, therefore, serve as a rich source of information for Jane's research.

(40) The correct answer is: (C) Reckless.

The reason (C) is the correct answer is that it is clear from the given statement that the word "foolhardy" has a negative connotation. The other three options do not have that negative quality.

(41) The correct answer is: (B) The word that is simplest.

The reason (B) is the correct answer is that whenever you are writing an essay or some other piece of prose, the main goal is to communicate to the reader; you want the reader to properly understand what you have written. As such, the simpler the words, the better.

(42) The correct answer is: (C) A word or phrase used for connection.

(C) is correct because once a word or phrase is used to connect different parts of speech, it is a transition word or phrase. For example, when you are reading a passage, the conjunctions you find are transition words.

(43) The correct answer is: (D) Nevertheless.

The reason (D) is correct is that it is a transitional word that helps the reader understand how the first and second sentence are related. A transition word does not have to appear in the middle of a compound or complex sentence. It can appear at the beginning of a sentence like in this question.

(44) The correct answer is: *(C) Refuge within Fiction; Not Factual.*

(C) is correct because the major issue discussed in the passage is post-apocalyptic science fiction, the environment within which the survivors exist and the grim scenario that might emerge if certain factors change—in this case, the capacity of the pumps to remove excess water from the subway tunnels.

(45) The correct answer is: (C) A table that shows the volume of water running through the subway system of New York City under varying conditions.

(C) is the correct answer because the writer has explained clearly how unsafe it would be for the apocalypse survivors to be underground during a terrible weather incident, such as a flood, in case there are no people working to pump out the water.

(46) The correct answer is: (C) A list of novels about people's lives in the subway tunnels.

The reason (C) is the correct answer is that normally the information contained in the sidebar is related to the same readers or audience the main story targets. As such, it is logical that a list of novels about subway-dwelling people would be in the sidebar.

(47) The correct answer is: (C) Up.

The reason (C) is correct is that it is generally accepted that the up side of the map represents the north direction; it is the convention. If the designers of the map defy this convention, they provide a compass rose with the map.

(48) The correct answer is: (C) Expounding on a theme.

(C) is the correct answer because themes are essentially messages that are not always named or spelled out explicitly in works of fiction, even though titles may give hints on what the respective themes are about.

(49) The correct answer is: (B) Hospital nurses are expected to keep their patients' personal information confidential.

(B) is correct because writing the sentence in plural form removes the gender issue; the plural of "his" or "hers" is "theirs." It is erroneous to assume that a certain career employs a particular gender, whether male or female.

(50) The correct answer is: (C) A statement expressing an opinion.

The reason (C) is correct is that a statement of opinion encompasses feelings or beliefs that do not have to be true or verifiable, but which are often based on reasoning that is valid.

(51) The correct answer is: (D) All of the above are incorrect; the paragraph's topic is implied.

(D) is the correct answer because none of the choices provided represent the paragraph's main topic. The author of the paragraph narrates the experience of a young woman who is fed up with listening to an older woman reminiscing about her children's youth. The topic is implied.

(52) The correct answer is: (C) Fiona gets frustrated listening to people nostalgically reminisce about taking care of little children.

(C) is correct because it encompasses the paragraph's core idea, which is the frustration Fiona was feeling listening to the nostalgic stories being told by the elderly woman, regarding her own experiences bringing up kids. According to the author, Fiona's personal experience was boring enough; she did not need to listen to someone else's.

(53) The correct answer is: (B) Speaking softly and gently.

The word "cooing" is used to denote a soft, gentle manner of speaking. In the context of the passage, it is easy to understand the description of the elderly lady admiring the baby in the sentence, "Fiona sighed as she watched the elderly woman cooing at the beautiful baby ..."

Math Section – Test 3 Answers

(1)   The correct answer is: (B) (4y-10) (y+5) (y-5).

There is not a lot of simplification that needs to be done here. Just divide out the 4. When you divide your numerator and denominator by 4, you get (4y-10) (y+5) (y-5).

(2)   The correct answer is: (D) 42%.

$20,400/35,000 = 0.583 \cdot 100 = 58.3\%$

$100 - 58.3 = 41.7\%$ or 42%.

(3)   The correct answer is: (D) $66.15 < p < 80.85$.

If the stock increases in value by 10%, its value will be 110% or $110/100 \cdot 73.50$, which is 80.85. If the stock drops in value by 10% then its value will be 90% or $90/100 \cdot 73.50$, which is 66.15. So p < \$66.15 and p < \$80.85.

(4)   The correct answer is: (A) \$662.50.

At company x, Joshua works for $15 \cdot 20$, which is \$300 per hour. At company y, he works from Monday to Friday for two hours daily. $5 \cdot 2 = 10$ hours for \$18.25 per hour. So $10 \cdot 18.25 = \$182.5$. He works for 37 hours and during the first two days he works for 25 hours. $37 - 25 = 12$ hrs. He gets \$15/hr, so $12 \cdot 15 = \$180$. Add the three salaries to get \$662.50.

(5)   The correct answer is: (B) 5 liters.

1 liter contains 1,000 cm³ and 6 bottles of 2 liters each means there was $6 \cdot 2 = 12$ liters of wine. When converted to cm³, 12 liters = 12,000 cm ³. So if the guests consumed 7,264 cm³ , then $12,000 - 7,264 = 4,736$ cm³ leftover. 4,736 cm³ = 4.736 liters, and when rounded to the nearest whole liter you will get the correct answer of 5 liters.

(6)   The correct answer is: (C) 3.5%.

To get the bonus and benefits, subtract 77,500 – 65,000 to get $12,500. Health benefits were 15% · 65,000, which is $9750. So the bonus was 65,000 + 9,750 – 77,500 = $2,750. Divide the bonus by the total compensation, then multiply by 100 to get the percentage: $2,750/77,500 · 100 = 3.5%.

(7)   The correct answer is: (A) 0.025.

The currency was trading at 1.32075 then dropped to 1.29620. To find the difference you need to subtract the second rate from the initial rate. The decrease was 1.32075 – 1.29620 = 0.02455. When you round this to the nearest thousandth, you get 0.025.

(8)   The correct answer is: (D) 73 deciliters.

If 1 liter covers 9 m² and there is 66 m² worth of surface to paint, then the painter will need 66 m² / 9 m², which is 7.3 m². 73 deciliters is the most accurate answer since 10 deciliters make 1 liter.

(9)   The correct answer is: (A) There is a negative covariance noted between the intake of coffee and the risk of diabetes.

There is a negative covariance noted between the intake of coffee and the risk of diabetes because as people increased their intake of coffee, type 2 diabetes cases were reduced. When there is a negative covariance, it means that once one variable goes in a particular direction, the corresponding variable moves in the opposite direction.

(10) The correct answer is: (B) 600.

To simplify this operation, round 0.049 to 0.05 so that you are left to divide 30 by 0.05. This gives you 600. Ordinarily, 30 ÷ 0.049 would be 612.24, but in this case the question not only asks for an estimate, but also for the answer to be in one significant figure.

(11) The correct answer is: (D) 63.

The average is obtained by dividing the total sum of the numbers by the number of values. We are given the average as 30 and one value as 27. When we write an equation, it will be: (m + n + 27) / 3 = 30. When we solve this equation, we get m + n = 63.

(12) The correct answer is: (D) 67.5.

Average = total sum of the numbers/number of the given values. We are given that (a + b + 27) / 3 = 30. When you solve this, you get a + b = 63. The mean of the five numbers is (a + b + m + n + 27)/5 = 45. So substitute the known values of a + b to get (63 + m + n + 27)/5 = 45. Solve this to get 135/2 = 67.5

(13) The correct answer is: (A) 7.

The median is the middle number in a sequence, so to get the median you should first arrange the numbers from the least to the highest in value, then look for the middle number. When arranged in order we have 1, 2, 4, 4 ,4, 7, 8, 8, 9, 9, 10, so the median is 7.

(14) The correct answer is: (C) 2.

A mode is the number that occurs most often in a sequence. In this case, 2 is repeated four times, so it is the modal score. 0 appears three times, as does 1, and 3 appears just once.

(15) The correct answer is: (D) Both scientists got a similar average weight and scientist y got a higher variability and range than scientist x.

The two scientists got the same average weight, which was 105 pounds. However, scientist x's range was four pounds while scientist y's range was eight pounds. (A), (B) and (C) are all incorrect as they do not accurately describe the results' variation or average.

(16) The correct answer is: (D) 22.

The 25 computers, 14 printers, 18 photocopiers, 12 staplers and 19 desks make up 100% of the inventory and only 25% of this inventory can be rented out. First, get the total items by adding all equipment together, then find 25% of that. 25 + 14 + 18 + 12 + 19 = 88. If 100% is 88, then 25% of 100 is 22.

(17) The correct answer is: (B) 2 p.m. to 9 p.m.

For you to convert 24 hr clock time to standard time, you should subtract 1200 from the 24 hr clock time that is given. In this case, 1400hrs will be 1400 − 1200, which is 2 p.m., and 2100hrs will be 2100 − 1200, which is 9 p.m. So, the doctor works from 2 pm to 9 p.m.

(18) The correct answer is: (A) 25%.

The 8 cows, 5 goats, 2 sheep and 5 pigs represent 100%. To get the percentage of the pigs, first identify what fraction of the total animals they represent, then get the percentage. To get the fraction, add 8 + 5 + 2 + 5 to get 20. Therefore, the pigs are 5/20 of the 100%. This can be calculated as 5/20 · 100, which is 25%.

(19) The correct answer is: (A) 37°C.

When you are converting °F to °C, you should subtract 32 from °F, then multiply by 5/9. So, in this case divide 98.6 by 32 to get 98.6 ÷ 32 = 66.6. Then multiply that by 5/9 to get 66.6 · 5/9 = 37.

(20) The correct answer is: (B) 1,967.

In Roman numerals, M = 1000, C = 100, L = 50, X = 10, V = 5 and I = 1. When C is placed before M it means that you should subtract C from M, which is 1000 − 100. So MCM is 1,000 + (1,000 − 100), which is 1,900. When you substitute each value in LXVII, you get 50 + 10 + 5 + 2, which is 67. Now add the two to get 1900 + 67, which is 1,967.

(21) The correct answer is: (D) 8.706.

Before adding decimals, make sure that you align them properly to avoid mistakes. To make decimals easier to add, give each value an equal number of decimal places. So in this case, add a 0 to 8.65. Now both values have two decimal places. Add them together to get 8.650 + 0.056 = 8.706.

(22) The correct answer is: (C) 1/10.

There are 10 millimeters in 1 centimeter. Therefore, for you to determine how many centimeters are in 1 millimeter, you should divide 1 millimeter by 10. In this case, we are looking for the number of centimeters in 1 mm, so 1 ÷ 10 = 1/10.

(23) The correct answer is: (C) 2.88 liters.

There are 32 oz in 1 quart. Therefore, 3 quarts contain 32 · 3 = 96 oz. 1 oz is an equivalent of 30 milliliters and 1000 milliliters = 1 liter. To get the amount in liters, first convert the 96 oz into millimeters by multiplying 96 by 30 to get 2,880 milliliters. To convert the 2,880 into liters, divide it by 1000 to get 2.88 liters.

(24) The correct answer is: (D) 440 ml.

First, convert all measurements into a common unit. 1 pint = 16 oz. Therefore, 2 pints = 16 · 2 = 32 oz. Add the liquids together to get 32 oz + 8 oz + 8 oz = 48 oz. Now convert these ounces to mm by multiplying by 30 since 1 oz = 30 millimeters. So 48 * 30 = 1,440 ml. The patient had therefore consumed 1,440 ml. To get the deficit, subtract 1,000 from 1,440 to get 440 ml.

(25) The correct answer is: (B) $408.04.

Total distance traveled is 2,727 miles, and for every 27 miles, the vehicle consumes 1 gallon. How many gallons were consumed? To find out, calculate 2,727 miles ÷ 27 miles = 101 gallons. Each of these gallons costs $4.04. Therefore, 101 gallons should cost 101 · $4.04, which is $408.04.

(26) The correct answer is: (D) 14.

Substitute x and y in both equations first. $3x^2 - 2y = (3 \times 3^2) - (2 \times 5)$, which is $(3 \times 9) - 10 = 27 - 10 = 17$. $2x^2 - 3y = (2 \times 3^2) - (3 \times 5) = (2 \times 9) - 15 = 18 - 15 = 3$. Now subtract the latter value from the former: $17 - 3 = 14$.

(27) The correct answer is: (A) 7.

First, get the unknowns on the left side; subtract 3x from the right and 3 from the left of the equation. Hence, from $2x + 3 = 3x - 4$ you get: $2x - 3x = -4 - 3$; $-x = -7$. Since you can get x by multiplying $-x$ by -1, do the same to -7. $x = 7$.

(28) The correct answer is: (B) 42.

Find the prime factors of every one of these numbers. $42 = 2 \times 3 \times 7$; $126 = 2 \times 3^2 \times 7$; $210 = 2 \times 3 \times 5 \times 7$; the prime numbers common to all three numbers are $2 \times 3 \times 7$ and their product is 42.

(29) The correct answer is: (B) $16 million.

Let the first year's sales be x. Hence, the second year's sales should be x + $3 million. The third year's sales were, therefore, (x + $3 million) · 2. If (x + $3 million) · 2 = $38 million, what is x? (x + $3 million) = $38 million ÷ 2. x = (19 − 3) million dollars = $16 million.

(30) The correct answer is: (C) 1,250.

Substitute x with 150 in $x^2/25 + 4x - 250$. This becomes $150^2/25 + 4 \cdot 150 - 250$, and now you can work that out like any other math problem. $150^2/25 + 4 \cdot 150 - 250 = (22,500/25) + 600 - 250 = 900 + 600 - 250 = 1,250$.

(31) The correct answer is: (B) $l = 2w - 3$.

Considering the length is given in terms of the width, let the width be represented by "w." Double width is $2 \times w = 2w$. The length that is less than double width must be $2w - 3$ inches, which is exactly the length of the box; $l = 2w - 3$.

(32) The correct answer is: (D) Infinite.

"Infinite" means that the number of irrational numbers within the range of 1 to 6 is extremely large; there will always be one more you can find. An irrational number is one that cannot be written as a ratio, and among its features is having endless decimals like pi = 3.14159265358 ...

(33) The correct answer is: (C) 54 pounds.

Confirm that one person now consumes a minimum of 67½ pounds of sugar annually, just like an average high school student. Since the plan is to reduce that amount by 20%, it means each successful individual will consume a maximum of 80% of 67½ lbs, since 67½ represents 100% consumption. 80% x 67½ = 54 lb.

(34) The correct answer is: (C) 20 turns.

In order for the screw to penetrate the wooden surface one inch, the screw would need to be turned 8 times, each with a lead of 1/8 inch (1 ÷ 1/8) Now that the length to be penetrated is as long as the screw whose length is 2.5 inches, the number of leads should be (2.5 ÷ 1/8) = 20

(35) The correct answer is: (C) 18.

Solve for y (Equation 1). xy = 144, so y = 144/x. Substitute for y (Equation 2). x + y = 30 means x + 144/x = 30. Multiply both sides by x; x^2 + 144 = 30x. Subtract 30x from both sides; x^2 − 30x + 144 = 0. Do factoring (x − 24)(x − 6) = 0. Remember, x > y.

(36) The correct answer is: (B) 2x − 5.

The reason (B) is the correct answer is that 2x − 5 is one of the factors of the polynomial, $2x^2$ − 3x − 5. The full expression, or the expanded form of the polynomial, is actually (x + 1) (2x − 5), which means (2x − 5) is one of the factors and (x + 1) is the other.

Science Section – Test 3 Answers

(1) The correct answer is: (C) The lymphatic system.

(C) is correct because it is in the same category as the lymph nodes, and it functions as the blood's filter. The spleen, acting as a filter, clears out whatever red blood cells are worn out, and does the same to any foreign organisms like germs. The spleen is part of the lymphatic system and drainage network.

(2) The correct answer is: (D) Every secretary is a great typist. Catherine is a secretary. Hence, Catherine is a great typist.

(D) is correct because it fits the working of deductive thinking, which begins with a number of premises considered to be factual or true, followed by a conclusion that is arrived at logically. The logical line of thinking in deductive thinking is that A leads to B, and C leads to A; and so C automatically leads to B.

(3) The correct answer is: (C) Whiplash.

(C) is correct because disc herniation results from a spinal disc's inner core leaking through the disc's outer part; a kind of injury to the spine often occasioned by injury to a person's back or spine or both. Any time someone suffers whiplash, there is a chance it could lead to disc herniation.

(4) The correct answer is: (B) It regulates the heart's, stomach's, lungs' and intestines' involuntary activity.

(B) is correct because it is the role of the autonomic nervous system to control digestion, heart rate, rate of respiration and perspiration, salivation and swallowing, breathing and other such involuntary actions. This system is different from the somatic nervous system, whose control is of voluntary actions.

(5) The correct answer is: (A) Water combines with carbon dioxide.

(A) is correct because the two compounds that are combined during photosynthesis are water with carbon dioxide. They combine as the plant absorbs both of them and converts them to glucose and oxygen. Photosynthesis is the process by which a green plant makes its nutrients out of the two compounds.

(6)   The correct answer is: (C) Neutrons and protons.

Only protons and neutrons can be found within the nucleus. Those electrons are in a cloud that surrounds that particular nucleus; hence, they cannot be located inside the nucleus.

(7)   The correct answer is: (D) Consumers at a tertiary level receive less energy than consumers at the primary level.

A decrease is always noted in the energy quantity transferred to a higher trophic level from a lower one. Generally, the higher the consumer is with regards to the trophic level, the less the amount of energy that is available overall. Logically then, consumers at the primary level receive higher amounts of energy than those at upper levels.

(8)   The correct answer is: (A) A dress has molecules with no capacity to absorb the wavelengths of red light.

Whenever light falls on an object, the object ends up absorbing some of the light and reflecting the rest. It is those wavelengths that the object reflects that determine the way we perceive color. As such, the reason a red dress is seen as red is because those are the wavelengths reflected.

(9)   The correct answer is: (C) Independent variable.

(C) is correct because when such an experiment is being done, the control factor used by the researchers is the independent variable—one that a scientist can change or control.

(10) The correct answer is: (B) The endocrine system.

(B) is correct because the endocrine system regulates the functions of metabolism, the rate of growth and the state of one's moods. It also controls other functions like how the tissues of the body work, and reproduction.

(11) The correct answer is: (B) The acceleration of both the big animal and the penny is 9.8 m/s².

(B) is correct because when a small thing like a penny and a big animal like an elephant fall freely within a vacuum, the acceleration rate for both of them remains equal. Owing to gravitational force, both of them drop at a rate of 9.8 m/s². Objects of greater mass drop faster only when there is significant air resistance.

(12) The correct answer is (A) A train that is 9,500 kg and traveling at 200 mph.

(A) is correct because an object's momentum equals the object mass times the object's velocity. The highest momentum would be observed in the train that weighs 9,500 kg and is moving at 200 mph.

(13) The correct answer is: (C) An inverse relationship.

(C) is correct because where a given factor has a specific effect on another, the two factors can be taken as having a powerful correlation. In this question, the population of the native salmon drops as the population of the new species rises; hence, the two species have a relationship that can be aptly described as inverse.

(14) The correct answer is: (B) A rise in the chemical reaction rate.

(B) is correct because the definition of a catalyst is an enzyme with the capacity to reduce the energy required to initiate a reaction. As such, adding a catalyst to a reaction that is already taking place has the effect of making that reaction faster, because compared to the energy previously needed, less is now required.

(15) The correct answer is: (A) Respiratory.

(A) is correct because it is part of a person's respiratory system. Even then, it is also one of the parts of the body that facilitates the process of digestion.

(16) The correct answer is: (D) They have mitochondria.

(D) is correct as eukaryotic cells have mitochondria, unlike prokaryotic cells, which do not. In addition to having mitochondria, eukaryotic cells also have nuclei, lysosomes and chromosomes.

(17) The correct answer is: (C) The element's neutron count.

(C) is correct because an element's neutron count is responsible for its isotope. The proton count determines what the element is. Meanwhile, the electron count is responsible for giving the element's atomic particle its specific charge; negative, neutral or positive.

(18) The correct answer is: (D) The sugar it has is much less than that of DNA.

The reason (D) is the correct answer is that the statement is untrue. The difference between RNA and DNA has nothing to do with the amount of sugar either of them has. Rather, it is the number of −OH groups each has. Ribose RNA has an extra −OH group as compared to the deoxyribose that DNA has.

(19) The correct answer is: (B) Toxic waste plus the pollution percentage in the air versus an organism's life span in that location.

(B) is correct because this is a scenario where a rise in toxicity in the atmosphere is likely to lead to decreasing number of organisms in the area; this is termed an inverse relationship. That eventuality automatically negates the possibility of normal distribution. The other three options have a chance for exhibiting normal distribution.

(20) The correct answer is: (D) The cytoplasm.

(D) is correct because the Golgi body is an organelle found within a cell's cytoplasm. Cytoplasm is a solution the cell membrane encloses; it is thick and comprises water, proteins and salts.

(21) The correct answer is: (C) Family.

The size of family is just a step away from "Order" in the declining sequence. Taxonomy is the process by which animals, plants and other things are named and classified into varying groups in the context of a bigger system. The taxonomic rank sequence is: kingdom, phylum, class, order, family, genus, species.

(22) The correct answer is: (B) Cytokinesis, the cell plate.

(B) is correct as cytokinesis takes place following the telophase stage, and it involves cells splitting into two. In the case of plants, cytokinesis entails the creation of a cell plate, but with animals this process is about forming a cleavage furrow.

(23) The correct answer is: (B) Uracil.

(B) is correct because uracil is not one of the nucleotides that DNA information is stored as. DNA information is stored as adenine, guanine, thymine and cytokine; the first two being categorized as purines and the latter two as pyrimidines. A replacement usually happens in RNA, with uracil taking the place of thymine.

(24) The correct answer is: (D) The thermosphere.

(D) is the correct answer because the layer at the topmost level within the atmosphere, just before getting to the exosphere, but beyond the mesosphere, is the thermosphere. That is the area where the molecules of the atmosphere drift freely within space. Within the thermosphere is ultraviolet radiation that creates ions within the ionosphere through photodissociation or photoionization.

(25) The correct answer is: (A) Parenchyma.

(A) is correct because the parenchyma is not in the group of four major categories of tissue, which are epithelial, connective, nervous and muscle.

(26) The correct answer is: (C) Superior.

(C) is correct because the position of a person's stomach is above the small intestine. In anatomy, the term "superior" denotes either "above" or "upper." The last stages of nutrient absorption occur in a person's small intestine, after receiving bile and pancreatic juice.

(27) The correct answer is: (C) 79.

In order to calculate an atom's atomic mass, you need to find the sum of protons and neutrons that are within the nucleus. The size of an electron is miniscule when compared to protons and neutrons, and therefore the outcome cannot contribute to the atom's mass. Hence, the atomic mass here is 42 + 37, which is 79.

(28) The correct answer is: (B) Hippocampus.

The reason (B) is the correct answer is that the hippocampus is a person's memory storage site. (A) is incorrect as the medulla oblongata deals with controls of an involuntary nature. (C) and (D) are incorrect because the corpus callosum deals with emotions; and a person's pituitary gland is part of the endocrine system.

(29) The correct answer is: (C) Magnetic bond.

A magnetic bond is not a type of chemical bond. An ionic bond involves the donation of electrons and their acceptance—a bond of a chemical nature with the capacity to generate two charged ions that are opposite to each other. The polar bond describes differences of an electronegative nature, whereas a covalent bond involves the sharing of electrons.

(30) The correct answer is: (D) Mass and density increase.

(D) is correct because air mass in a set volume increases as its molecule number rises, and this causes its density to also increase. Since (A), (B) and (C) do not satisfy both of those conditions, they are incorrect.

(31) The answer is: (D) 120 grams.

A solution of 60% sodium chloride can be prepared by dissolving 60 grams of sodium chloride in slightly less than 100 milliliters of water, and subsequently adding enough water to reach 100 milliliters. If there had been 200 milliliters of a 60% sodium chloride solution, the dissolved NaCl would have been 120 grams.

(32) The correct answer is: (B) 24.

(B) is correct because a reaction of a chemical nature is balanced only when the reactants' amount is the same as that of the products. In the reaction there are 24 carbons in total, and as such it is necessary to also have 24 carbons on the side of the products.

(33) The correct answer is: (D) c = b/a.

The reason (D) is correct is that power equals energy divided by time. You can also work with the formula that energy is equal to power multiplied by time. Energy uses joules as its unit, power uses watts and time uses seconds.

(34) The correct answer is: (C) 2 diploid cells

(C) is correct because the process of mitosis ends up producing two diploid-daughter cells, with similar genetic matter to that of their parent cell. Mitosis is the cell division process where one cell produces two daughter cells, and each of the new cells has a similar chromosome number as that in the nucleus of the mother cell.

(35) The correct answer is: (A) Kingdom.

(A) is correct because the three animals indicated fall under the category "animalia," which means "kingdom." Cheetah, rainbow trout and inchworms are so different that they cannot be put in the same phylum class. The first two belong to the phylum Chordata, and inchworms fall under the phylum Arthropoda.

(36) The correct answer is: (B) ANP

(B) is correct because ANP, or Atrial Natiuretic Peptide, is a hormone the body releases to respond to an increase in the volume of blood and pressure known to cause vasodilation. Owing to vasodilation, the body increases its sodium and water excretion, restoring its homeostatic condition.

(37) The correct answer is: (C) The left ventricle.

The heart's right ventricle pumps blood poor in oxygen into the person's lungs via the pulmonary valve, and the heart's left atrium takes the blood with oxygen out of the lungs, pumping it into the heart's left ventricle. This left ventricle then pumps the oxygenated blood out via the heart's aortic nerve for distribution to the entire body.

(38) The correct answer is: (B) Dopamine.

(B) is correct because production of dopamine is done by the hypothalamus, within the brain's substantia nigra and ventral tegmental. Dopamine is specifically a neuro-hormone, though it works as an inhibitor hormone. Melatonin is mainly produced in the pituitary gland, hepcidin is produced by the liver and calcitonin is produced by parafollicular cells.

(39) The correct answer is: (A) Myoglobin.

(A) is correct because myoglobin is the primary muscle tissue pigment that carries oxygen. When myoglobin in the cells is in high concentration, it enables an organism to hold its breath for a longer duration. Mammals that dive, like seals or whales, possess muscles that have significantly higher myoglobin levels.

(40) The correct answer is: (B) Hypoglossal nerve.

The reason (B) is correct is that the hypoglossal nerve is responsible for innervating every extrinsic and intrinsic muscle the tongue has, apart from the palatoglossus. The hypoglossal nerve is essentially the twelfth nerve of the cranium.

(41) The correct answer is: (D) Mongoose.

The reason (D) is correct is mongooses have actual placenta, like humans. That placenta is where offspring develop within the uterus.

(42) The correct answer is: (B) Habitat destruction.

A habitat is said to have been destroyed when it has ceased to have the capacity to sustain the species within it. Such destruction results in the habitat's diversity of plants and animals also being destroyed. Habitat destruction can be exemplified by the harvesting of fossil fuel, dredging of rivers, deforestation, urbanization and other such activities.

(43) The correct answer is: (A) Cow.

(A) is correct because a prion is an agent that causes a neurological disorder in a cow. This agent is taken to be a form of modified prion protein and the disorder it causes in the cow is progressive; it is known as Bovine Spongiform Encelopathy—BSE. It's also known as "mad cow disease."

(44) The correct answer is: (C) Leukocytes.

Leukocytes are white blood cells (WBCs). These cells help protect the body's immune system. They are the largest blood cells, have no color and do have a nucleus. They are located not only in a person's blood but also within the lymph.

(45) The correct answer is: (D) Bacillus thuringiensis.

(D) is correct as Bacillus thuringiensis is found in the soil. BT Brinjals are made through the insertion of the bacterium in the brinjal cultivar's genome. The reason the transgenic brinjal was developed was to create a plant that was resistant to insects like the fruit and shoot borer.

(46) The correct answer is: (B) Protozoa.

(B) is correct as nosema belongs to a parasite genus, and nosema bombycis is the cause of pebrine among silkworms. This parasite is not a virus, bacteria or a fungus, but is a protozoa. A protozoa is a eukaryote that is single-celled and parasitic, and feeds on organic matter like other microorganisms or debris.

(47) The correct answer is: (A) Gustatory receptors.

(A) is correct because gustatory receptors enable a person to detect taste; they are found within the taste buds. They are normally close to the tongue surface, the soft palate, the upper section of the esophagus, the epiglottis and within the cheeks. They can detect bitter, salty, sour, sweet and umami.

(48) The correct answer is: (D) Gums.

(D) is correct because pyorrhea, which is also referred to as periodontitis, is a grave infection which causes damage to the gums and sometimes even destroys a person's jawbone. Ordinarily people suffer from pyorrhea due to poor oral hygiene. The infection increases the risk of heart and lung disease.

(49) The correct answer is: (D) Sodium benzoate.

The reason (D) is correct is that sodium benzoate, due to its anti-fungal properties, has the capacity to preserve food. Fungi is known to make food go bad, but once sodium benzoate has penetrated the various cells of the food, it balances the food's pH and makes it unfavorable for fungi.

(50) The correct answer is: (B) Light Amplification by Stimulated Emission of Radiation.

The reason (B) is correct is that the meaning of LASER is "Light Amplification by Stimulated Emission of Radiation." The device is used for the purpose of emitting light using the optical amplification process whose basis is the stimulated discharge of electromagnetic radiation.

(51) The correct answer is: (C) Goiter.

(C) is correct because a goiter is an abnormal increase in the size of the thyroid gland, whose cause is an iodine deficiency, or just thyroid gland inflammation. It is not a disease transmitted to a person by a mosquito.

(52) The correct answer is: (C) Virus.

(C) is correct because the cause of smallpox is a virus. The disease was officially eradicated in 1980, but people still receive vaccinations to prevent it. Symptoms of the disease include ones similar to the flu, and people affected also develop rashes on the face, hands and torso.

(53) The correct answer is: (B) Blood.

The reason (B) is the correct answer is that thalassemia is a hereditary health condition that affects hemoglobin, whose main role is transporting oxygen all over the body. People with this condition are likely to be seriously anemic.

English and Language Use Section – Test 3 Answers

(1)   The correct answer is: (B) As the researchers' control group continued as normal with no change in behavior, the test group reported several significant changes. This observation led the scientists to assume they were dealing with a viable hypothesis.

(B) is correct because words such as "researchers," "scientists" and "hypothesis" are all likely to be found in an academic journal, or an academic report. (A) is likely to be found in a newspaper, (C) in an advertisement and (D) in a novel.

(2)   The correct answer is: (B) She let out a sigh of relief and allowed her entire upper body to fall back onto the sofa.

The third person does not use the pronouns "I" or "you" that are used for the first- and second-person, respectively. (B) is correct because it uses the pronoun "she," which marks the third-person.

(3)   The correct answer is: (B) Hastily.

The word "hastily" modifies the verb "moved" to provide more information about that action. It is because of this added information that you can tell the manner in which James shifted the books. Modifiers of verbs are referred to as adverbs.

(4)   The correct answer is: (B) Snacks, children.

The word "snacks" represents the direct object, because it is the one that experiences the direct impact of the verb or action. The buying happened to the snacks. After what happened to the snacks/direct object, the children benefitted from the action of buying.

(5)   The correct answer is: (D) I should begin working on the project now, without further procrastination.

To determine whether a text is written formally or informally, check for idioms or casual expressions. Formal writing is straightforward in the manner it delivers information, unlike informal writing, where more generalized or idiomatic language is often used.

(6)   The correct answer is: (C) But.

The reason (C) is the correct answer is that the clause that follows after the conjunction "but" introduces a contrast in what the reader would expect of a receptionist. "So" is incorrect because what comes after the conjunction does not depend on what has happened before it.

(7)   The correct answer is: (D) Were good sports.

Being a good sport is an informal expression used when a person remains polite despite things becoming awkward or unpleasant. In this case, Jane's friends played along as she pretended to be a health-care provider even though they understood it was not real.

(8)   The correct answer is: (B) She never eats them.

The reason (B) is the correct answer is that the conjunction "but" introduces the answer. This means that for the sentence to be logical, it must be completed with something contradictory.

(9)   The correct answer is: (A) To find your way around something as you sail.

In this situation, you need to consider the various parts that form the word "circumnavigate." "Circum" connotes a circle, while "navigate" means to travel. With these two clues, it is easy to pick (A) as the appropriate answer.

(10) The correct answer is: (C) Although.

A transitional word makes it easy to move from one part of the sentence to the next. (C) is the best answer because it helps to clearly connect two contradictory clauses.

(11) The correct answer is: (C) The (before "chimpanzee"); fascinating

Articles indicate whether the noun that follows is specific or one among many. In this case, "the" is an article that indicates the chimpanzee is being referred to as an individual or specific animal. "Fascinating" is the complement that provides information about the specified noun, the chimpanzee.

(12) The correct answer is: (A) The sheriff explained that the suspect had not broken any criminal law, although there were myriad unsettled traffic tickets in his file.

In (B), the error falls in the use of the verb form "were" instead of "was," since it is in reference to the singular pronoun "it." In (C), the phrase "secured in the police department" should not be enclosed in commas—only the second comma is necessary. The sentence in (D) is incomplete.

(13) The correct answer is: (B) Break, loose.

Although the word "break" can serve as a verb meaning to snap into pieces, in the context of running, it serves as a noun that means a pause. Also, in this context the word "loose" means "not tight," but in other contexts it could mean to misplace something.

(14) The correct answer is: (C) Menagerie.

The word "menagerie" is used in reference to many animals assembled together to be exhibited. An arboretum is a garden of trees; milieu has to do with one's social environment and a sanctuary is an animal's natural habitat that is legally protected.

(15) The correct answer is: (B) Dilapidated.

If houses are dilapidated, it means they are rundown and almost falling apart. They could be mediocre but still strong structures that do not require restoration; and if they are demolished they cannot be restored, and only new ones can be constructed. Also, buildings cannot be said to be effervescent. Hence, (A), (C) and (D) are incorrect.

(16) The correct answer is: (B) Remove the capitalization from "Political Statements."

The words "Political Statements" are general and do not represent the name of an organization or any other specific thing. As such, capitalizing them is erroneous. No comma is required in the sentence, and "preachers" should not have an apostrophe because there is no possessiveness being shown. To change "political statements" to singular, the noun phrase would require the article "a."

(17) The correct answer is: (B) Returning.

The preposition "of" helps to pick the verb that is in the correct form, which is "returning." The infinitive "to return" would mean to erroneously have two prepositions together. (C) is incorrect because the scary event is in the future as denoted by the auxiliary "has" in "has been," which means the scare is still continuing.

(18) The correct answer is: (C) More challenging.

The word "challenging" is an adjective that modifies the noun "exam," and it is developed from the noun "challenge." It is, therefore, not a conventional adjective like "big" or "tall" that only needs "-er" at the end to form a comparison. So its magnitude is expressed in terms of "challenging, more challenging, most challenging."

(19) The correct answer is: (B) Reputable, admire.

The comma that comes immediately after the first dash indicates that whatever comes next is meant to enhance the meaning of what you fill in that first gap. In the case of (B), a breeder who is reputable is admired and respected not only by customers but by his peers.

(20) The correct answer is: (D) Integrity, intelligence and courage.

The best answer, which is (D), is the one whose adjectives are in the same form. The uniformity should be evident as you read he is a man of integrity, intelligence and courage.

(21) The correct answer is: (C) Carefully, drastically.

The adverb "carefully" fits well in the first gap, showing how meticulous the sailors had been in planning the voyage. Phrases like "well-illustrated maps" and "provisions for any problems" confirm the careful planning. "Drastically" serves to show how badly the ship was derailed from its course, which corresponds to the sentence's conclusion that they could not arrive in time.

(22) The correct answer is (B) Adverb.

An adverb provides more information regarding a particular verb, and in this case the word "extensively" gives information pertaining to how the subject (she) carried out the action of researching.

(23) The correct answer is: (A) American Idol

Since *American Idol* is the name of a television program, the name should be capitalized.

(24) The correct answer is: (D) Conjunction.

The underlined word "since" is a conjunction normally used to connect two clauses, one independent and the other dependent. In this case, as in all others, the underlined conjunction comes immediately before the dependent clause. It is also correct to begin the sentence with such a dependent clause as long as "since" maintains its position as the starting word.

(25) The correct answer is: (D) Constitution.

The word "constitution" in the context of the given sentence means the make-up of the animal species. However, "constitution" is also used in reference to a document of a legal nature, on whose basis a country or organization is governed.

(26) The correct answer is: (C) One version of a written document, such as an assignment or research findings.

Although the word "draft" can be used in reference to air circulating within a small area, in the context of this sentence the word means a copy of a written document.

(27) The correct answer is: (C) Change.

The reason (C) "Change" is the correct answer is that it is a fact that the temperatures did not remain constant. However, (A) and (B) cannot be correct because the word "fluctuate" would be used when the temperatures rise as well as when they drop.

(28) The correct answer is: (C) When speaking to a new coworker.

Whenever you meet a person for the first time, it is preferable to use formal language, especially at work.

Practice Test 4: Questions

Reading Section – Test 4

(1) Which of the following answers has no sign of gender bias?

(A) From the beginning of humankind, there has not been a time when man has ceased to wonder about stars

(B) From the beginning of mankind, there has not been a time when man has ceased to wonder about stars

(C) From the beginning of humankind, there has not been a time when people have ceased to wonder about stars

(D) From the beginning of humankind, there has not been a time when man's imagination has not been captured by stars

(2) The word "_____" is used to mean a certain form of bias that is harmful.

(A) Overgeneralizing

(B) Opinion

(C) Assuming

(D) Stereotype

(3) Which of the following terms best defines "bias"?

(A) A community that is often a victim of prejudice

(B) A belief that is preconceived and at times unfair

(C) A statement that is generalized and sometimes untrue

(D) An idea that is implied in an argument

(4)   Which of the following does not show gender bias?

(A)   Any parent feeding her own child organic food is mindful of her child's physical development

(B)   Any parent feeding his own child organic food is mindful of his child's physical development

(C)   Any parent feeding a child organic food is mindful of the child's physical development

(D)   Any parent feeding their child organic food is mindful of her child's physical development

Read the paragraph and then answer the four questions that follow.

The entire theater was full. The attentive audience witnessed the characters losing their own homes, jobs, feelings of security and even the fundamental beliefs they had held. Only a few characters succeeded in saving at least one member of their family. The majority of characters retained small souvenirs in their pockets. Ultimately, they all had close to nothing remaining of their worldly possessions by the time disaster befell them. Once the show ended, the entire audience walked out smiling. Nothing beats a story where the world is ending—so long as it is entirely fictional.

(5)   Which of the following states the paragraph's major idea?

(A)   A new disaster film has been released and is showing in theaters

(B)   Anyone who has experienced a disaster has to be extra strong

(C)   Somehow, people are fascinated by disaster films

(D)   Anyone who enjoys disaster films is abnormal

(6)   Which of the following explains the role the last sentence plays in the paragraph?

(A)   An idea that is implied

(B)   The topic sentence

(C)   A support detail

(D)   An introduction

(7)   What is the reason the writer waited till the final sentence to make a clear point?

(A)   It produces the greatest impact

(B)   It is distracting to the person reading the passage

(C)   It has the effect of altering the subject

(D)   It ensures the reader is not offended

(8)   If the writer was interested in extending the paragraph further, and wanted to say that people are naturally vicious, what detail would be best added to subsequent paragraphs to support that allegation?

(A)   An argument about censoring violence

(B)   Examples of aggression-based entertainment throughout history

(C)   A review on the most recent disaster film

(D)   Acts of valor and generosity exemplified within disaster films

(9) _____ idea is only suggested and not outright mentioned.

(A) An informational

(B) An explicit

(C) A persuasive

(D) An implied

(10) Different economic activities contribute to the state of the economy at any one time. Which graphic diagram best represents the economy as a combination of different economic sectors in varying proportions?

(A) A bar graph

(B) A sketch

(C) A flowchart

(D) A pie chart

(11) Which of the following accurately describes a summary?

(A) It provides judgment regarding the original text

(B) It is an implicit restatement of ideas stated in the text

(C) It is a collection of words drawn from the original text

(D) It is a paragraph that excludes the text's major idea

(12) Which of the following best represents a graphic element used within a text?

(A) The spaces in between one paragraph and another

(B) A major idea communicated differently

(C) A number of concepts arranged in sequential order

(D) Information that is communicated visually

(13) When a writer uses a quote in text, he/she does not have to _____.

(A) Indicate where that quote has been taken from

(B) Provide an explanation on how useful that quote is in supporting a particular point

(C) Include a citation

(D) Restate that same quote in other words

(14) The financial crisis of 2008 can be aptly described in a paragraph using a _____ textual structure.

(A) Descriptive

(B) Compare and contrast

(C) Sequential

(D) Cause and effect

Read the passage and then answer the six questions that follow.

The train didn't go "choo choo," but the girl loved it anyway. It was the best train in the world. She screamed the sound, "Chooo chooo! Choooooo!" For hours, she played with the trains. At the height of her excitement, the toddler then lost her favorite pacifier. Subsequently, after noticing that her pacifier was missing, the girl became hysterical. Her wailing could be heard three floors down. Usually the girl loved to wave to Hank, the garbage man, but this time she was too distraught to do so. It was evident that the toddler was not about to recover from the heavy loss anytime soon; very likely never. Some moments later, she could be seen playing at the nearby park.

(15) Identify the adjectives that describe the tone of the passage.

(A) Ironic and humorous

(B) Earnest and annoyed

(C) Earnest and humorous

(D) Ironic and angry

(16) Which of the following is an example of irony?

(A) She screamed the sound, "Chooo chooo! Choooooo!"

(B) Subsequently, after noticing that her pacifier was missing, she became hysterical.

(C) Her wailing could be heard three floors down.

(D) Some moments later, she could be seen playing at the nearby park.

(17) To establish a tone of hyperbole from the very beginning, the writer of the passage _____.

(A) Describes how the child headed to the nearby park to play

(B) Refers to the train as the "best train in the world"

(C) Pretends the small girl can create train sounds

(D) Erroneously claims the girl lost her pacifier when she actually lost her doll

(18) Consider the sentence, "It was evident the toddler was not about to recover from the heavy loss anytime soon; very likely never." Based on context, what can you expect a reader to feel when he/she reads that line?

(A)   Horrified

(B)   Amused

(C)   Excited

(D)   Worried

(19) Which of the following is not used as a transition within the passage?

(A)   Below

(B)   Subsequently

(C)   Some moments later

(D)   At the height of her excitement

(20) The transition "later" in the passage connects ideas by indicating _____.

(A)   When particular events took place

(B)   The contrast between two particular ideas

(C)   Exemplified ideas

(D)   Relationships of cause and effect

Read the pair of sentences and then answer the question that follows.

"Stephen chose to join friends who wanted to spend the entire day playing football, as opposed to studying for the upcoming science test. He scored very poorly on his exam."

(21) Which of the following answers, if used at the start of the second sentence, would serve as a good transition word?

(A) For instance

(B) As a result

(C) Similarly

(D) However

(22) Literature can be categorized into what two genres?

(A) Technical, expository

(B) Fables, myths

(C) Sequence, description

(D) Fiction, nonfiction

(23) Which of the following exemplifies persuasive writing?

(A) A book of history

(B) An autobiography

(C) An op-ed article

(D) A user manual

(24) An essay on WWI and WWII can be analyzed within a structure best described as
_____.

(A) Cause and effect

(B) Technical

(C) Compare and contrast

(D) Expository

(25) Jean found a video presentation on a conference linked to the scientific topic she is dealing with for her research, and she is interested in finding out how credible the video is. Which of the following would be a reason not to trust the video as a credible source?

(A) The person giving the address makes arguments that are greatly emotional

(B) The person giving the address is a professor at Harvard whose specialization is related to Jean's area of research

(C) The date of the conference is as recent as two years ago

(D) The people who created the video are reputable, well-known people in the scientific field Jean is researching

(26) Susan is carrying out research on how parenting techniques have changed over the past fifty years. Which of the following research sources would be least credible?

(A) A 1990 publication on how best to bring up your child

(B) A long op-ed article regarding the difficulties a parent faces when bringing up an adolescent

(C) An article published recently in *Parents* magazine comparing the parenting experience of the 1990s to today.

(D) A pediatrician's interview published in a reputable magazine discussing the importance of positive discipline

(27) A student whose major is art has found a video presentation involving a number of people making comments on some work done by a renowned artist whom she has studied for some time. Which of the following will not help the student determine whether or not the presentation is a credible research source?

(A)   That video is two years old

(B)   A professor of art history comments on the video

(C)   There are original paintings of an artist shown in the video

(D)   That video is visibly edited, with some of the speakers cut off midway through their comments

Read the passage and then answer the three questions that follow.

Do you feel tired of having your children not pay attention to what you are saying? Do you find your kids distracted whenever you ask them to carry out some task? Do you find yourself facing stares from their glassy eyes whenever you address them? The problem is partially excessive screen time.

There are benefits to using technology, but there is also plenty of damage it causes to children's ability to focus. Flashing lights, excessively bright colors, copious hyperlinks— it is a miracle children can still manage some level of focus!

It would work wonders for your children if you could limit their screen time. Create opportunities for them to engage in normal conversations where people face one another. Such activities are bound to help your children practice how to listen to each other and will help them develop their communication skills. Give your kids a book! This can help them practice sitting still and focusing on a single thing for a specific duration of time.

Technology is not going to go away, yet it is possible for you to set some limits that can help your children focus and listen, and even be better at engaging with you.

(28) The audience for the above passage is intended to be _____.

(A) Teachers

(B) Parents

(C) Policymakers

(D) Children

(29) The writer of the article has made the assumption that _____.

(A) Children don't like following directions from parents

(B) Parents get frustrated when kids don't listen

(C) Children prefer to read instead of use electronic devices

(D) Parents have more screen time than their kids

(30) Which of the following is a conclusion that cannot be supported with information from the passage?

(A) It is the author's view that parents should do more to help their children spend less time with their electronic devices

(B) It is the author's view that children have excessive screen time

(C) It is the author's view that parents have no clue how children should be disciplined

(D) It is the author's view that technology is having a negative impact on children

Read the next passage and then answer the five questions that follow.

The survey brought to the fore a wide-ranging pattern of bias expressed unconsciously against minority students on campuses dominated by white students. To start with, a shocking proportion of respondents from the minority groups, 83%, said they regularly experienced marginalization or being overlooked by people in the majority of the campus community.

In an interview on phone, Aida Green, a sophomore of African American descent at Iowa's Stanmore University, explained that she often receives questions from students such as, "Where are you visiting from?" She noted that though the encounters are friendly in tone, the underlying connotation is clear: she is not recognized as someone who belongs to her own community.

When asked the reason it matters, Green's frustration was evident in her voice. "I observe as people pass me over when putting together study groups. I'm forced to draw attention to myself." She lets out a sigh. "That is when I am aware there is an opportunity somewhere which I may be missing out on."

Similar comments were made by other minority students who were interviewed. A common sentiment expressed was fatigue; minority students are tired of being overlooked and ignored. And several students ended up echoing the concern expressed by Green that there is a great likelihood that opportunities are passing them by.

Clarity Ferrer, a black woman from Puerto Rico and a senior at Vermont's Northeastern College, stated, "My sorority sisters began to hold informal lunches where they met alumni to discuss jobs and internships, but I was never invited. Every other senior was informed about these events. But I was forgotten."

(31) The basic purpose of the passage is _____.

(A) To provide entertainment

(B) To provide information

(C) To cause annoyance

(D) To be persuasive

(32) The writer of the passage is likely to concur with which of the following statements?

(A) Though students in the minority experience prejudice, their suffering is not mitigated by affirmative action.

(B) Probably Clarity Ferrer was excluded from the lunch meetings for reasons unrelated to race

(C) White students actively coordinate initiatives meant to suppress minority students

(D) There is a possibility the reason racism is unconsciously practiced on campuses in different colleges is that there is an income gap between graduates from the minority groups and those from the white community

(33) Which of the following is an argument that can be supported using information from the passage?

(A) Colleges should ensure that all students have equal opportunities

(B) If minority students can cease to be marginalized, racism in the US will come to an immediate end

(C) It should be a requirement on every campus that all students undergo training about biases that manifest themselves unconsciously

(D) Students from minority groups should receive training and support to help them endure racism

(34) The comments Aida Green made were included in the passage so as to
_____.

(A)   Include an emotional element about the proportion of students from minority communities who feel marginalized

(B)   Act as a distraction from the most important idea of the passage, so that ultimately the reader will believe something that has no evidence

(C)   Demonstrate how marginalization is just of myriad problems black students face

(D)   Capture the reasoning of the readers by providing additional data of a statistical nature to support a stance many respondents of the survey have shared

(35) The reason the actual proportion of marginalized students is indicated is _____.

(A)   To introduce a point to counter an argument that favors training about recognizing biases

(B)   To provide evidence that marginalization is widespread

(C)   To ignore the fact that 17% of students from minority communities did not experience marginalization

(D)   To make the reader fear he/she may be inadvertently racist

(36) The opinions a writer holds on a particular subject are known as _____.

(A)   Reasoning

(B)   Point of view

(C)   Purpose

(D)   Major idea

(37) What is the purpose of a diabetic diet recipe cookbook likely to be?

(A) To persuade

(B) To help in decision-making

(C) To entertain

(D) To disseminate information

Read the next passage and then answer the two questions that follow.

During the last quarter of the year, India's economy grew at a rate less than anticipated, continuing to put pressure on the country's Central Bank to persist with its record increases in interest rates even in the face of a weakening global recovery. There has been an increase in the yields of stocks and bonds, as well as in the country's currency, the rupee.

According to a report from the country's Central Statistical Office in New Delhi, the country's GDP increased by 7.7% within three months that ended on June 30. This compares well with the 7.8% increase in the preceding three months. A total of twenty-six predictions from a survey done by Bloomberg News produced a median 7.6% gain.

India's consumption level has been consistently strong owing to increased salaries, but inflation is likely to remain stagnant within the near future. This was the observation made by India's Reserve Bank.

(38) Which of the following is an inference that can be drawn from the passage?

(A) India's economy is on the decline

(B) Bloomberg News overestimated how India's economy is growing

(C) India's economy slowed down in the current quarter compared to the last quarter

(D) India's Reserve Bank is not presently concerned about over inflation

(39) Which of the following has no supporting material in the passage?

(A) Inflation levels and consumption cannot be affected by similar factors

(B) The recovery of the global economy is weak

(C) India's currency is becoming stronger

(D) It is necessary for interest rates to rise if the economy is to experience growth

(40) Read the next sentence and then answer the question that follows.

"Her ideas are set regarding the way parents ought to behave."

Which of the following is the dictionary definition of the word "set"?

(A) An increasing number

(B) Fixed or solidly established

(C) Circling back around

(D) Being prepared

(41) Read the next sentence and then answer the question that follows.

"Following years of community service, owing to a fund shortage the local clinic will soon be closed."

Identify the misplaced phrase in the sentence.

(A) Following years of

(B) Community service

(C) Owing to a fund shortage

(D) Will soon be closed

Read the next passage and then answer the two questions that follow.

In 1876, Melvil Dewey developed the eponymous Dewey Decimal System for book classification. Before then, books in libraries were arranged according to the time they were received. Dewey's system organized titles under ten classes, each one of them with ten divisions, and each division having ten sections.

The starting set, 000, has computer plus informational titles or volumes. The group in the 300s covers social sciences, while the very last of the categories, the 900s, covers history and geography. The 500s section is mathematics. The 516 section is dedicated to geometry, while 516.3 denotes analytic geometry specifically.

Although some libraries still use the Dewey Decimal System, many libraries used for research and academics prefer the Library of Congress' classification system, where works of a general nature are put under Class A, yearbooks are in sub-class AY and dictionaries are under AG.

(42) Based on the passage, the Dewey Decimal System puts every book under the category of ____.

(A) A single general class

(B) A single general class plus a single division

(C) A single general class plus a single division plus a single section

(D) A single general class inclusive of AG

(43) Which of the following meanings is closest to that of the word "eponymous"?

(A) Of utmost importance

(B) Named after a person

(C) Innovative

(D) Logical and simple

Read the next paragraph and then answer the question that follows.

The bonobo great ape's primary habitat is the Congo Basin Forest. The bonobo is considered to be one of the species which most closely resembles human beings. Bonobos are not only social but also expressive, and they form societies that are matriarchal, where males assume their position within the group as per their own mothers' status. Females provide all parental care.

(44) Based on the passage, identify the correct inference from the following answers.

(A)   Among bonobos, the status of males is lower than that of their own mothers

(B)   Female bonobos are most similar to human beings

(C)   The bonobo great apes are the main occupants of the Congo Basin Forest

(D)   The expressive bonobos can show different emotions

Read the next passage and then answer the question that follows.

Camp Lily is the best place to spend your holiday with your family. We have a wide range of accommodations to suit your tastes and budget. If your family wants to enjoy some traditional camp fun, we have expansive campsites whose grounds are nicely level to hold your tents, and we also offer hookups for electricity as well as water access. Our rural campsites can accommodate not only pop-ups and most mid-sized RVs, but also trailers. If you prefer to camp indoors, we provide a variety of cabins, starting from ordinary bungalows to cozy luxury cottages. Any camper who stays during the off-season months, meaning from October to May, can expect to enjoy a generous discount of 20% on every accommodation. Call us today and make arrangements for your next vacation with your family!

(45) Based on the passage, which of the following camping options would be cheapest?

(A)   Ordinary bungalows in March

(B)   Ordinary bungalows in June

(C)   Rural campsite in September

(D)   Rural campsite in February

Read the announcement provided next and then answer the question that follows.

We have the pleasure of welcoming Dr. Emily Alberto as the new head of research at Marco-Polo Biometrics. Over the last sixteen years, Dr. Alberto has continued to be a great asset to the team at J.T. Laboratories, where she has been serving as laboratory director and special coordinator for unique research projects. Before joining J.T. Laboratories, Dr. Alberto served as a Bright University adjunct professor, where her exemplary work saw her lead a study, alongside some graduate students, which was a trailblazer on how to use markers of biometric identification within the criminal forensics arena. Considering her knack for innovation, leadership full of vision, and expertise equal to none, we at J.T. Laboratories are excited to have Dr. Alberto guide us toward new exciting possibilities within the scope of biometrics.

(46) According to the announcement, which of the following was Dr. Alberto's first job?

(A)   Head of research

(B)   Adjunct professor

(C)   Laboratory director

(D)   Graduate student

Read the next two sentences and then answer the question that follows.

(i)   Most students read books to expand their knowledge.

(ii)   Some students read strictly to pass exams.

(47) Which of the following shows the correct relationship between the two sentences?

(A)   No. (i) shows the cause while No. (ii) shows the effect

(B)   No. (ii) contrasts No. (i)

(C)   No. (i) states a concept while No. (ii) expounds on that concept

(D)   No. (ii) is a repetition of No. (i)

Read the next two sentences and then answer the question that follows.

(i) Allocating some time to charity work is vital to Company A.

(ii) Company A gives its employees days off to volunteer and still pays them in full.

(48) How is Statement (ii) related to Statement (i)?

(A) Statement (ii) is a contradiction of Statement (i)

(B) Statement (ii) is a reinforcement of Statement (i)

(C) Statement (ii) is the solution

(D) Statement (i) is a revelation

(49) A reader can tell the tone of a passage by noticing the ____.

(A) Setting

(B) Choice of words

(C) Characters' feelings

(D) Conjunctions used

(50) Identify the term for the feelings created in a reader by a text.

(A) The tone

(B) Irony

(C) The mood

(D) The theme

(51) Authors can use varying techniques in support of their arguments when developing their main idea. Identify one phrase from those listed below that describes one such technique.

(A) Viewpoint

(B) Fallacy

(C) Statistical analysis

(D) Rhetoric

(52) A writer's point of view can be described as _____.

(A) His/her lack of direction

(B) His/her general outlook

(C) His/her rhetorical strategy

(D) Appealing to emotions

(53) The reason an author decides to write can be described as his/her ____.

(A) Purpose

(B) Viewpoint

(C) Rhetoric

(D) Subject

Math Section – Test 4

(1)   There are _____ grams in one kilogram.

(A)   2,000

(B)   1,000

(C)   16

(D)   100

(2)   How many centimeters are in 1 meter?

(A)   10 cm

(B)   100 cm

(C)   1,000 cm

(D)   10,000 cm

(3)   Anita was given $100 by her mother to buy some clothes. She went to a clothes store and bought a black dress worth $64.57 and a red dress worth $26.82. How much was Anita left with after the purchase?

(A) $9.61

(B) $37.75

(C) $91.39

(D) $8.61

(4) What is the product of 78 and 0.91?

(A) 64.68

(B) 70.98

(C) 73.24

(D) 78.45

(5) Alex has been advised by his doctor to reduce the amount of diet soda that he consumes by 25%. If he currently consumes four cans of soda and each can contains 12 ounces of soda, how much ounces of soda will he be consuming once he reduces his consumption as per the doctor's orders?

(A) 24 ounces

(B) 12 ounces

(C) 40 ounces

(D) 36 ounces

(6) What do you get when you subtract 0.130 from 11.013?

(A) 11.143

(B) 11

(C) 10.883

(D) 10.013

(7) There are _____ milliliters in one liter.

(A) 30

(B) 100

(C) 3,000

(D) 1,000

(8) A ranch owner sells 10 different breeds of animals on a daily basis. On average, his daily sales are 2 breeds of horses, where he sells 20 of every breed; 3 breeds of cattle, where he sells 15 of every breed; 1 breed of pigs, where he sells 7 per day; and 4 breeds of sheep, where he sells 6 of every breed. How many animals does the rancher sell in a day?

(A) 116

(B) 48

(C) 29

(D) 11.6

(9) If Kevin's waist measures 88.9 centimeters, calculate his waist measurement in inches.

(A) 225 inches

(B) 35 inches

(C) 22.5 inches

(D) 40 inches

(10) If a bartender makes one type of cocktail juice in 50 minutes, how many types of cocktail can the bartender make in 7.5 hours?

(A) 12

(B) 9

(C) 10

(D) 11

(11) Which answer choice correctly arranges the following variables from smallest to largest?

A= 0.0002; B=-0.02; C=0.2; D=-200; E=1/2

(A) CDEBA

(B) ABCED

(C) DBACE

(D) CEDAB

(12) Calculate the percentage of black cars in a garage if there are 29 red cars and 32 black cars. Round to the nearest tenth.

(A) 52.5%

(B) 50.5%

(C) 46.5%

(D) 48.5%

(13) Solve for y in the following equation: $\left|14y - 1/3\right| = 2$

(A)   -1/6, -5/42

(B)   32 1/3, -23 1/3

(C)   32 1/3, -32 1/3

(D)   1/6, -5/42

(14) A new toaster costs $800. Sandra has insurance on her toaster and in the event that the toaster is broken or stolen, the insurance will cover 73% of the value of a new toaster. How much would she need to pay for the new toaster?

(A) $164

(B) $200

(C) $216

(D) $237

(15) When you multiply two numbers, you get a value that is six times less than the value you would get from adding the two numbers together, and when you calculate the difference between these two numbers, you get 12. Which of these correctly expresses that information?

(A) $2a^2 - 24a + 72 < 0$

(B) $a^2 - 24a + 72 < 0$

(C) $a^2 + 72 < 0$

(D) $2a^2 + 72 < 0$

(16) If 1 inch is equivalent to 2.54 cm, how many inches are equal to 395 cm?

(A) 155.51 inches

(B) 395.21 inches

(C) 143.62 inches

(D) 310.43 inches

(17) If one cup holds 0.289 liters of tea, approximately how many cups would be needed to fill a teapot that holds 3.4 liters?

(A) 8 cups

(B) 15 cups

(C) 13 cups

(D) 10 cups

(18) If Alex ran at a speed of approximately 4 mph for a period of 1 hour 20 minutes, how much distance did he cover in miles?

(A) 6.3 miles

(B) 5.3 miles

(C) 4.5 miles

(D) 5.67 miles

(19) Simplify the following expression: 9 11/21 + 3 5/7

(A) 13 5/21

(B) 5 7/21

(C) 13 7/3

(D) 13 7/21

(20) Which of these is equal to 0.38201?

(A) 38,201%

(B) 382.01%

(C) 38.201%

(D) 3.8201%

(21) Susan is a tailor who has been asked to make table runners that are to be used to decorate tables at a wedding. There will be 12 short tables that measure 6 feet each and twice that number of long tables that measure 10 feet each. If each runner is supposed to overhang the table on every side by 8 inches, how many yards of fabric does Susan need for the table runners if no material is to be wasted?

(A) 104 yards

(B) 120 yards

(C) 114 yards

(D) 110 yards

(22) If Richard is travelling at 60 miles/hr, calculate his speed in feet per second given that 5,280 ft is equal to 1 mile.

(A)   88 ft/sec

(B)   4.4 ft/sec

(C)   44 ft/sec

(D)   8.8 ft/sec

(23) In a seminar, there were 28 ladies and 21 gentlemen. Calculate the ratio of gentlemen to ladies and the ratio of ladies to the total number of people in that seminar.

(A)   4:3 and 7:4

(B)   3:2 and 4:7

(C)   3:4 and 1:7

(D)   3:4 and 4:7

(24) The ratio of nurses to doctors in a hospital is 5:4. If there are 72 nurses and doctors in total, how many doctors are there in the hospital?

(A)   72

(B)   32

(C)   36

(D)   40

(25) Miss Mary has a bag full of toy blocks labeled E, F, G and H in her class and the ratio of these blocks, E:F:G:H, is 4:7:3:1. If there are 50 more blocks labeled E than there are those labeled G, how many blocks labeled F are there?

(A) 350

(B) 300

(C) 450

(D) 200

(26) The ratio of blueberries to strawberries is 5:8. If there are 30 blueberries, how many strawberries are there?

(A) 13

(B) 48

(C) 30

(D) 20

(27) Kelly mixed 45 liters of paint in the ratio of red paint to blue paint as 1:2. How much red paint will she need to add to achieve a ratio of 2:1?

(A) 30 liters

(B) 15 liters

(C) 45 liters

(D) 3 liters

(28) A recipe requires that for every 6 kilograms of wheat flour, 3 kilograms of sweet syrup should be added. How much sweet syrup should be used to yield 60 kilograms of this treat?

(A)   15 kilograms

(B)   30 kilograms

(C)   9 kilograms

(D)   20 kilograms

(29) If there is 12% of glucose in 60 ml of drinking water, what amount of water should be added to have an 8% glucose concentration?

(A)   30 ml

(B)   90 ml

(C)   7.2 ml

(D)   12 ml

(30) In a map, 1 centimeter is used to represent 12 kilometers of actual distance. If the distance between point A and point B is 96 kilometers, what is the representation of this distance on the map?

(A)   12 cm

(B)   96 cm

(C)   10 cm

(D)   8 cm

(31) If Sandra can type 360 words over a period of 4 minutes, how long does it take her to type a total of 900 words?

(A) 10 minutes

(B) 90 minutes

(C) 9 minutes

(D) 15 minutes

(32) Arrange these ratios in descending order: 3:4, 2:3, 1:5, 5:6

(A) 1:5, 2:3, 3:4, 5:6

(B) 5:6, 3:4, 2:3, 1:5

(C) 5:6, 1:5, 3:4, 2:3

(D) 3:4, 1:5, 5:6, 2:3

(33) Identify the value of two numbers that are in the ratio 3:4 and whose sum when added together is 63.

(A) 7 and 56

(B) 3 and 4

(C) 4 and 59

(D) 27 and 36

(34) Charles divided some money among Terry, Bridget and Simon in a ratio of 2:3:5. How much money did Charles give the three if Simon received $150?

(A) $300

(B) $259

(C) $350

(D) $500

(35) In a conference, the ratio of men to women is 4:3. How many men are in the conference and what is the total attendance if there are 18 women?

(A) 18 men, total attendance is 36

(B) 26 men, total attendance is 44

(C) 24 men, total attendance is 42

(D) 12 men, total attendance is 30

(36) Find the value of x, where x is the second number in the geometric series:

1/4+ x + 1/36 + 1/108 + ...

Keep in mind that the ratio from one term to the next in a geometric series remains constant.

(A) 1/9

(B) 1/18

(C) 1/12

(D) 1/3

Science Section – Test 4

(1) Oxygenated blood is produced by which of the following organs?

(A) The heart

(B) The stomach

(C) The kidneys

(D) The lungs

(2) Which of the following activities is carried out by the blood?

(A) Regulating the wound-healing process

(B) Aiding in the removal of waste products from the body

(C) Controlling the population of leukocytes found inside the buffy coat

(D) Defending the body against any foreign substances

(3) After blood has flowed through the pulmonary vein, where does it go next?

(A) Into the left atrium

(B) Into the aorta

(C) Through the superior vena cava

(D) Through the arteries

(4)   After observing a cell under a microscope, a researcher determined that the cell had a diameter of no more than half a millimeter and that its cell wall was surrounded by pili. What should this cell be classified as?

(A)   Eukaryote

(B)   Autotroph

(C)   Prokaryote

(D)   Heterotroph

(5)   For different biological functions to be performed, a cell has to convert carbohydrates into ATP. In which part of the cell does that conversion occur?

(A)   Mitochondria

(B)   Vacuole

(C)   Golgi apparatus

(D)   Lysosome

(6)   After a protein is synthesized inside the ribosome, it travels to _____.

(A)   The lysosome

(B)   The Golgi apparatus

(C)   The vacuole

(D)   The endoplasmic reticulum

(7) During which phase do chromosomes line up?

(A) Interphase

(B) Anaphase

(C) Telophase

(D) Prometaphase

(8) Which of the following is the correct order of the phases that occur in mitosis?

(A) Prophase, metaphase, anaphase, telophase

(B) Metaphase, prophase, telophase, anaphase

(C) Telophase, prophase, metaphase, anaphase

(D) Anaphase, metaphase, telophase, prophase

(9) At what point are sister chromatids formed?

(A) After chromosomes elongate

(B) After chromosomes replicate

(C) After chromosomes separate

(D) After chromosomes condense

(10) Which of these measuring tools is used to determine how sunlight impacts the growth of plants?

(A) A barometer

(B) A triple-beam balance

(C) A clock

(D) A thermometer

(11) Electric balances are used to measure the _____ of an object.

(A) Temperature

(B) Mass

(C) Volume

(D) Length

(12) Which relationship is described by a variable increasing when another increases?

(A) A negative variation

(B) A positive variation

(C) An indirect correlation

(D) An inverse correlation

(13) How does the human body respond to growth hormones?

(A) It increases the production of insulin

(B) It increases the production of melanin

(C) It increases protein synthesis

(D) It increases its mitochondrial synthesis

(14) Blood sugar levels in the body are regulated in the negative feedback loop when insulin is released to help the body use the digestion products. When levels of blood sugar are low, what is secreted in the pancreas?

(A) Glycogen

(B) Glucagon

(C) Glucose

(D) Glycolysis

(15) Hormone secretion should be regulated in order to _____.

(A) Promote metabolism

(B) Enable cell division

(C) Maintain homeostasis

(D) Develop maturity

(16) Which hormone is responsible for secreting cortisol?

(A) Luteinizing

(B) Thyroid

(C) Adrenocorticotropic

(D) Prolactin

(17) Where does the cardiac sphincter open into?

(A) The stomach

(B) The gallbladder

(C) The pancreas

(D) The liver

(18) Which enzyme, produced inside the pancreas, completes protein digestion when it is secreted into your small intestine?

(A) Maltase

(B) Lactase

(C) Peptidase

(D) Pepsin

(19) Which disorder results from the death or damage of the liver?

(A) Hepatitis

(B) Cirrhosis

(C) Vomiting

(D) Ulcer

(20) Transcription produces _____ in eukaryotes.

(A) Pre-mRNA

(B) mRNA

(C) tRNA

(D) rRNA

(21) What does a peptide bond do?

(A) It connects nucleic acids

(B) It connects amino acids

(C) It connects proteins together

(D) It connects nucleotides together

(22) When you touch a hot object, your immediate response is to jump. Which skin layer is responsible for this response?

(A) The dermis

(B) The stratum lucidum

(C) The hypodermis

(D) The stratum basale

(23) Which molecules are primarily found in the fluid that is produced by sweat glands?

(A) Protein

(B) Salt

(C) Sugar

(D) Fat

(24) When you are anxious, the sweat that travels via the eccrine glands is usually released from your _____.

(A) Scalp

(B) Underarms

(C) Groin area

(D) Forehead

(25) When using the scientific method, researchers are required to carry out which of the following activities immediately after they propose a scientific question?

(A) Analyze data so as to observe patterns or trends

(B) Carry out background research on that topic

(C) Communicate the results in a presentation or an article

(D) Gather data or information through an experiment

(26) Which of these traits distinguishes a living thing from a non-living thing?

(A) Homeostasis

(B) Size

(C) Environment

(D) Genetics

(27) How does HIV/AIDS disable a person's immune system?

(A) It blocks T cells from acting

(B) It causes B cells to be produced

(C) It triggers genetic mutations

(D) It destroys macrophages and T cells

(28) The human body fights against pathogens that threaten to invade the body with the help of _____, which signal an alarm, and _____ that activate T-helper cells.

(A) Macrophages, antibodies

(B) Proteins, B cells

(C) Proteins, antibodies

(D) Macrophages, proteins

(29) As sarcomeres contract, actin myofilaments are moved closer to _____.

(A) The I-band

(B) The M-line

(C) The A-band

(D) The Z-disc

(30) Which body system works together with the muscular system to help in the movement of the body?

(A)   The digestive system

(B)   The cardiovascular system

(C)   The skeletal system

(D)   The respiratory system

(31) Which of the following activities is aided by the frontal lobe?

(A)   Hearing noises as you walk along the street

(B)   Remembering major events that occurred when you were a child

(C)   Solving word puzzles in a short amount of time

(D)   Watching birds as they catch insects

(32) Which of these structures is divided into hemispheres and contains gray matter?

(A)   The spinal cord

(B)   The cerebral cortex

(C)   The cerebellum

(D)   The brainstem

(33) If a person has trouble speaking and problems remembering some things, which lobe of his brain is likely to have been damaged?

(A)   Occipital

(B)   Frontal

(C)   Temporal

(D)   Parietal

(34) A person's body temperature may rise when in hot areas and drop when in cold areas. This means that body temperature is _____.

(A)   A factor

(B)   A cell

(C)   A chemical

(D)   A variable

(35) Which tissues in the body resemble long threads?

(A)   Muscle tissue

(B)   Connective tissue

(C)   Neural tissue

(D)   Epithelial

(36) Where are the ova produced?

(A)   In the vagina

(B)   In the ovaries

(C)   In the fallopian tube

(D)   In the uterine wall

(37) Semen is formed through the combination of sperm and other components. Where are the other components formed?

(A)   In the penis

(B)   In the female accessory glands

(C)   In the glans penis

(D)   In the male accessory glands

(38) The reproductive system of a female includes_____.

(A)   The ovaries, vagina and prostate glands

(B)   The cervix and uterus

(C)   The ovaries, corpus cavernosum and uterus

(D)   The fallopian tube and epididymis

(39) Which of these statements is true about gas concentration in the blood coming from the left side of the heart?

(A) Carbon dioxide and oxygen levels are usually high

(B) The level of oxygen is high

(C) The level of carbon dioxide is high

(D) Carbon dioxide and oxygen levels are usually low

(40) Blood that is rich in oxygen _____.

(A) Leaves the heart from the right side

(B) Is also rich in carbon dioxide

(C) Flows out and into systemic circulation

(D) Has a low pH

(41) Why do lungs vary in size?

(A) Because of the alveoli sacs that are found in the lungs

(B) Because of the anatomical position in the chest cavity

(C) Because the diaphragm needs space as it changes shape

(D) Because of the expansion of the heart while it is pumping blood

(42) Which part of the atom has zero charge?

(A) The nucleus

(B) The proton

(C) The neutron

(D) The electron

(43) Which boron isotope is largest and why?

(A) Boron-11; it is closest in mass to the average atomic mass in the periodic table

(B) Boron-10; it is closest in mass to the average atomic mass in the periodic table

(C) Boron-11; it is farthest in mass from the average atomic mass in the periodic table

(D) Boron-10; it is farthest in mass from the average atomic mass in the periodic table

(44) In an atom, which part has the greatest mass?

(A) The neutron

(B) The proton

(C) The electron cloud

(D) The nucleus

(45) Which of these bones falls under the category of irregular bones?

(A) The humerus

(B) The coccyx

(C) The nasal bone

(D) The kneecap

(46) What are bones mainly made of?

(A) Sodium

(B) Phosphorus

(C) Chloride

(D) Magnesium

(47) When carrying out a procedure, Angela found that she needed 0.0505 grams of sodium. This unit of measurement is used to describe _____.

(A) Mass

(B) Length

(C) Time

(D) Volume

(48) What is the role of glomerular filtrate?

(A) It reabsorbs urea through the force of blood pressure

(B) It makes solutes diffuse into the renal artery

(C) It increases urine concentration inside the collecting duct

(D) It secretes nitrogenous wastes for excretion through the urine

(49) Where do filtered fluids travel through in tubular reabsorption?

(A) The ureter

(B) The nephrons

(C) The urethra

(D) The glomerulus

(50) When urine reaches the bladder, it flows through tubes that are known as
_____.

(A) Capillaries

(B) Nephrons

(C) Arteries

(D) Sphincters

(51) Which statement accurately describes the movement of urine via the nephron?

(A) Distal convoluted tubule, proximal convoluted tubule, collecting duct, loop of
Henle, glomerulus

(B) Glomerulus, proximal convoluted tubule, loop of Henle, distal convoluted tubule,
collecting duct

(C) Collecting duct, glomerulus, proximal convoluted tubule, distal convoluted tubule,
loop of Henle

(D) Loop of Henle, distal convoluted tubule, glomerulus, proximal convoluted tubule,
collecting duct

(52) The kinds of plants categorized as fungi lack _____.

(A) Nitrogen

(B) Oxygen

(C) Chlorophyll

(D) Moisture

(53) Which of the vessels listed is the smallest in diameter?

(A) The arterioles

(B) The venules

(C) The capillaries

(D) The lymphatic

English and Language Use Section – Test 4

(1) From the sentences listed below, identify the one that is most informal.

(A) We shall come to see you on Friday.

(B) See you sometime.

(C) I will pass by in the afternoon.

(D) Jane and I will hang out this Saturday.

(2) Which of the following comprises common nouns from the given sentence?

"The fans chanted in jubilation as the captain of their team lifted the trophy."

(A) Fans, jubilation, team, trophy

(B) Fans, captain, team, trophy

(C) Chanted, jubilation, team, trophy

(D) Chanted, jubilation, team, lifted

(3) How many pronouns does the following sentence have?

"Jane, Mary and Susan inquired about you."

(A) 3

(B) 1

(C) 2

(D) 0

(4) Which sentence is correctly punctuated?

(A) I woke up early so I could arrive on time.

(B) I woke up early so, I could arrive on time.

(C) I woke up early so I, could arrive on time.

(D) I woke up early, so I could arrive on time.

(5) A person is said to be amicable if he/she is _____.

(A) Friendly

(B) Unsure

(C) Timid

(D) Responsible

(6) Which of the following answers means the same thing as the word that is underlined in the given sentence?

"James has always been intransigent regarding his position on the matter."

(A) Clear

(B) Passionate

(C) Stubborn

(D) Indecisive

(7) The word "reinstated" has the prefix "re-." In reference to a person's job position, identify the answer that explains what has happened.

(A) The job has been assigned to someone else again

(B) The job has been reestablished

(C) The job has been scrapped

(D) The job has been advertised again

(8) The word "miscreant" can best be defined as _____.

(A) Villainous

(B) Careless

(C) Opinionated

(D) Ignorant

(9) Which of the following has a meaning closest to the word "color"?

(A) Vide-

(B) Chrom-

(C) Vid-

(D) Therm-

(10) The plural form of the word "half" is _____.

(A) Halfs

(B) Halves

(C) Halfes

(D) Hooves

(11) Identify the best pair of words to complete the sentence.

"Immediately, the ship set sail; the department of meteorology ___ that there ___ a hurricane coming."

(A) Announce, was

(B) Announced, was

(C) Announces, was

(D) Announced, is

(12) Choose the correct verb form to complete the sentence.

"The musicians ____ lined up behind the dais playing melodious tunes all along."

(A) Is

(B) Are

(C) Were

(D) Was

(13) Which of the following conjunctions best completes the sentence?

"Do you think we should order a soup ____ salad?"

(A) Yet

(B) But

(C) Or

(D) Since

(14) Read the two sentences given next, and then identify the answer that best combines them.

"The two had a long chat. They enjoyed their dinner that evening."

(A) The two had a long chat, but they enjoyed their dinner that evening.

(B) The two had a long chat, yet they enjoyed their dinner that evening.

(C) The two had a long chat or they enjoyed their dinner that evening.

(D) The two had a long chat, and they enjoyed their dinner that evening.

(15) Which of the following answers correctly identifies the dependent clause in the sentence?

"Madison always prays before she goes to sleep."

(A) Goes to sleep

(B) Before she goes to sleep

(C) Madison always prays

(D) Always prays

(16) Choose the answer that corrects the sentence fragment.

"After leaving the conference room."

(A) After leaving, the conference room he headed straight to the party.

(B) After leaving, the conference room, he headed straight to the party.

(C) After leaving the conference room, he headed straight to the party.

(D) After, leaving the conference room he headed straight to the party.

(17) Which of the following answers correctly completes the sentence grammatically and keeps it a simple sentence?

"The shrine with a sculpture of a woman and a baby _____."

(A) It is feared by the local people

(B) Is meant to remain sacred

(C) Is ancient, though it still remains beautiful

(D) It is used by Christians

(18) Choose the answer that creates a complex, grammatically correct sentence.

"I enjoy spending my holidays in countries along the equator, _____."

(A) The sun can sometimes be very hot

(B) But, the sun can sometimes be very hot

(C)   Nevertheless, the sun can sometimes be very hot

(D) Although the sun can sometimes be very hot

(19) Identify the most grammatically correct answer to the question:

"Where were you when they announced the city council voting results in 1996?"

(A) I went home.

(B) I am at home.

(C) I was at home.

(D) I have been at home.

(20) The answers listed below are from a research report. Identify the one that should have a citation.

(A)   The symptoms of asthma are wheezing, difficulty breathing, tightness of the chest and coughing

(B)   The most recent report by the WHO states that there is a chance of asthma becoming worse during the night or when one exercises

(C)   Contrary to the findings by the WHO as indicated in the second paragraph, the conclusion of this paper is that symptoms of asthma can be reduced by exercising regularly

(D)   This paper seeks to explore the link between a person exercising and developing asthma

(21) Choose the answer that identifies the antonym of the word underlined in the given sentence.

"His eyeglasses had accumulated so many specks that they had turned opaque."

(A)   Clear

(B)   Oval

(C)   Transparent

(D)   Antique

(22) What is the meaning of the word "polysemy"?

(A)   Having varied forms

(B)   Being of a single color

(C)   Having varied meanings

(D)   Having different husbands

(23) Identify the meaning of the word "semi" from the context of the given sentence.

"Because the patient had been semiconscious, the nurses were doubtful if he could remember what they had said to him on admission."

(A) Prior

(B) Half

(C) Not

(D) After

(24) Which of the following best defines "theocracy"?

(A) A government with many rulers

(B) A political system controlled by the rich

(C) A government where the ruler is a religious authority

(D) A state of absolute sovereignty

(25) Which of the following is appropriate for an official document?

(A) Please do yourself a favor and do what is required if you want to be hired

(B) Unless you apologize, your job is kaput

(C) Failure to adhere to the stipulations laid down by the company will lead to the termination of the employee's contract

(D) If you find it difficult to match our demands, we are very sorry to declare you are ineligible to be hired

(26) Choose the answer that best completes the sentence.

"I now remember what an odd _____ Tom was; he never acknowledged my presence whenever we met outside the office."

(A) Person,

(B) Person;

(C) Person

(D) Person and

(27) Choose the answer that best completes the sentence.

"Cuban coffee is so ___ that people who drink it in the evening hardly sleep four hours."

(A) Fragrant

(B) Sweet

(C) Strong

(D) Hot

(28) Identify the answer that best completes the sentence.

"The reality that she has been promoted every two years ___, all the more, her excellence and continued diligence."

(A) Highlight

(B) Had highlighted

(C) Will be highlighting

(D) Highlights

Practice Test 4: Answers

Reading Section – Test 4 Answers

(1)   The correct answer is: (C) From the beginning of humankind, there has not been a time when people have ceased to wonder about stars.

The reason (C) is the correct answer is that the use of "man" or "mankind" makes the writer biased towards the male gender, but the use of "people" is all-inclusive with no gender bias. Although (A) and (D) have avoided gender bias by using "humankind," they remain gender biased because later they include the word "man."

(2)   The correct answer is: (D) Stereotype.

The reason (D) is correct is that the word "stereotype" applies to a form of bias that is used against a given community or group of people. A good example is when people assume that members of a community all exhibit a particular behavior, ignoring their individuality.

(3)   The correct answer is: (B) A belief that is preconceived and at times unfair.

(B) is correct because a bias is always preconceived, which means it is not based on any fact regarding the current situation and is therefore likely to be unfair. Bias can target an individual and not necessarily the group or community to which that person belongs.

(4)   The correct answer is: (C) Any parent feeding a child organic food is mindful of the child's physical development.

(C) is correct because the writer uses the article "a" to avoid using the pronoun "his" or "her." It is acceptable to use "a," "an" or "the" in place of some pronouns. It is also acceptable to use gender-neutral words such as "one" for the sake of avoiding gender bias.

(5)   The correct answer is: (C) Somehow, people are fascinated by disaster films.

(C) is correct because the beginning of the paragraph focuses on an audience's interest in watching a disaster film, and the ending depicts the audience being fascinated with disaster films.

(6)   The correct answer is: (B) The topic sentence.

The reason (B) is the correct answer is that it summarizes the paragraph's core idea. The paragraph details a movie where characters are actively involved in surviving multiple crises, yet the audience enjoyed it.

(7)   The correct answer is: (A) It produces the greatest impact.

The ending referred to is the sentence, "Nothing beats a story where the world is ending—so long as it is entirely fictional." That sentence encompasses the gravity of the events in the film, yet it also portrays the joy of the audience as they enjoy the movie.

(8)   The correct answer is: (B) Examples of aggression-based entertainment throughout history.

The reason (B) is the correct answer is that if the author included a long list of violent movies, followed by examples of people acting out violently after watching the films, it would support the notion that people enjoy violence and are naturally vicious.

(9)   The correct answer is: (D) An implied.

An idea is implied when it is not explicitly spelled out in text.

(10) The correct answer is: (D) A pie chart.

(D) is correct because in a pie chart you can see the percentage every sector contributes to the economy, and you can compare its contribution to the economy as a whole. Not only are you able to view the performance of the economy, but also the distinct contribution of each economic sector.

(11) The correct answer is: (B) It is an implicit restatement of ideas stated in the text.

(B) is correct because a summary must accurately describe ideas from the original text.

(12) The correct answer is: (D) Information that is communicated visually.

(D) is correct because a graphic element is meant to communicate certain information visually. Elements of this nature are normally used as backup for information already transmitted in text or audio form. One such graphic is a pie chart, where data is often displayed in percentages.

(13) The correct answer is: (D) Restate that same quote in other words.

(D) is correct because although it is fine to introduce a quote and to explain how it helps drive home a point, it is unnecessary to rewrite the quote in different words.

(14) The correct answer is: (D) Cause and effect.

(D) is correct because the scenario described is about something that happened as a result of something else; what happened first was the cause and what followed was the effect. Essentially, if there had not been an economic crisis, employees would not have lost their jobs in such large numbers; declining profits led to company layoffs.

(15) The correct answer is: (A) Ironic and humorous.

The tone of the passage is not only ironic but also humorous. The humor can be found in the manner the girl pounds on the railing as she produces train sounds. As for irony, the fact that the author declares the girl might never be happy again and moments later is seen playing at the park is ironic.

(16) The correct answer is: (B) Subsequently, after noticing that her pacifier was missing, she became hysterical.

Irony is when what is being said cannot be taken literally, although it may appear true at the moment. In this case, losing the pacifier seems like the worst thing that could ever happen to the girl (from her perspective). Yet, some moments later she is seen having fun at the nearby park, indicating that the pacifier wasn't all that important after all.

(17) The correct answer is: (B) Refers to the train as the "best train in the world."

The reason this part of the sentence is hyperbolic is that a model train cannot be the best one ever available; the writer has chosen to exaggerate something merely ordinary.

(18) The correct answer is: (B) Amused.

From the moment the author expresses the magnitude of the child's loss, it is evident it is exaggerated, and the reader cannot help but be amused by the exaggeration. In fact, the reader is vindicated for his/her disbelief regarding the seriousness of the loss when it is learned the child has, within no time, proceeded to play at the park.

(19) The correct answer is: (A) Below.

A transition word or phrase helps to link an idea that has been expressed to another one being stated. For example, the word "subsequently" serves as such a link in: "At the height of her excitement, she lost her pacifier. Subsequently, after noticing her pacifier was missing, the toddler became hysterical."

(20) The correct answer is: (A) When particular events took place.

(A) is correct because transitions like "later" link ideas that are related to time. Not only do they indicate the event timing, but also the sequence in which the events happened; hence, they are ordinarily considered transitions of time and sequence.

(21)   The correct answer is: (B) As a result.

The reason (B) is correct is that if the transition phrase "As a result" is used, the ideas in the two sentences would be linked in a logical way, where one thing happened on the basis of another: the student didn't study; therefore, he scored poorly on the test the next day.

(22)   The correct answer is: (D) Fiction, nonfiction.

(D) is the correct answer because every piece of literature can fit in either of the two genres, fiction or nonfiction.

(23)   The correct answer is: (C) An op-ed article.

(C) is the correct answer because considering an op-ed article is written to express a particular opinion, it is only logical that it should be written in a manner that is persuasive. The other three answers, user manual, a book of history and autobiography are all factual; which means they are not meant to sway anyone.

(24)   The correct answer is: (C) Compare and contrast.

(C) is the correct answer because it provides the right structure for a piece about comparisons. Identifying and analyzing the similarities and differences between World War I and World War II can only be done using a compare and contrast structure.

(25) The correct answer is: (A) The person giving the address makes arguments that are greatly emotional.

(A) is correct because whenever a person makes arguments that are greatly emotional, it sounds like he/she has some vested interest in the topic. Thus, the person loses credibility. In short, it is difficult to believe a person is being logical when his/her presentations are laden with intense emotions.

(26) The correct answer is: (B) A long op-ed article regarding the difficulties a parent faces when bringing up an adolescent.

The research Susan is doing must be backed up with credible material and verifiable data, yet an op-ed article is likely to be biased. This means you can expect to read innuendos from the writer's perspective as opposed to neutral facts or balanced arguments. After all, op-ed pieces are expected to express the opinions of the respective contributors.

(27) The correct answer is: (D) The video is visibly edited, with some of the speakers cut off midway through their comments.

The reason (D) is correct is that when a video is heavily edited, there is a likelihood that some parts have been deliberately cut in order to distort the original message or spirit of the speaker. In short, highly edited videos may not portray the information originally recorded in an objective manner; hence, they are not recommended for research.

(28) The correct answer is: (B) Parents.

(B) is the correct answer because in the passage there are places where the writer has used the second-person possessive pronoun and directly spoken of who the children belong to. A good example is the opening sentence of the passage, "Do you feel tired of having your own children not pay attention to what you are saying?"

(29) The correct answer is: (B) Parents get frustrated when kids don't listen.

(B) is correct because the way the writer has suggested solutions to the problem of children spending too much time on electronic devices is an indication of an underlying assumption that parents are frustrated by their children tuning them out.

(30) The correct answer is: (C) It is the author's view that parents have no clue how children should be disciplined.

(C) is correct because there is no mention in the passage about parents' capacity or skill to discipline children. It is all about the time kids spend using technology and how it affects their capacity to stay focused on things such as normal conversation.

(31) The correct answer is: (B) To provide information.

(B) is correct because, though the writer of the passage would support any measures with the potential to eliminate community-based biases, he/she avoids saying so in the passage. Instead, the passage provides the results of surveys conducted at various colleges whose campuses are dominated by white students.

(32) The correct answer is: (D) There is a possibility the reason racism is unconsciously practiced on campuses in different colleges is that there is an income gap between graduates from the minority groups and those from the white community.

(D) is the correct answer because from the results of the interviews with students from the minority groups, it would be understandable if the same subtle bias was found in the job arena.

(33) The correct answer is: (C) It should be a requirement on every campus that all students undergo training about biases that manifest themselves unconsciously.

(C) is correct because it is clear that racial bias exists in college campuses, but it is also acknowledged by interviewees that such biases seem to be manifested unconsciously. For that reason, it makes sense to help make students aware of behavior that is tantamount to racial bias, albeit subtly.

(34) The correct answer is: (A) Include an emotional element about the proportion of students from minority communities who feel marginalized.

(A) is correct because it is true that the responses given by Aida Green and other students interviewed inject an emotional element into the study results. The researchers already had statistics to support their study, but by interviewing people within the communities being studied, they gave a human face to the problem of unconscious racism on college campuses.

(35) The correct answer is: (B) To provide evidence that marginalization is widespread.

(B) is correct because it is accurate that the statistic of minority students on campuses in white-dominated colleges who feel marginalized is high. The higher the statistic, the greater the chances of college authorities becoming proactive in taking steps to reduce unconscious racial discrimination or marginalization.

(36) The correct answer is: (B) Point of view.

A person's point of view, and in this case the author's, is portrayed by the kind of opinions he/she holds on an issue. Reasoning, as in (A), falls under point of view, because one's perception can affect a person's line of thinking.

(37) The correct answer is: (D) To disseminate information.

(D) is correct because a cookbook is factual and has important information meant to educate people; in this case, it educates people who are diabetic on how to eat right in order to stay healthy.

(38) The correct answer is: (C) India's economy slowed down in the current quarter compared to the last quarter.

(C) is correct because it is clearly stated in the passage that "According to a report from the country's Central Statistical Office in New Delhi, the country's GDP increased by 7.7% within three months that ended on June 30. This compares well with the 7.8% increase in the preceding three months."

(39) The correct answer is: (D) It is necessary for interest rates to rise if the economy is to experience growth.

The reason (D) is correct is that there is no information in the passage to show it is a correct premise. Instead, it is indicated in the passage that "During the last quarter of the year, India's economy ... with its record increases in interest rates even in the face of a weakening global recovery."

(40) The correct answer is: (B) Fixed or solidly established.

The reason (B) is correct is that it suggests a fixed belief; in this case, the person has such a strong belief on how parents should behave.

(41) The correct answer is: (C) Owing to a fund shortage.

The reason (C) is the correct answer is that it is in the wrong section of the sentence; it could cause confusion, appearing as though many years of service was provided because there was a scarcity of funds. The sentence should read: "Following years of community service, the local clinic will soon be closed owing to a fund shortage."

(42) The correct answer is: (C) A single general class plus a single division plus a single section.

(C) is correct because it is true that the Dewey Decimal System is detailed in its order of classification, titles filed under ten classes that have ten divisions each, and which in turn have ten sections each. The reason (A) and (B) are incorrect is that they have omissions. (D) belongs to the Library of Congress Classification system.

(43) The correct answer is: (B) Named after a person.

The meaning of the word "eponymous" in the context of the passage is "being named after a person." This deduction can be made after observing that as soon as the passage introduces Melvil Dewey, it proceeds to introduce the library organization system that bears his name.

(44) The correct answer is: (A) Among bonobos, the status of males is lower than that of their own mothers.

(A) is correct because besides being told in the passage that the bonobo apes have a matriarchal society, it is also indicated that the status of the male is dependent on the position his own mother holds in that society. Note that a question of inference calls for you to make a deduction.

(45) The correct answer is: (D) Rural campsite in February.

(D) is the correct inference after considering the information provided. It is said that rates are low from October to May, which is off-season at Camp Lily. Consider also that accommodation in (A) is cheaper than that in (B); and that of (D) is cheaper than that of (C). Choose between (A) and (D) and (D) is cheaper.

(46) The correct answer is: (B) Adjunct professor.

The writer has explained the roles Dr. Emily Alberto has held in her career in reverse chronological order; and adjunct professor comes last, meaning it was her earliest position.

(47) The correct answer is: (B) No. (ii) contrasts No. (i).

The reason (B) is the correct answer is that it is the one that portrays the closest relationship the two sentences have. The message in the second sentence is in contrast to the message in the first sentence; in the first sentence, students want to be knowledgeable, but in the second sentence they are only interested in passing exams.

(48) The correct answer is: (B) Statement (ii) is a reinforcement of Statement (i).

(B) is correct because it is accurate that the second statement reinforces the first one; it actually provides evidence that the company values volunteering.

(49) The correct answer is: (B) Choice of words.

Word choice, and the manner in which those words are delivered, is a good way to help determine the tone of a passage. The tone of a passage is the attitude the author has toward the subject matter being discussed.

(50) The correct answer is: (C) The mood.

(C) is correct because the mood of a piece of writing refers to the feeling the reader develops after reading the text. *Mood* should not be confused with *tone*, which refers to the attitude the author has toward the text subject; instead, mood should be viewed as the emotional reaction elicited in the reader.

(51) The correct answer is: (D) Rhetoric.

(D) is correct because rhetoric is used by the author in support of his/her argument.

(52) The correct answer is: (B) His/her general outlook.

(B) is correct because the view of the author is how he/she looks at the subject overall.

(53) The correct answer is: (A) Purpose.

(A) is correct because the purpose is the reason an author decides to write a specific piece. It is different from a viewpoint, which is the author's outlook.

Math Section – Test 4 Answers

(1) The correct answer is: (B) 1,000.

One kilogram contains 1,000 grams. When you are asked to convert kilograms into grams, multiply the number of kilograms given by 1,000. When asked to convert grams into kilograms, divide the grams given by 1,000.

(2) The correct answer is: (B) 100 cm.

There are 100 centimeters in one meter. When you are asked to convert centimeters into meters, divide the number of centimeters given by 100. When converting meters into centimeters, multiply the meters given by 100.

(3) The correct answer is: (D) $8.61.

Anita had $100 and she bought two items. First, calculate the total amount she spent by adding the cost of the two dresses together. $64.57 + $26.82 = $91.39. If Anita spent $91.39 and she initially had $100, what she was left with is the difference between $100 and $91.39. $100 − $91.39= $8.61.

(4) The correct answer is: (B) 70.98.

To make this calculation easier, you can first remove the decimal in 0.91 so that you are left with 91. Now, multiply 78 by 91 to get 78 · 91 = 7,098. Next, return the decimal point and since there were two decimal places, place your decimal point two places to the left to get 70.98.

(5) The correct answer is: (D) 36 ounces.

To get the total amount of soda that Alex drinks, multiply 12 oz by 4 to get 12 · 4 = 48 oz. A 25% reduction means Alex should cut 25/100 of 48. 25/100 · 48 = 12 oz. He needs to reduce the total by 12 ounces, so 48 ounces − 12 ounces = 36 ounces.

(6) The correct answer is: (C) 10.883.

When you are adding or subtracting decimals, always ensure that the decimals are properly aligned to avoid confusion. Where necessary, add the required number of zeros after the last digit to have uniform decimal places. Here, $11.013 - 0.130 = 10.883$.

(7) The correct answer is: (D) 1,000.

There are 1,000 milliliters in one liter. When you are asked to convert milliliters into liters, divide the number of milliliters by 1,000. When asked to convert liters into milliliters, multiply the number of liters by 1,000.

(8) The correct answer is: (A) 116.

Use multiplication to determine how many animals of each type were sold, then add all the animals together. Horses: 2 breeds $\cdot$ 20 = 40 horses; cattle: 3 breeds $\cdot$ 15 = 45 cattle; pigs: 1 breed $\cdot$ 7 = 7 pigs; sheep: 4 breeds $\cdot$ 6 = 24 sheep. Now add all the animals together to get 40 horses + 45 cattle + 7 pigs + 24 sheep = 116 animals.

(9) The correct answer is: (B) 35 inches.

You first need to know how many inches are in 1 centimeter. Since there are 0.394 inches in 1 centimeter, multiply 88.9 centimeters by 0.394. $88.9 \cdot 0.394 = 35.02$ inches. Rounded off to the nearest whole number, this is 35 inches.

(10) The correct answer is: (B) 9.

Here you have a proportion/ratio problem. 1 cocktail = 50 min, so y cocktails = 7.5 hours. Convert the 7.5 hours to minutes by multiplying by 60 to get $7.5 \cdot 60 = 450$ min. Now write this information as a ratio, 50:1 = 450:y. As a fraction, this is 50/1 = 450/y. Cross-multiply to get $50 \cdot y = 450 \cdot 1$, which is 50y = 450. Divide both sides by 50 to get 50y/50 = 450/50. So y = 9.

(11) The correct answer is: (C) DBACE.

First ensure that all the variables are written in a common form, so convert variable E into a decimal to get 1/2 = 0.5. Now your variables are 0.0002, -0.02, 0.2, -200 and 0.5. Next, place these values from the smallest to the largest: -200, -0.02, 0.0002, 0.2 and 0.5, where D = -200, B = -0.02, A = 0.0002, C = 0.2 and E = 0.5.

(12) The correct answer is: (A) 52.5%.

Use the formula part/whole = y/100 where part is 32 black cars and whole is the sum of all the cars. 29 + 32 = 61, so 32/61 = y/100. To solve this, cross-multiply to get $61 \cdot y = 32 \cdot 100$ as 61y = 3,200. Divide both sides by 61, so 61y/61 = 3200/61 gives y = 52.459. 52.459 rounded to one decimal place is 52.5.

(13) The correct answer is: (D) 1/6, -5/42.

The absolute value symbol | | indicates the number inside can either be negative or positive, so solve 14y − 1/3 for both possibilities. Solve as a positive: 14y − 1/3 + 1/3 = 2 + 1/3 to get 14y = 2 1/3. Divide both sides by 14 to get 14y ÷ 14 = 7/3 ÷ 14 as y = 1/6 when simplified. Assume the problem is a negative and do the same: 14y + 1/3 = 2 will be 14y + 1/3 − 1/3 = 2 − 1/3 solve to get y = -5/42.

(14) The correct answer is: (C) $216.

The toaster costs $800, and 73% of that cost would be covered by insurance. So Sandra would cover 100% − 73%= 27%. Therefore, calculate 27/100 of 800 (which is Sandra's cost to cover) to get $216. You can also calculate how much the insurance would cover, which is 73/100 of $800. 73/100 * 800 = $584. Then subtract this cost from the total cost to get $800 − $584 = $216.

(15) The correct answer is: (B) $a^2 − 24a + 72 < 0$.

Let a and b represent the two values. According to the information, a − b=12. Solve to get a − b + b = 12 + b. So a = 12 + b further solved, a − 12 = b. b = a − 12. The second equation will be ab < 6(a + b). Replace b with its value: ab<(a + a − 12), so a^2 − 24a<-72. In the choices, there is a 0 to the right of the inequality, so move 72 to the left and make the right side 0.

(16) The correct answer is: (A) 155.51 inches.

1 inch is equal to 2.54 cm. Therefore, to get how many inches are equal to 395 cm, divide 395 cm by the equivalent of 1 inch, which is 2.54cm. So, 395 cm ÷ 2.54 = 155.5118. The answer choices are rounded off to two decimal places, so round off this figure to get 155.51 inches.

(17) The correct answer is: (D) 10 cups.

Since we are estimating, round off each value then divide the required amount by the capacity of the cup. 3.4 will become 3 since the number after the decimal is less than 5. In 0.289, the second number after 2 is more than 5, so add 1 to 2 to get 0.3. When you divide 3 by 0.3 you get 3 ÷ 0.3 = 10.

(18) The correct answer is: (B) 5.3 miles.

Distance = rate · time. Here, rate = 4 miles/hour while time =1 hr 20 min. First, convert the 20 minutes to hours by dividing the 20 min by 60 to get 1/3 hrs. Our time, therefore, is 1 1/3 hrs. Next, multiply the rate by the time. 4 · 1 1/3 will give you 5.3 miles.

(19) The correct answer is: (A) 13 5/21.

Add the whole numbers first. 9 + 3 = 12. Now, add 11/21 + 5/7 by first finding the LCM of 21 and 7, which is 21. Divide each denominator by 21, then multiply each answer by the numerator in that fraction. Next, add the two values together, (11 + 15)/21 = 26/21. Turn this into a mixed fraction to get 1 5/21. 1 5/21 + 12 = 13 5/21.

(20) The correct answer is: (C) 38.201%.

Here, the answers have been given in percentage, meaning that you should convert 0.38201 to a percentage. To do this, you should multiply 0.38201 by 100. When you have a decimal and you are required to multiply it by 100, it is the same as moving your decimal point two places to the right. This will give you 38.201%.

(21) The correct answer is: (B) 120 yards.

12 short tables and twice that number of long tables means 12+ (12 · 2) = 36 tables. Short tables measure 6 feet, so 12 · 6 = 72 feet. Eight inches of extra fabric on both ends means 36 tables will have (8 · 2) · 36 = 576 inches. 1 foot = 12 inches, so 576/12 = 48 feet. Long tables need 10 feet of fabric each, so 24 · 10 = 240 feet. 72 + 48 + 240 = 360 feet. 3 feet = 1 yard, so divide 360 by 3 to get 120.

(22) The correct answer is: (A) 88 ft/sec.

This problem is testing you on your conversion knowledge. You should first convert miles to feet and hours into seconds. 5280 ft = 1 mile, while 1 hour = 3,600 seconds. So, convert 60 miles into feet by multiplying 60 by 5280 to get 60 · 5280 = 316,800 ft. Divide this by 3600 seconds to get 316,800/3600 = 88 ft/ sec.

(23) The correct answer is: (D) 3:4 and 4:7.

The ratio of gentlemen to ladies is 21:28. Simplify this by dividing both portions by the GCF of 21 and 28, which is 7, to get 3:4. The ratio of ladies to the total number of people is 28: (28 + 21) or 28:49. Simplify by dividing both portions by 7 to get 4:7.

(24) The correct answer is: (B) 32.

Convert the ratio into fractions by giving both portions of the ratio a denominator. To get the denominator, add the two ratios together to get 5 + 4 = 9. Therefore, the nurses are 5/9 of the 72 and doctors are 4/9 of the 72. Since we want the number of doctors and they are 4/9 of 72, we multiply 4/9 · 72 to get 32.

(25) The correct answer is: (A) 350.

Let each ratio be represented by letter y so that we can get the value of y in 4y:7y:3y:y. If 4y has 50 more blocks than 3y, create an equation to look like this: 4y = 3y + 50. Solve that to get 4y − 3y = 50, so y = 50. If y is 50, then the blocks labeled F, which we have represented as 7y, are 7 · y or 7 · 50, which is 350.

(26) The correct answer is: (B) 48.

To find the number of strawberries, first create fractions for the two portions by getting a denominator for both. Add the two portions to get the denominator as 5 + 8 = 13. If blueberries are 5/13 = 30, what is 8/13? Get the value of 1/13 first, then multiply that by 8. If 5/13 = 30, then 1/13 = 30/5, which is 6. So, if 1/13 is 6, then 8/13 is 6 · 8 = 48.

(27) The correct answer is: (C) 45 liters.

The ratio in which she mixed the paints was 1:2, so the red paint was 1/3 of 45, which is 15. The blue paint was 2/3 of 45, which is 30. The ratio was therefore 15 liters:30 liters. To achieve a ratio of 2:1, let the additional red paint be y. (15 + y)/30 = 2/1. Therefore, 45 liters of red paint will be needed.

(28) The correct answer is: (D) 20 kilograms.

The ratio of wheat flour to sweet syrup is 6:3. If the total amount of flour and sweet syrup in the treat is to be 60 kilograms, then we need 3/9 of 60 kilograms of sweet syrup. This is 3/9 · 60, which is 20 kilograms.

(29) The correct answer is: (A) 30 ml.

There is 12/100 in 60 ml. 12/100 · 60 = 7.2 ml. If there is 7.2ml of glucose in 60 ml of water, then how much water will be needed to have 8% of glucose? If 12% = 7.2 ml, then 8% is equal to 8/100 = 7.2/x. When you solve this, you get x = 90 ml. If 90 ml is the total amount, then the amount you should add to the original 60 ml is 90 – 60 = 30 ml.

(30) The correct answer is: (D) 8 cm.

If 1 cm represents 12 km, then how many cm represent 96 km? First, create an equation. Let y represent the distance in cm, which represents the 96 km on the map. 1 cm/12 km = y cm/96 km. Solve this to get y cm = 96 km/12 km, which is 8 cm.

(31) The correct answer is: (A) 10 minutes.

If it takes 4 minutes to type 360 words, how long will it take to type 900 words? First, determine how many words are written in 1 minute by dividing the 360 words by 4 to get 360/4 = 90 words. If 1 min = 90 words, then x minutes = 900 words. Divide 900 by the words per minute to get 900/90 = 10 minutes.

(32) The correct answer is: (B) 5:6, 3:4, 2:3, 1:5.

These ratios as fractions are 3:4= 3/4; 2:3=2/3; 1:5=1/5 and 5:6=5/6. Next, get the LCM of the denominators 4, 3, 5 and 6, which is 60. 3/4 · 60 = 45; 2/3 · 60 = 40; 1/5 · 60 = 12 and 5/6 · 60 = 50. Now the fractions read 45/60, 40/60, 12/60 and 50/60. Arrange them in descending order to get 50/60, 45/60, 40/60, 12/60, then replace these fractions with the initial ratios.

(33) The correct answer is: (D) 27 and 36.

First, write the two ratios as fractions. When you add 3 and 4 together to get a common denominator, you get 3/7 and 4/7 as the ratios. We are given that the sum of the two values is 63, so multiply each fraction by the sum to get 3/7 · 63 = 27 and 4/7 · 63 = 36. The two numbers are therefore 27 and 36.

(34) The correct answer is: (A) $300.

First, write the three ratios as fractions by adding the ratios to get a common denominator. 2 + 3 + 5 = 10, so 10 is the common denominator. The fractions will then be 2/10, 3/10 and 5/10. If 5/10 = $150, how much is 10/10? First, get the value of 1/10. Then multiply the answer by 10. So 150/5 · 10 = $300.

(35) The correct answer is: (C) 24 men, total attendance is 42.

Write the ratios as fractions first. Add the ratios together to get a denominator, so 4 + 3 = 7. The fractions are now 4/7 and 3/7. If there are 18 women, then 3/7 = 18. To get the number of men, get the value of 1/7 by dividing 18 by 3 to get 6. If 1/7 = 6, then 4/7 is 6*4 = 24 and total attendance is 6 * 7 = 42.

(36) The correct answer is: (C) 1/12.

The reason (C) is correct is that it is clear from the third and fourth terms that the denominators are being multiplied by 3; 36 x 3 = 108. If you use the same factor, 3, to get the second term represented by x, 4 x 3 = 12, and so that second term should be 1/12.

Science Section – Test 4 Answers

(1)   The correct answer is: (D) The lungs.

Blood enters the right atrium, then moves through the right ventricle. From there, the right ventricle is responsible for pumping the blood to the lungs, where it is oxygenated. This oxygenated blood is then returned to the heart through the pulmonary veins that enter the left atrium.

(2)   The correct answer is: (D) Defending the body against any foreign substances.

White blood cells, which are also known as leukocytes, are immune system cells. These cells protect the body against foreign invaders and infectious diseases. When there is a threat, the white blood cells multiply and work to fight the infection or foreign substance that has been detected in the body.

(3)   The correct answer is: (A) Into the left atrium.

Blood enters the heart through the inferior and superior vena cava. The deoxygenated blood is then emptied into the right atrium and passed through the right ventricle. From there, the right ventricle pumps the blood to the lungs, where it is oxygenated. This oxygenated blood is returned to the heart through two pulmonary veins that enter the left atrium.

(4)   The correct answer is: (C) Prokaryote.

Prokaryotes are unicellular organisms that do not have mitochondria, a membrane-bound nucleus or any kind of membrane-bound organelles. These cells have hair-like structures known as pili surrounding the cell wall. Prokaryotes are usually categorized into two domains—bacteria and archaea.

(5)   The correct answer is: (A) Mitochondria.

The main role of mitochondria is to take in the nutrients from the cell and turn those nutrients into energy by breaking them down. The chemical energy that is produced from this process is stored in a tiny molecule known as adenosine triphosphate (ATP).

(6)   The correct answer is: (B) The Golgi apparatus.

The Golgi apparatus is where proteins are modified, sorted and packaged in vesicles that are membrane-bound inside the cell before they are sent to their final destination. The sacs that are found in the Golgi apparatus are known as cisternae.

(7)   The correct answer is: (D) Prometaphase.

Prometaphase is usually the second phase of mitosis. Here, the duplicated genetic material that is found inside the nucleus of the parent cell is separated into two identical daughter cells. The spindle fibers pull these duplicated chromosomes closer to the cell's poles.

(8)   The correct answer is: (A) Prophase, metaphase, anaphase, telophase.

The mitosis phase starts after the interphase stage where the cell copies its DNA. The first phase of mitosis is prophase, where the chromosomes start to migrate toward the center of the cell. Metaphase is the second phase, followed by anaphase, where the paired chromosomes separate. Then, finally, there are two identical daughter cells in the telophase.

(9)   The correct answer is: (C) After chromosomes separate.

During the interphase, the spindle fibers, joined to the chromosome's centromeres, pull the chromosome apart. This pull makes the chromosomes separate and two sister chromatids are formed. These two sister chromatids remain joined by one common centromere until the anaphase.

(10) The correct answer is: (D) A thermometer.

A thermometer is used to measure how hot or cold an object or environment is. Sunlight produces heat, so for you to determine the impact that sunlight has on the growth of plants, you should use the thermometer.

(11)   The correct answer is: (B) Mass.

We use a balance to determine the mass of a particular object. There are different types of balances that are used when measuring mass such as electric balances, analytic balances, trip balance scales, platform scales, spring balances, triple-beam balances and many more.

(12)   The correct answer is: (B) A positive variation.

When one variable increases as the other increases or when two variables move in the same direction, the relationship is referred to as a direct correlation, positive variation or positive correlation. In a negative correlation, two variables move in opposite or inverse directions.

(13)   The correct answer is: (C) It increases protein synthesis.

Generally, growth hormones stimulate protein anabolism in tissue, and this means that there is an increased uptake of amino acids, an increase in protein synthesis and a decrease in the oxidation of proteins. The anabolic hormone stimulates human muscle growth by increasing protein synthesis and reducing the breakdown of protein.

(14)   The correct answer is: (B) Glucagon.

Glucagon is produced in the alpha cells of the pancreas. This peptide hormone raises the glucose concentration as well as the fatty acids concentration in your bloodstream. It is considered the main catabolic hormone in the body and is used to treat several health conditions.

(15)   The correct answer is: (C) Maintain homeostasis.

To maintain homeostasis, various organs and systems are required to coordinate. The cells responsible for secretion of hormones are usually located in organs known as endocrine glands, and the endocrine system is made up of organs, cells, and tissues that are involved in the secretion of hormones.

(16) The correct answer is: (C) Adrenocorticotropic.

The adrenocorticotropic hormone (ACTH) is produced in the pituitary gland inside the brain. This polypeptide tropic hormone stimulates the secretion of the glucocorticoid hormone that is known as cortisol which is released from the adrenal cortex cells.

(17) The correct answer is: (A) The stomach.

The lower esophageal sphincter, which is also referred to as the cardiac sphincter, is located at the top of the stomach. The role of the cardiac sphincter is to prevent stomach contents from pushing upward and entering the esophagus.

(18) The correct answer is: (C) Peptidase.

A peptidase, also referred to as proteolytic or protease, is an enzyme that plays an important role in protein hydrolysis. This enzyme acts as a catalyst in breaking down proteins into single amino acids or smaller polypeptides. The breakdown occurs when the enzyme cleaves the peptide bonds that are within the protein through a process known as hydrolysis.

(19) The correct answer is: (B) Cirrhosis.

Cirrhosis refers to a condition in which a person's liver fails to function properly due to damage that occurs over a period of time. This condition is characterized by scarring of the liver and it may be caused by a variety of liver conditions and diseases such as hepatitis and chronic alcoholism, among others.

(20) The correct answer is: (A) Pre-mRNA.

In the nucleus, the production of a pre-mRNA occurs when a part of DNA from a liner chromosome goes through transcription. When it is still inside the nucleus, in order to become mRNA, the transcript has to go through processing, which involves splicing and adding of the poly-A tail and 5' cap.

(21) The correct answer is: (B) It connects amino acids.

The bond that holds two amino acids together is referred to as a covalent chemical bond or a peptide bond. This bond happens when a reaction between the carboxylic group of one of the molecules and the amino group of the other occurs. When these two molecules link together, a water molecule is released.

(22) The correct answer is: (A) The dermis.

The dermis is the second layer of skin and it contains hair follicles, sweat glands and tough connective tissue. The topmost skin layer is the epidermis and it is responsible for creating the skin tone as well as providing a barrier against water, while the innermost layer is the subcutaneous tissue, which is made of connective tissue and fat.

(23) The correct answer is: (B) Salt.

The fluid that is produced by the sweat glands is known as sweat or perspiration and it mainly consists of electrolytes and water. These electrolytes primarily consist of sodium and chloride, or what we generally refer to as salt.

(24) The correct answer is: (D) Forehead.

The eccrine glands produce a clear and odorless fluid that may be secreted due to intense heat, exercise, anxiety and fear. Generally, the kind of sweat that is involved in hyperhidrosis is eccrine sweat. When you are anxious, the eccrine glands release sweat through the forehead.

(25) The correct answer is: (B) Carry out background research on that topic.

When you are using the scientific method of research, the first thing you should do is state a problem or question based on what you have observed. After that first step, you should do thorough research and gather more knowledge on the topic that your question originates from.

(26) The correct answer is: (A) Homeostasis.

Homeostasis refers to the ability that a living thing has to maintain an internal state that is relatively stable even when the environment changes. All living organisms have the ability to regulate their internal environment and this helps them to survive.

(27) The correct answer is: (D) It destroys macrophages and T cells.

The HIV/AIDS virus multiplies actively and begins to infect and kill the immune system cells known as CD4+T cells. These are the main infection fighter cells in the immune system. Once the HIV virus enters the human body, it starts to destroy and disable these cells even when an infected person is not experiencing symptoms.

(28) The correct answer is: (A) Macrophages, antibodies.

Macrophages are produced by the white blood cells known as monocytes, while antibodies are produced by white blood cells known as B lymphocytes. Both macrophages and antibodies are able to trace and destroy foreign bodies such as viruses, bacteria and parasites.

(29) The correct answer is: (B) The M-line.

The filaments move toward the M line as the actin is pulled. This type of movement is known as a power stroke since it is where the production of force occurs. The sarcomere becomes shorter and your muscles contract.

(30) The correct answer is: (C) The skeletal system.

In the musculoskeletal system, both the skeletal system and the muscular system work in tandem to move and support your body. The bones that make up the skeletal system protect your body organs, give your body shape and support your body weight.

(31) The correct answer is: (C) Solving word puzzles in a short amount of time.

There are four major lobes in your brain and the frontal lobe is the largest among the four. It is the lobe that is responsible for controlling cognitive skills such as problem solving, emotional expression, language, memory, sexual behavior and judgment.

(32) The correct answer is: (B) The cerebral cortex.

The cerebral cortex is the outermost layer of the neural tissue found in the cerebrum of the human brain. It is divided into two hemispheres by a longitudinal fissure and it is gray in color since the nerves in that area are deprived of the insulation that the rest of the brain gets.

(33) The correct answer is: (C) Temporal.

The temporal lobe is situated behind the ears, under the lateral fissure which extends to both ends of your brain. Sounds, speech, comprehension and auditory language systems are all processed in this lobe. If a person has trouble speaking or finds it hard to remember things, then this is the lobe that is most likely damaged.

(34) The correct answer is: (D) A variable.

Body temperature may be classified as a variable because it changes depending on the environment. If you are in a warm area, then your temperature is likely to rise. If you are in a cool area, your temperature is likely to drop since temperature does not remain constant.

(35) The correct answer is: (A) Muscle tissue.

Muscle tissue is comprised of thread-like cells called fibers which specialize in contraction. There are three types of muscle tissue: smooth tissues, cardiac tissues and skeletal tissues. The main role of the muscular system is to facilitate movement.

(36) The correct answer is: (B) In the ovaries.

The ovum is the female reproductive cell that develops into a new organism when fertilized. The ovum is produced by the ovaries after which it is carried to the fallopian tube, where it awaits fertilization by a sperm. If the egg is fertilized, it moves to the uterus, where it is incubated.

(37) The correct answer is: (D) In the male accessory glands.

The male accessory glands are comprised of the prostate gland, bulbourethral glands and seminal vesicles. These specialized structures produce fluids such as fructose, alpha-glucosidase, bicarbonate, citric acid and prostaglandins, among others that are essential for nourishment, protection and sperm motility.

(38) The correct answer is: (B) The cervix and uterus.

The female reproductive system carries out various functions. The ovaries produce an ova that is transported to the fallopian tubes, where fertilization by a sperm usually takes place. If the egg is fertilized, it is implanted into the uterus wall, but if fertilization does not occur, the uterine lining is shed through a process called menstruation.

(39) The correct answer is: (B) The level of oxygen is high.

The pulmonary vein transports oxygen-rich blood to the left side of your heart from where it is pumped into the aorta. The right side of the heart receives deoxygenated blood from the vena cava and then pumps it into the pulmonary vein.

(40) The correct answer is: (C) Flows out and into systemic circulation.

In systemic circulation, oxygenated blood is carried from your left ventricle to the capillaries inside your body tissue through the arteries. Deoxygenated blood returns from the tissue capillaries through a network of veins to the right atrium of your heart.

(41) The correct answer is: (B) Because of the anatomical position in the chest cavity.

Your lungs do not have an equal size because of the placement of certain organs in the body. The right lung is broader than the left lung, but it is shorter since the liver occupies a larger space under the rib cage. And the left lung tends to be smaller since the heart takes up most of the space.

(42) The correct answer is: (C) The neutron.

The neutron is a small particle that has a slightly higher mass than the proton, but no electric charge. Neutrons are produced through nuclear fusion and, together with protons, they make up the nuclei of atoms.

(43) The correct answer is: (A) Boron-11; it is closest in mass to the average atomic mass in the periodic table.

Boron-11 is a stable or non-radioactive isotope of boron. This metal occurs naturally, but it can also be produced through fission. Boron-11 has 5 protons and 6 neutrons and that is why it has an atomic mass number of 11.

(44) The correct answer is: (D) The nucleus.

The nucleus contains the DNA of eukaryotic organisms. It occupies about one tenth of the total cell volume and this makes it the largest organelle in the cell. The nucleus facilitates replication and transcription processes which help in maintaining the integrity of the cell.

(45) The correct answer is: (B) The coccyx.

Other irregular bones include the vertebrae, temporal, sacrum, ethmoid, sphenoid, maxilla and mandible. The coccyx or tailbone is the attachment site for ligaments, tendons and muscles and it also serves as the insertion point of several muscles located in the pelvic floor.

(46) The correct answer is: (B) Phosphorus.

Tissue contains elements such as phosphorous, calcium, magnesium, sulfur and trace elements like zinc, iron and magnesium. Collagen forms the soft framework of bones and this framework is hardened and strengthened by calcium phosphate.

(47) The correct answer is: (A) Mass.

Simply put, mass is a measure of how much matter is in an object and the common units that are used to measure mass are grams and kilograms. When measuring mass, you should use a balance to compare known amounts of matter to unknown amounts of matter.

(48) The correct answer is: (C) It increases urine concentration inside the collecting duct.

Filtration is an important process since it introduces the many steps that take place along the nephrons, whereby water and other solutes are reabsorbed back into the bloodstream, causing an increase in urine concentration. The glomerular filtrate contains glucose, water, urea and salts.

(49) The correct answer is: (B) The nephrons.

Tubular reabsorption takes place in the nephrons of your kidneys. Here, fluid travels through several components that are found in the nephrons. It travels through the proximal convoluted tubes from the glomerulus before arriving at the loop of Henle, where necessary substances are reabsorbed back to the bloodstream. What is not reabsorbed is then excreted in the form of urine.

(50) The correct answer is: (D) Sphincters.

Sphincters are the muscular tubes that are located in your bladder. When these tubes contract, they squeeze urine to your urethra from your bladder and this facilitates the excretion of urine. After excretion, the tubes relax.

(51) The correct answer is: (B) Glomerulus, proximal convoluted tubule, loop of Henle, distal convoluted tubule, collecting duct.

Fluid travels through several components that are found in the nephrons. It travels through the proximal convoluted tubes from the glomerulus before arriving at the loop of Henle, where necessary substances are reabsorbed back to the bloodstream. What is not reabsorbed is then collected in the collecting duct and excreted in the form of urine.

(52) The correct answer is: (C) Chlorophyll.

(C) is correct because although it is known that most plants do not rely on other organisms for food, but rather manufacture their own, fungi have no capacity to make their food as they lack one essential ingredient—chlorophyll. Chlorophyll is a green-colored pigment which facilitates plants' absorption of sunlight for food preparation through photosynthesis.

(53) The correct answer is: (C) The capillaries.

(C) is the correct answer because although the human body has other small blood vessels, such as the arterioles, none are as tiny as the capillaries, whose function is to deliver blood to every cell of the body. While their diameter is in the range of 5 to 10 micrometers, that of arterioles is around 30 micrometers.

English and Language Use – Test 4 Answers

(1) The correct answer is: (B) See you sometime.

(B) and (D) sound informal, but (B) stands out as the most informal for its incompleteness as a sentence. It can be described as being fragmented, meaning that it does not qualify as an independent sentence or clause.

(2) The correct answer is: (B) Fans, captain, team, trophy.

Common nouns are words used to refer to things in general. These are in contrast to the proper nouns that are specific to individual things. For example, "president" is a common noun while "President Bob" is a proper noun.

(3) The correct answer is: (B) 1.

The reason (B) is correct is that the only pronoun in the sentence is "you." A pronoun is a word that stands in place of a noun, and in this case, instead of mentioning your name, we are simply saying "you" because it is self-explanatory.

(4) The correct answer is: (A) I woke up early so I could arrive on time.

(A) is correct because no comma is necessary within that sentence, not even before the conjunction "so." Although a comma is required before a conjunction when the two clauses being joined are independent, it is not required if such clauses are very short. You can tell when you read the sentence to yourself that no pause is necessary.

(5) The correct answer is: (A) Friendly.

Amicable people are friendly. They behave in a manner to avoid discord. Being unsure does not guarantee friendliness, and being timid simply means that one is nervous or shy. While being responsible is a positive quality, it does not necessarily go hand in hand with friendliness or amicability.

(6) The correct answer is: (C) Stubborn.

The word "intransigent" means "stubborn," or not willing to yield to a different opinion or position. It is the opposite of "flexible." Although usually, when people are intransigent about something they are also passionate about it, it is possible to be passionate and still be willing to be open to other's opinions.

(7)   The correct answer is: (B) The job has been reestablished.

Considering the prefix "re-" stands for "again," it means if the job was originally scrapped, it has now been reestablished, and if the person had been removed from the job but the position still remained, the person has been given back his/her job.

(8)   The correct answer is: (A) Villainous.

Someone is described as a miscreant when his/her behavior is terrible and/or unlawful.

(9)   The correct answer is: (B) Chrom.

"Chrom," a word derived from the Greek word "chroma," is ordinarily used alongside other terms to form a whole word, with "chrom" denoting "color." Such words include chromatography, chromatic and chromogenic.

(10) The correct answer is: (B) Halves.

Ordinarily, nouns that end with "-f" have their plural form ending with "-ves," hence, getting rid of the "-f." Similar nouns include "shelf – shelves"; "hoof – hooves" and "leaf – leaves." However, there are nouns that end with "-f" but are uncountable and so remain as they are in their plural form, such as "beef."

(11) The correct answer is: (B) Announced, was.

The sentence requires consistency of tenses, and so, since the "ship set" indicates the action has happened, the action of the meteorology department should also show completion; meaning the past tense.

(12) The correct answer is: (C) Were.

"Were" is the correct answer because it fulfills the subject-verb agreement and also matches the tense reflected in the rest of the sentence. "Musicians" being in plural cannot go with "is" or "was." The phrase "all along" indicates an ongoing period, so from the choices, "were" is the most appropriate.

(13) The correct answer is: (C) Or.

The reason "or" is the best answer is that it helps to make the two combined choices well understood. The other answers—(A) (B) and (D)—do not logically combine the choices of appetizers.

(14) The correct answer is: (D) The two had a long chat, and they enjoyed their dinner that evening.

The reason (D) is the correct answer is that what is provided are two simple sentences, each of them independent, without either of them relying on the other for completeness. Also, neither of them contrasts the other. For that reason, the most appropriate conjunction to join them into one sentence is "and."

(15) The correct answer is: (B) Before she goes to sleep.

(B) is the dependent clause whose main characteristic is not having the capacity to stand on its own despite having a subject, verb and complement. Also, the presence of the word "before" should provide a hint because the word is normally used at the beginning of a dependent clause.

(16) The correct answer is: (C) After leaving the conference room, he headed straight to the party.

(C) is correct not only because, like the other answers, the comma is followed by an independent clause, but also because the comma marks the end of the dependent clause. In this case the dependent clause is an adverbial of time (describing when), but the sentence would still be correct if it had been another type of adverbial phrase.

(17) The correct answer is: (B) Is meant to remain sacred.

The reason (B) is correct is that it keeps the sentence simple. The answers that begin with the pronoun "it" end up creating a compound sentence that is ungrammatical. (C) creates a grammatical sentence but it is complex, and the requirement in the question is a simple sentence.

(18) The correct answer is: (D) Although the sun can sometimes be very hot.

(D) is the correct answer because it is a dependent clause that is added to an independent clause, and that is what creates a complex sentence. Moreover, the two clauses are appropriately joined by a conjunction that is preceded by a comma.

(19) The correct answer is: (C) I was at home.

A simple question like "where were you" requires a simple answer of the form "I was at ...," and that is what (C) provides. (A) corresponds to a question of the form "what did you do?" while (B) corresponds to a question of the form "where are you?" (D) corresponds to a question like "where have you been?"

(20) The correct answer is: (B) The most recent report by the WHO states that there is a chance of asthma becoming worse during the night or when one exercises.

Citations are required when writers use material from other people. The fact mentioned in (B) is not the writer's own. Hence, it requires a citation. (A) contains common knowledge and needs no citation. (C) and (D) do not require any citation as (C) references a paragraph in the report and (D) references the report in general.

(21) The correct answer is: (C) Transparent.

Something "opaque" is impossible to see through because it does not permit light to penetrate it. As such, its antonym is "transparent." (A) refers to something you can easily see through—more of a synonym to transparent. (B) is incorrect since it is about shape. (D) is incorrect because it is in reference to age (something historic).

(22) The correct answer is: (C) Having varied meanings.

Polysemy can be exemplified by the verb "get," which not only means to procure, but also to understand. The word that fits (A) is polymorphous, while the one that fits (B) is monochromatic. The word for (D) is polyandry.

(23) The correct answer is: (B) Half.

A patient is said to be semiconscious when his/her consciousness is partial. None of the other options are appropriate.

(24) The correct answer is: (C) A government where the ruler is a religious authority.

(C) can be explained in that "theo" in "theocracy" stands for "God," whereas "-cracy," in the same word, stands for "government" A situation like in (A) is defined as "polyarchy," whereas a situation as in (B) is defined as "plutocracy." The (D) situation is defined as "autarchy."

(25) The correct answer is: (C) Failure to adhere to the stipulations laid down by the company will lead to the termination of the employee's contract.

Administrative language should be impersonal, and that is the reason the passive voice is preferred. (A) and (B) are too informal, and though formal, (D) is somewhat too friendly.

(26) The correct answer is: (C) Person.

(C) is the correct answer as there is no need for any punctuation mark in that part of the sentence. A semicolon would have been correct if the sentence read something like: "I now remember Tom was an odd ____; he never acknowledged my presence whenever we met outside the office."

(27) The correct answer is: (C) Strong.

(C) is correct because terming the coffee strong means it is potent. It is logical that a person would find it impossible to sleep for long after consuming it. Flavor, as depicted in the words "sweet" and "hot" has no effect on one's capacity to sleep; the same case applies to fragrance.

(28) The correct answer is: (D) Highlights.

(D) fits the gap very well. It fulfills the subject-verb agreement, because the pronoun "she" is singular, and the verb "highlights" corresponds accordingly. It also matches in tense because "highlights" is in the present and "has been" indicates a current situation.

Made in the USA
Middletown, DE
26 September 2020